NEW HAVEN

A Guide to Architecture and Urban Design

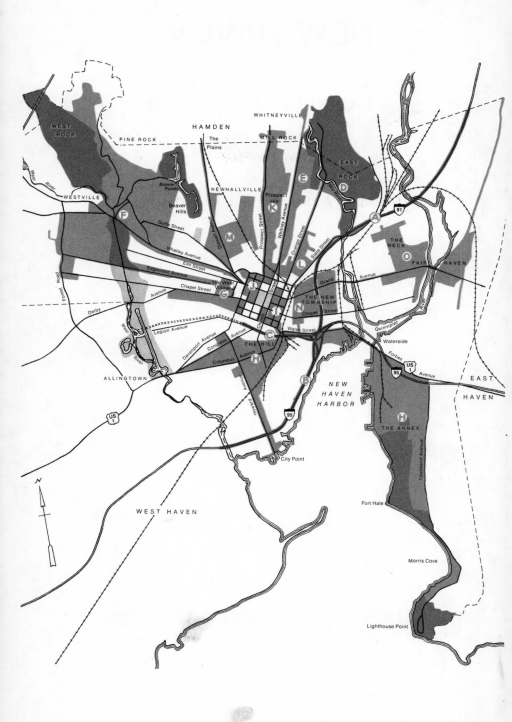

NEW HAVEN

A Guide to Architecture
and Urban Design

Elizabeth Mills Brown

New Haven and London, Yale University Press

Designed by John O. C. McCrillis
and set in Helvetica type by
Eastern Typesetting Company, Hartford, Conn.
Preparation by Jay's Publishers Services.
Printed in the United States of America by
Eastern Press, Inc., New Haven, Conn.

The photographs for this book were taken by Gilbert Kenna,
Ray Schmakel, and Lee Tabor.

13   12   11   10   9   8   7   6   5   4

Contents

Preface

Designed originally to be the capital city of a large colony, New Haven began life on a high plane, and although it lost this exalted independent status almost at once, it soon made up for the loss by becoming the seat of a college. For two and a half centuries Yale has given the city a special flavor, drawing to it people of cultivation and influence. Although never rich—at any rate never as rich as it has constantly dreamed of being—it has maintained a cosmopolitan style rare in a town its size.

As a result, architectural patronage, while seldom pretentious, has been discriminating, and down the years the city has collected samples of the work of many of the country's well-known architects: Asher Benjamin, Ithiel Town, A. J. Davis, Peter B. Wight, Russell Sturgis, Cass Gilbert, James Gamble Rogers, Eero Saarinen, Paul Rudolph, Philip Johnson, Louis Kahn, and others. In addition, it has long had an able architectural profession of its own, which deserves more recognition.

Also worthy of more recognition is New Haven's brilliant urbanist tradition. It is here that the genius of the city lies. The town plan of 1637–38, the monumental redesign of the central city in the Federal period, and the Redevelopment program of modern times are all landmarks in American urbanist history. In addition there is the work of Donald Grant Mitchell, Frederick Law Olmsted, Jr., and Maurice Rotival; and the campus planning of John Trumbull, John Russell Pope, and James Gamble Rogers. Between these peaks lies a disciplined tradition of vernacular urbanism, carried on mostly by private speculators and builders, which created the whole web of streetscapes and landscapes that made New Haven known in the 19th century as one of America's most beautiful cities.

This urbanist tradition, today largely forgotten, needs rediscovery. Streets as well as buildings are *made,* and, like buildings, they embodied when they were first designed certain visions of art and order. If we can learn to read them better—to understand what they started out to be and how they have changed—much that is incoherent in the modern city becomes intelligible.

It is this quality of the urban scene rather than the landmark that needs to be highlighted in our cities today when the engines of demolition are barging blindly into old neighborhoods, and when preservationists, alert but harried, are darting about trying to save one fragment here, another fragment there, out of once well-knit complexes. As we are beginning to learn, the fragment saved with loud hurrahs often turns out to be disappointing when we see it by itself or when it is moved to another site, and we learn too late that what we had liked about it was not what it *was* but what it *did:* the role it played in a larger scheme where movement, rhythm, repetition and contrast, exit and approach were related to one another in a purposeful way. We need to rediscover what the intentions of the urban designers of our existing cities were, and to become more sensitive to the urbanist intentions of today's designers, if we are ever going to achieve a viable synthesis of the old and the new.

A handbook as small as this one, dealing simply with what presents itself to the eye, cannot attempt to explore the history of streets and neighborhoods or the programs that created them. But it can, I hope, at least suggest a *way of looking.*

Material for the book is drawn from research for a forthcoming history of architecture and urbanism in New Haven. Although historical information is included here, this guide is not a history: it is simply a camera's eye, catching the city as it happens to look at a particular moment in time—the start of the year 1975. Many of the works observed here in their fortuitous relationships to one another —the old and the new thrown together on the city streets by the accidents of time—will be studied in the context of their own periods in the later volume.

Although designed as a field book, the guide is also intended to be of use to scholars. Dates and attributions, as explained in the introduction, have been documented, and traditional attributions that turned out to be dubious have been discarded. For those who may want to use the material of the book for a study of building history, a subject index is provided and also a chronological breakdown.

One of the disappointments of writing a book like this is the number of buildings one wants to include but cannot. Selection is limited by the routes and by the size of the book. Many things that are interesting or pleasing have had to be left out, especially from the great amount of contemporary building, which is not only abundant but is scattered to the four corners of the city. This body of work, backing up the fireworks of the big-name architects from out of town who have taken the limelight, deserves a study of its own.

Many people have been helpful in the production of this book, and it is a pleasure to remember their support and friendliness.

My first acknowledgment is to the New Haven Bicentennial Commission and to its chairman, William Ogden Ross, for the substantial grant which the Commission has made toward publication, and also to the New Haven Preservation Trust for its supporting grant. The staff of the New Haven Colony Historical Society has shown me kindnesses for which I cannot find adequate words of appreciation. Ottilia Koel, Harriet Bishop, and Lysbeth Andrews-Zike have so facilitated my work that it has been possible to learn and record things which under a less generous administration might never have been found. I also recall with gratitude the help of Lydia Wentworth and Dorothy Armistead who were with the society during the early stages of this work. In the Yale Archives and Manuscripts Room, Herman Kahn and Judith Schiff and all other members of the staff have been unfailingly helpful.

Equally cordial and constructive have been all the members of the city government to whom I have gone for material: William Donahue, Executive Director of the Redevelopment Agency; John McGuerty, Director, City Plan Department; David A. Storrs, Program Coordinator. Patricia Smith, Anita Palmer, and Catherine Trentini in the Public Information Office were not only helpful in answering questions but lent many photographs from the Agency's splendid collection, and Edward Hogan in the City Plan Department supplied maps. Orlando Silvestri, Building Official, gave me free access to the city's permit files.

Marjorie Noyes deserves a special kind of appreciation, for without her professional skill and steadying hand the complex job of assembling 500 photographs on time might never have got done. To the three photographers who have taken pictures for the book— Gilbert Kenna, Ray Schmakel, Lee Tabor—I also extend particular thanks not only for their pictures but for their interest and their willingness to handle rush orders, and to Herbert Noyes for drawing the plan of University Quadrangle and taking on a few emergency assignments; and to Karl Rueckert for drawing the maps. Other photographs have come from the Yale News Bureau, where Stephen Kezerian and Mary Sullivan were extremely obliging about handling a taxing order.

Many people have helped with information, among whom I would especially like to express my thanks to Norris Andrews, Director of the Regional Planning Agency of South Central Connecticut; to John B. Kirby, Jr., Doris B. Townshend, and Gilbert Kenna. My research assistants, Margaret LaFarge and Diane Renshaw, have earned the gratitude of others besides myself for their work of indexing the early building permits. To H. Ward Jandl I am indebted for information about Henry Austin's work in New Jersey, and to A. Tappan Wilder for countless insights from his extensive research in New Haven's early 20th-century building and planning history. Lila

Freedman has kindly contributed information about Yale sculpture. And finally I am especially beholden to George L. Hersey, for the present book has grown out of an earlier project which we set out to do together several years ago. I am most grateful to him for his continued interest and help.

Introduction

1637–1665 *First Maritime Period: the Independent Colony.* New Haven was founded, like many New England plantations, both as a Puritan community and a mercantile enterprise. But under the leadership of two forceful men, Theophilus Eaton and the Reverend John Davenport, it carried both ideas to their extreme development: in New Haven Puritanism can be seen at its most pure, and a merchant adventure at its most adventurous.

Founded as the capital of an independent colony, the town began with dreams of empire and of a fortune to be made in the beaver-skin trade. But these dreams soon foundered, and by 1660 the colony was in ruin. The merchant adventurers died or left, and their poorer followers remained to face a future of farming and isolation. The final blow came in 1665 when New Haven lost its independence and was swallowed up by the Colony of Connecticut. Not until 1701 did it regain its status and become, with Hartford, joint capital of the colony.

1665–1750 *Lean Years.* Connecticut was the edge of the wilderness, far from the urban culture of both New York and Boston. Life was poor, provincial, and raw, marked however by one dramatic achievement, the founding of Yale College in 1701. Trailing William and Mary by eight years, Yale was the third college in America. In 1717, after a furious fight with Hartford, New Haven succeeded in being chosen as its seat.

1750–1835 *Second Maritime Period.* As New England entered its great maritime era, New Haven shared in the increase in trade. The port came back to life, and by the time of the Revolution signs of prosperity were beginning to appear, heralding the boom that was to follow.

The Federal period is the beginning of the city's golden age, a rising curve that would last until the Civil War. Chartered as a city in 1784, New Haven was made joint capital with Hartford of the State of Connecticut, and with an explosion of energy it rushed into the new century. With the best harbor in western New England, it was soon a major port. At the same time, tanning and shoemaking flourished, and small shops making carriages and hardware began to appear.

1

This period is the formative moment in New Haven's physical history, a time of enormous florescence and urban creation which laid the base on which the 19th-century city developed. In this complex background four figures stand out: James Hillhouse, U.S. senator, capitalist, owner of vast lands in the northern part of town, and a man passionately driven by a vision of New Haven as a rich and beautiful city; Ezra Stiles, president of Yale from 1778 to 1795; Timothy Dwight, his successor from 1795 to 1817; and Eli Whitney, inventor and landowner, who opened a gun factory in New Haven in 1798 and there introduced a system of production which was to make industrial history. Under the leadership of these men and their circle, New Haven became the foremost city in Connecticut and Yale became the largest college in America, no longer a regional but now a national institution. Sparked by Yale's pioneering work in science and by the celebrated presence of Whitney, the city also became a center for inquiring minds interested in inventions and practical scientific thought. This would bear fruit in another generation.

Prosperity was interrupted by the Embargo and the War of 1812, which nearly ruined the port. Recovery dragged until 1825 when, gathering up all its resources in a massive bid to recapture its trade, the city set out to build a canal, designed to bypass Hartford and reach to the far edge of Massachusetts and ultimately Canada. This heroic undertaking proved to be more than a small city could handle: the Farmington Canal, though functional for a while, was never a financial success and in 1846 it was abandoned. But the exciting decade that saw its inception set off such an expansion of the city and gave it such a special glow that it may fairly be set apart as New Haven's Canal Age.

1835-1860 *Manufacturing Town.* The failure of the Farmington Canal virtually ended New Haven's maritime career, but by this time carriage shops and other small factories were growing fast, and the shift from a mercantile to a manufacturing economy took place smoothly. In a climate that stimulated invention and experiment, New Haven suddenly stepped onto the frontier of the new age, becoming one of the foremost manufacturing towns of New England, making carriages, guns, rubber boots, clocks, and hardware.

The leading figure now is James Brewster, whose carriage company opened far-flung markets for a line of fleet and elegant sulkies, phaetons, barouches, and rockaways. It was also Brewster who built the first railroad to New Haven (1833–39) and did much to develop the city's manufacturing potential. By 1860 New Haven was carriagemaker to the world.

1861-1880 *War and Reconstruction.* The Civil War was a disaster for New Haven for its largest market had been the South. It was nearly 1880 before the city recovered and, when it did, it had lost ground that could never be regained. Although prosperity would revive—indeed wealth on an unheard-of scale still lay ahead—a corner had been turned: Detroit, not New Haven, would become the inheritor of the carriage industry.

In 1873, in a bitter episode, New Haven lost its position as co-capital of the state, and Hartford pulled ahead as the first city of Connecticut.

1880-1929 *Industrial City.* The transition from antebellum manufacturing to the new giant scale of post-Civil War industry, with its sprawling plants, railroad tracks, smokestacks, and ever-mounting demand for cheap foreign labor, was made gradually from the '70s on, and by the '90s New Haven had confidently joined the march of American imperialism and wealth. Four new sources contributed: the Winchester Repeating Arms Company, maker of the famous "rifle that won the West" and soon the city's biggest industry; the consolidation of a network of railroads into a single system with New Haven as headquarters; the invention of the world's first telephone exchange and establishment of the Southern New England Telephone Company in New Haven; and finally a new escalation of Yale College which in 1887 legally became Yale University, and by the end of the century numbered a faculty-student community of nearly 3000 and was on its way to becoming one of the city's biggest businesses.

To a town heavily involved in guns, the years from 1898 to 1918 were fruitful, and New Haven once again began to boom, the turn of the century becoming its third great period of expansion. A sizeable proportion, in fact, of today's city was built at that time, in the short space of about fifteen years between 1895 and 1910. Growth continued all through the palmy days of the '20s, but as the city filled, it went increasingly to the suburbs.

1929-1975 Meanwhile, below the surface all the now-familiar problems of the American industrial city were accumulating, and the Depression opened Pandora's box. There is no need to go on with the story, for the urban crisis of our times is well known. In 1953 Richard C. Lee was elected mayor and launched a full-scale program of redevelopment. By this and other means the city has since been trying to build a new urban community on the remains of the old.

ARCHITECTURAL NOTE

Aside from the first buildings of the merchant adventurers, about which little is known except that a dour Bostonian said they were extravagant, New Haven built almost nothing of note in the Colonial period. All that remains today are Yale's Connecticut Hall (J 2) and four or five houses (H 44, H 49, I 3, I 5, 0 23). The houses are conservative and plain, suggesting the narrow horizon that still bounded this provincial community.

The Federal period brought an architectural explosion as the newly rich town rushed to catch up with fashion. Outside architects were imported for major programs, and such figures as John Trumbull, Peter Banner, Asher Benjamin, and young Ithiel Town now appear on the scene. Yale embarked on a whole new campus—the celebrated Brick Row, which was probably the first planned campus in the country—and in one of America's outstanding urbanist programs of the time the Green was legally reserved as a public space and redesigned as a monumental civic center, the climactic event being the building of the three churches (Itinerary I). Led by James Hillhouse, and drawing on concepts of planning expressed by his friend Timothy Dwight, a program to remake and beautify the city makes the Federal period the high tide of New Haven urbanism, and the urbanist standards set at this time survived for two or three generations, identifying New Haven as one of the most charming cities of 19th-century America. In a mass movement, also led by Hillhouse, elm trees were planted at private expense around the Green and along the major streets.

In architecture a vernacular developed with its own regional flavor: still conservative by comparison with Bulfinch's Boston, but graceful and ornamental. Most of this work is anonymous, although in modern times the name of David Hoadley has often been associated with it. But Hoadley's role has probably been somewhat misunderstood. He was more a builder and joiner than what is meant today by an architect, and he usually worked to plans by others. In New Haven now the only known building built by him is the United Church. Other examples of his work are in Bethany and Orange.

New materials and techniques appeared at this time: flushboarding, stucco, and traprock. Traprock came from a new quarry on East Rock, and for another forty years or so it was used for foundations, giving New Haven's Federal and Greek Revival architecture a special character. Houses were commonly painted white or what was called a "lively cream," and the street was given linear precision with fences painted white.

New Haven's Canal Age was also its Periclean Age. Around the Hillhouse set and the College, a cultivated society grew up whose patronage of Ithiel Town and his partner Alexander Jackson Davis introduced the Greek Revival in a pure and sophisticated form, and established New Haven as the Athens of Connecticut. From having so recently been a conservative outpost, New Haven quickly became one of the most modern cities of New England.

New wealth brought a larger scale, as well as increased use of stucco, now "penciled" to resemble ashlar, and of brick, now painted to resemble stucco. White was still the dominant color, with softer hues evoking marble or granite. Shutters became popular.

In urbanism, as the thriving city expanded, the impetus and discipline of the Federal period were carried over into the projects of many private developers, producing such varied works as Jocelyn, Spireworth, York and Wooster Squares, Custom House Square which is now gone without a trace, and a protoindustrial park near Collis Street.

The Greek Revival is a high moment in the city's architectural history, and one that is almost singly attributable to the firm of Town and Davis and to the builders who carried out their designs and learned to copy them: Nahum Hayward, Charles Thompson, Sidney Mason Stone, Elihu Atwater, Ira Atwater, and Atwater Treat. Although Ithiel Town came to live in New Haven in 1837, the firm's practice was in New York, and New Haven's Greek Revival flowering cannot exactly be called native.

Of an original thirty to forty prominent buildings known to have been built by these men, seven or eight remain today in fairly good shape. But all are bereft of their setting, and little is left to show one of the characteristic features of the Greek Revival: the creation of urban *scenery*—a romantic suburban landscape in which white porticoes are glimpsed through dark glades. The naked aridity of Hillhouse Avenue today—Town and Davis's masterpiece—is a travesty of the original concept.

Building continued to boom in the antebellum period as a new manufacturing class rose to wealth. In this boisterous climate the classical restraint of the Greek Revival could not long survive, and the exaggerated outlines and more exotic imagery of the Italian Villa style began to replace it. Built in great numbers in the many

5

prosperous quarters of the town in the two decades before the Civil War, the Italian Villa became New Haven's symbol of a proudly successful, aggressive, but still traditionally oriented society. A wealth of fine examples remains today, often quite disregarded because still so common, as souvenirs of New Haven's most golden days.

Materials became richer: brownstone trim began to appear on the finer houses and basements of beautifully dressed masonry, sometimes still of traprock but now often of brownstone. Colors deepened to tans and ochers and other "stone colors" as they were called, and roofs were sometimes a Mediterranean red—Raynham still gives a superb example (H 47). Black cast iron replaced white fences, bringing an air of opulent sobriety; Orange Street today, where its fences survive, still gives a hint of the sort of streetscape the age aspired to (Itinerary L). In urbanism a new romanticism appeared, represented by the picturesque layouts of Highland Park and Evergreen Cemetery, while Clinton Park carried on the old classical tradition.

The elm trees now had reached maturity and become the glory of the town, making New Haven famed as the City of Elms. Dickens, visiting in 1842, was charmed. "The effect is very like that of an old cathedral yard in England," he wrote of the Green, "seeming to bring about a kind of compromise between town and country." He pronounced it "novel and pleasant."

The two architects who dominate this period are Henry Austin and Sidney Mason Stone, and with them New Haven architecture comes of age, for this marks the moment when a local architectural profession is born. Austin, who had worked in Town's office and began his career in classical villas, became adept in all the latest modes: Italianate, Tudor, Egyptian, and in due course French Empire and High Victorian Gothic. In much of his work there is a vein of fantasy and exaggeration that is his personal stamp. Stone, who had begun as an itinerant carpenter and worked his way up through the building trades, is mainly associated with the more academic Renaissance Revival of the '50s, but he too adds a personal note in his feeling for rich but restrained detail. Of the enormous output of these two men, scarcely more than a dozen or so known examples remains today. Both worked out of town as well as in New Haven, and Austin's work has been found as far as Maine and New Jersey.

Building declined after the Civil War, and few examples of the French Empire style, then making its gaudy appearance in so many other cities, were ever built in New Haven. Mansard roofs appeared in large numbers, but even these were often thrifty modernizations of old flat-topped villas.

However, while the city coasted, Yale in the late '60s embarked on a mammoth building campaign which would transform the northwest side of town. The old practice of bringing in big-name architects was resumed, notably Peter B. Wight, Russell Sturgis, Richard Morris Hunt, and J. Cleveland Cady. A critic from the *American Architect and Building News* visiting in the '70s remarked snobbishly that outside of the Yale buildings New Haven could not boast a single "artistic structure."

Row houses were introduced in the '60s, and a tentative apartment house appeared in the '70s. Brownstone also arrived in a big way, and for the first time in decades brick began to be left unpainted and used for polychromatic effect. After the soft tonalities of the Villa Style, a deeper range of earth colors began to take over. Buildings became higher, and the silhouette began to erupt with spiky projections, gables, and turrets. A vast new restlessness and disturbance reigned.

Henry Austin continued to practice at least into the '70s, but the principal architects of the period are David R. Brown, Rufus G. Russell, and, somewhat later, Leoni W. Robinson—all three apprentices of Austin. Brown and Russell are mainly identified with the High Victorian Gothic style of the '70s and the early Queen Anne of the '80s. Of Brown's work not a great deal is known, but several hundred of Russell's drawings are preserved in the collection of the New Haven Colony Historical Society, providing a good record of the period.

Of greater fame than the architects was the landscape designer and author, Donald Grant Mitchell, who had moved to New Haven after having had a landscape practice in New York (in formal or informal association with the architect Richard Morris Hunt), and who soon achieved national popularity as a writer of rural essays under the name of Ik Marvel. Mitchell was involved in the layout of Edgewood and the western end of the city as well as in numerous private estates, but his principal contribution was the design of the new city parks—a varied group of inland, wetland, shorefront, and mountainous pieces of land which he made into one of the most distinguished park systems in the country. Not all of his designs were carried out, and most that were have now been altered or destroyed, but several of his drawings are preserved in the New Haven Colony Historical Society. The park program (including Edgewood Avenue), which was concentrated mainly between 1885 and 1895, is the only significant urbanist enterprise in New Haven in the second half of the 19th century.

Prosperity returned to New Haven in the '90s, and building once again began to boom. This period is noted mainly for an outburst of popular domestic architecture as an upward social explosion into the middle class produced a demand for large, splendiferous, but not too costly, frame houses. Queen Anne, Romanesque, Chateauesque, Baronial, Colonial—all the dreams are there. The profusion of detail seems almost infinite, but it has a mass-produced air about it, reflecting the advent of both machine production and architectural magazines. Upper Orange Street, Sherman Avenue, and Howard Avenue are the special preserves of this architectural extravaganza, but lesser examples fill street after street throughout the city, marking one of New Haven's greatest building periods. It is revealing of the income level on which expansion was taking place that many of these houses were designed for multiple occupancy. The '90s in fact are the heyday of that special phenomenon, the two-family house.

Leoni Robinson became the dean of the local architects in this decade, building extensively for corporations and the gentry, and he remained the acknowledged leader of the profession until his death after World War I. The largest volume of business however seems to have gone to the partnership of William H. Allen and Richard Williams and to Ferdinand VonBeren who, under the firm name of Brown and VonBeren,· inherited David R. Brown's practice. These men were adept at supplying whatever the market or the mode might require, from a Colonial cottage to a towered castle, from a tenement to a Roman mansion. They rode out many whirlwind fashions and dominated popular and political patronage into the 1920s.

The architecture of the early 20th century is a kaleidoscope of changing images. There is a general sobering up after the riotous excursions of the '90s, but this assumed many forms. Yale took off on a Beaux-Arts flight of new magnificence, launched by Carrère and Hastings, and the state and federal governments matched it with a Greek courthouse and a Roman post office. The city's first two skyscrapers were built, one Adamesque, one Tudor; also a Spanish synagogue, a Venetian office building, several English parish churches, and the two most sumptuous private houses New Haven had yet seen, one Elizabethan and one Palladian. The apartment house also arrived, sometimes California-Spanish, sometimes Georgian or Tudor, sometimes a stretched-up palazzo. At the same time an austere kind of Edwardian Gothic appeared and, along with the Arts and Crafts movement, a heightened interest in workmanship and materials.

Through all this, one theme finally became dominant: the Colonial Revival. Given the pride and conservatism of New Haven, now looking back to greater days, it seems inevitable that the Colonial Revival should have become an intense experience—not only an architectural fashion but also a pervasive attitude giving rise to historical studies, the creation of culture heroes, and the beginnings of the preservation movement. Besides producing numberless red brick Georgian houses and white frame Colonial houses, the revival set off a fad for Colonializing (or more often Federalizing) Victorian houses which would complicate the course of future architectural history by grafting 18th-century details salvaged from the wrecker onto 19th-century buildings.

By 1900 industrialization had begun to take its toll of the city: buildings were dirty, slums were spreading, streets were hung with wires and choked with trolleys and traffic. Worst of all, the elms had begun to die. Inspired by the City Beautiful movement emanating from the Chicago fair of 1893 and by the hope of restoring New Haven's onetime charm, in 1907 a group of citizens led by George Dudley Seymour, a local lawyer, formed the Civic Improvement Committee and hired Cass Gilbert and Frederick Law Olmsted, Jr., to make a city plan, a plan which was presented in 1909–10 and almost totally ignored by the city. It was Seymour also who organized a drive to save the elms—this too in vain.

The corps of local architects by this time was large and included men of considerable sophistication—R. W. Foote (who followed Robinson as acknowledged leader of the profession), Charles Scranton Palmer, George H. Gray, Lester Julianelle, J. Frederick Kelly, Dwight E. Smith, the firm of Norton and Townsend, and the landscape architects Ernest F. Coe (an apprentice of Donald Grant Mitchell's) and Frederick A. Davis Jr. are among the most conspicuous—but the list of members of the New Haven Architectural Club, founded at this time, is considerably longer. Because the city by now was filling up, much of their domestic work is in the suburbs and does not appear in this book.

Depression and war brought a lull of almost 25 years. The interval, at Yale, belongs to James Gamble Rogers who in the mid-1920s had begun to line the city streets with a superbly integrated fabric of buildings and spaces, and locally to Douglas Orr. Orr worked in a transitional style, often using a Colonial-Federal format and streamlining it with stripped trim or flattened ornament, sometimes *moderne*

9

or Art Deco. This was striking but economical. It had great appeal for businesses and institutions, and Orr's practice was immense, including not only work in New England but such nationally known commissions as the remodeling of the White House and the Taft Carillon in Washington. In 1947–49 he served as president of the American Institute of Architects. Orr died in 1966, but the firm has been carried on in his name by the succeeding partners.

Modern architecture came late to New Haven but when it did it came with revolutionary fervor. In 1951, under President A. Whitney Griswold, Yale commissioned Louis Kahn to do the New Art Gallery, and soon thereafter Mayor Lee initiated a policy of engaging eminent outside architects for city projects. Since then there has been a galaxy of big names and an outburst of monumental buildings that have made New Haven one of the pilgrimage centers of modern architecture. In this dynamic environment, enhanced by the presence of the Yale School of Art and Architecture, a new crop of resident architects has grown up to whom the systematic job of modernizing the city has largely fallen. Now beginning to react against the exaggerated hero-worship and the self-centric monuments of the 1950s and '60s, they are increasingly concerned with the problem of preserving or reestablishing the urban fabric as a humane and workable environment. Much of their work will be found in the following pages.

Along with the postwar resurgence of architecture came a sudden resurgence of urbanism as New Haven's urban renewal program was galvanized into vivid action by the election of Richard C. Lee as mayor in 1953 and presently the appointment of Edward J. Logue as Development Administrator. With a background of planning going back well before the war, formulated by Maurice Rotival and later by Norris Andrews, the city was ready for action when federal funds began to be available in the 1950s, and federal money poured in, making New Haven one of the first and most spectacular showcases of urban renewal in the country. At the same time came the superhighways.

From Rotival, the Redevelopment Agency inherited a Corbusian legacy—a vision of towers lined up with vast interspaces and highways sweeping off into the distance—and this sort of dream colored early plans. The scope of the programs that involved actual demolition and new construction in the downtown area alone is shown on maps I 15 and H 35. This amounts to a radical transformation of the architectural imagery of the central city and a restructuring of movement around automobile–truck patterns rather than those of pedestrians, street cars, trains, and boats. Not since the Federal period has the city experienced such a convulsion.

New Haven's redevelopment has since been much publicized and emulated, and like most pioneers it has also been increasingly criticized. It has suffered from its own precocity, revealing by experience some of the pitfalls of hopeful early postwar thinking. In the two decades since, America has learned to question the role of the superhighway in the city, as well as the obliteration of established neighborhoods in the name of slum clearance and the destruction of 19th-century architecture in the name of modernity.

In New Haven today redevelopment is controversial. While some complain because the Agency has not been resilient enough in responding to experience and changing attitudes, others complain because completion drags and businesses die in the meantime. One thing however is certain: New Haven is a major demonstration of postwar American urban renewal, conducted on a high level.

TOPOGRAPHICAL NOTE

New Haven was laid out in the form of a large square divided into nine smaller squares—the central one reserved as common land—with a tenth square going off at a diagonal to meet the harbor. This compelling diagram is recognized today as one of the earliest and most important in American planning history. This is not to say that it is unique as is sometimes claimed, for the grid with central square is a commonplace of European planning and had in fact already tentatively appeared in New England: New Haven added little that was new. But what it did was perhaps more important. It summed up a decade of trial and error in an unfaltering diagram of great scale and brought it to its final lucid conclusion. Far from being unique, its importance lies in the fact that this is the classic statement of the Puritan town.

The city was set on a great plain bounded by rivers and rock ridges. Surrounding the square of the town, a starburst of radial roads ran out across the plain, straight as arrows. One went to the mill, two went to the bridges over the West and Mill Rivers (US 1 and I 91 today still set their courses by these river crossings). But chiefly the radial roads gave access to outlots, dividing the plain into long radial wedges which in turn were subdivided into private fields.

A glance at the map in the front of the book will show that the colonial radial roads are still in use today and have provided the armature on which the city has been built.

Fields were laid in strips *across* the radial wedges. Later, when the city began to grow, the boundaries between fields tended to become streets, and as fields were of different sizes and their boundary lines were discontinuous from one wedge to the next, this gave rise to the curious spiderweb street pattern that has made modern New Haven a city that even its own inhabitants have trouble circumnavigating.

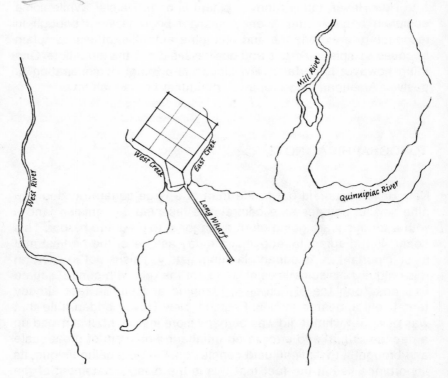

Originally the town stood by the harbor (a fact that today is often forgotten as the shoreline is increasingly filled and moved farther out—see Itineraries B and H). It was placed as close to the water as firm ground would allow and wedged into the angle of two creeks, giving maximum exposure of streets to waterways. Docks were built in the creeks. The little channel of the creeks crossed the mud flats to join the main channel far out in the harbor, and out there ships were unloaded by lighter.

The creeks were Main Street. The best merchants' houses were built along them, and all the daily life of the town plied up and down them in canoes and shallops. At their confluence, at the end of the 17th century, the first harborside wharf was built, becoming in time the Long Wharf, which by 1815 had been extended all the way across the flats to reach the channel. Around this point the economic life of the city revolved. In the 19th century railroads converged here, and the Long Wharf continued to play a vital part until the ocean-going vessels of modern times, with their deeper draft, made it obsolete. In 1949 the farther side of the harbor was dredged, and the Long Wharf was buried under the fill.

The creeks have left a more lasting mark. The West Creek from the earliest colonial times had been a place of tanneries, and tanneries and shoemaking continued to function in the area through the 19th century, giving their name to Morocco Street—later called Oak Street. Perhaps because of the tanneries and the marshes, this early became a poor quarter, and when the creek was filled in in 1875 it soon developed into a slum. The whole neighborhood was obliterated and redeveloped in 1959, and nothing now remains of Oak Street. But the West Creek, like a ghostly presence, continues to function in the life of the city much as it always has, serving as the channel for the Oak Street Connector.

The East Creek, and State Street beside it, remained important well into the 19th century (I 48). In 1825 it became the bed of the Farmington Canal, and in 1847 the canal in turn became the bed of a railroad, the second line in the city. This road in time became the main line of the consolidated system connecting New York, Boston, and Hartford. Thus, like the West Creek, the ghostly presence of the East Creek continues to impose its ancient course on the modern city.

Functionally, New Haven began in effect with two centers. The lower town along the creeks and harbor was the center of daily activity and economic energy, while in the upper town the square reserved as common land became the institutional center. Called the Market Place, it was used for the meeting house, town meetings, military drill, and other public functions (Itinerary I). Later, when Yale College was built, it too was on the Market Place (Itinerary J).

When the town began to grow, this duality at first increased, and throughout the 18th century the upper town around the Market Place remained sparsely inhabited and remote while wealth and fashion and urban density developed on the creeksides and waterfront—along State Street, George Street, and Meadow. It was the inspired and vigorous planning of the Federal period that finally integrated the city into the shape we know today, consolidating the Market Place—which began to be called the Green—and its surrounding streets into both institutional and functional center, and unifying the city at last around a single core. The organization of functions that then took place has to a large extent served ever since. The area south and east of the Green became downtown, Yale came to occupy an increasing part of the north and west, fine houses were built across the top of the Green, and behind them the city's most fashionable neighborhood spread northward (Itineraries K and L). By 1835 the Green had become the undisputed psychological center, and the corner of Church and Chapel had become the crossroads of the city, as it still is. State Street and the lower town gradually developed as the wholesale district, and the waterfront disappeared behind railroad yards, docks, and warehouses.

When growth beyond the original town began, it came in four major waves. The first was immediate. Within one generation both creeks had been bridged and new streets had been laid on the far banks.

The second wave began before the Revolution and corresponds to the city's second maritime era. Its main thrust was to the east along the shore, where fine merchants' houses were built facing the harbor and new streets were ambitiously projected behind them. By 1775 this area had been tellingly named the New Township (Itinerary N).

The third wave, reflecting the euphoria of the Canal Age, came with explosive force. In the hinterland two new towns crystallized— Fair Haven on the Quinnipiac River and Westville on the West River (Itineraries O and F). The city itself burst its bounds on all sides, forming a loose circle of satellite centers on its edges. Of these the New Township, blest with the canal, was the most vigorous, and its merchant owners began to think of it almost as a rival community, creating Wooster Square as their own counterpart of the Green. The canal as it turned out was short-lived, but it was quickly replaced by railroads, the first (1839) coming down from Hartford along the Mill River to meet the steamboat pier, the second (1847) following the canal. With two railroads, the steamboat, and the Long Wharf, the New Township swiftly developed as New Haven's main manu-facturing center.

Besides the New Township, three other principal clusters formed: to the southwest, the area across the West Creek (Itinerary H); to the west, the area now called the West Village (Itinerary G); and to the northeast, the Orange Street area (Itinerary L). All were much alike in makeup: self-contained village structures, each with its own rich and its own poor, its own broad base of small tradesmen and artisans, its own manufactories, and in time its own churches. Today the West Village, Orange Street, and the New Township still remain as examples of the tightly meshed urban mix that a pedestrian society creates.

On the fringes of this new growth ring, from the 1820s on, we hear of a number of darkietowns and, as the first Irish arrived to dig the canal, shantytowns: New Guinea and Slineyville in the New Township, Poverty Square on Whalley Avenue (F 4), Sodom Hill across the West Creek (H 16). At the same time, outside of town a new phenomenon appeared: the rural estate.

The rural estate had its origins in New Haven in the latter part of the 18th century, when a combination of romanticism and wealth began to open people's eyes to the beauty of the scenery surrounding the city—the drama of the great red rocks presiding over the plain, the long radiant harbor, and the arcadian charm of the rivers winding through salt meadows. Men of wealth began buying up large properties and retiring to lead the lives of gentlemen farmers, while at the same time laying out their grounds with a sharp eye to future development when the city should grow out to them. Examples spanning a century are Raynham (H 47), Sachem's Wood (K), Edgewood (F 28), and Lucerne (E 2).

The fourth and last wave of expansion occurred at the end of the century. Although the horse car had come in the '60s, its real impact was not apparent until the industrial boom of the '90s. Acres of new streets were built in the next two decades, filling the Howard Avenue area to the southwest (Itinerary H), the Sherman Avenue area to the west (Itinerary G), the Winchester Triangle to the northwest (Itinerary M), the Prospect Street, Whitney Avenue, and outer Orange Street areas to the north (Itineraries K, E, L), and Westville to the west (Itinerary F).

These developments differed from the earlier village complexes, reflecting a different society. The city by now was being physically changed by the new industrial scale and its blighting impact on the urban environment, and at the same time the once nearly homogeneous population was being changed (and threatened) by massive new waves of cheap foreign labor. A major regrouping of functions and people took place, in which the old self-contained pedestrian village clusters began to be replaced by separate zoning of working and dormitory areas, connected by public transportation; and in which the class or national or ethnic enclave began to replace the old social mix.

New wealth produced an upward social rush, and immigrants of the second generation from the New Township and Oak Street leap-frogged over the earlier growth ring to new rows of solid two-family houses in streetcar suburbs sprouting up on former rural estates. Patterns are not precise, but generally speaking the Irish went east and the Germans went west while the old town-born families went north. Later the Italians followed the Irish to the east, and Central European Jews followed the Germans to the west.

The town of the canal days was left to become the home of each new wave of incoming foreigners, and by 1900 three slums were well defined: Oak Street and the Hill (Jewish), the New Township (Italian), Dixwell Avenue (black). Since then all three have spread, forming a middle band which, except for the north corridor, almost surrounds the old colonial center, now filled by Yale and downtown. Beyond, the outmost band is still the territory of the middle classes. This pattern reverses the earlier one, in which the rich held the center and the poor were on the fringe.

In 1800 the built-up part of town covered about a third of a square mile. In 1950 it covered about 65 times that area, and, except for the old common to the northwest (F 13), the city was nearly filled. Since 1950 there has been little growth but great change. It is too soon to assess the impact that redevelopment, the automobile, modern construction technology, and other forces of urban change will have on the shape of the city, but in some of the more redeveloped parts of New Haven today (Itineraries C, H, I, M, N) there are illuminating insights into a new urban scale, a new concept of the street as divider rather than connector, a new fragmentation of neighborhoods and functions into "projects," "complexes," and "centers" which suggest that the city of the future may have a markedly different form from the city of the past.

ABOUT THE ITINERARIES

Itineraries have been mapped in accordance with the city's own patterns, not with a view to what can be covered in a set time. As a result, because New Haven grew on a spoke plan, many of the itineraries are radial salients, which in some cases are quite long and have been planned more with a view to driving than walking.

The tours cover a broad mix of the city scene. This guide is not the traditional kind that concentrates on the historic sights and screens out everything else. Rather it is an attempt to take New Haven architecture as the product of an urban community—not just the landmarks but also the everyday things, not just the work of big-name architects but also the rows of anonymous buildings that provide the scenery of urban life. It is an attempt to look at the city itself, and to notice some of the tides of urban change that have brought certain things to pass in certain places. Some of the itineraries go to rather ordinary places—in their very ordinariness is their historic eloquence; two or three others go to places that are sad or frightening. The casual sightseer looking for a Sunday afternoon walk should read the captions of the itineraries first and choose accordingly.

Calling the tours "itineraries" is a sentimental salute to Ezra Stiles (1727–95), who was one of Yale's greatest presidents and whose *Itineraries* and other writings show him also to have been one of America's greatest sightseers, one of the earliest and surely one of the most inquisitive. Stiles was followed in the presidency by Timothy Dwight (1752–1817), who was another of Yale's most important presidents and also, as it happens, another great sightseer. Perhaps it is to the inquiring eye and perceptive mind of these two influential men that New Haven owes the highly developed urbanist sensibility that made it one of the best-planned cities in America in the 19th century.

Urban Design. The term "urban design" in the title is used loosely, not confined to formally planned spaces but including a variety of vernacular street effects. Urban "context" might have been a better word. Work of this sort is hard to isolate or photograph and so it is seldom given a separate heading in the text but is referred to in many places. These side glances have been indexed as far as possible.

DATES

Building is a slow process, and in published architectural dates there is often a discrepancy of a year or more. Dates given here, where known, are roughly for the start of construction (Yale dates however follow official University listings).

With two exceptions, no date is given that has not been searched and documented. Traditionally accepted dates have been reexamined and in a number of cases changed. The two exceptions are: (1) Yale buildings, all of which have already been meticulously recorded in university publications, most recently in *Yale, A Pictorial History,* by Reuben A. Holden (Yale University Press, 1967); and (2) the city's scant half dozen Colonial buildings, which have long been assigned dates that seem authoritative, although the records on which they were based are no longer available.

New Haven city records have turned out to be discouragingly inadequate. By an incredible feat of bureaucratic stupidity, the 19th-century tax records—that mine of historical information—were thrown away eight years ago. The building records are woefully scant. With the exception of a lone surviving early ledger, permits do not begin until 1894 and are not indexed (hence are all but unusable) until 1905. Even thereafter many are sketchy. Early ones are sloppily written, and the personality of the harried clerk, eager to go home to his dinner, emerges clearly: when an out-of-town architect turns up whose name threatens to be difficult to spell, it is apt to be omitted.

In the absence of these two prime sources, one is thrown back on land records, maps, and the City Directory—a cumbersome and not always precise process. As a result there is much that will never be known about New Haven's building history.

Fortunately the inadequacy of the city records is partly compensated by a good series of 19th-century maps. While not yielding a precise date, they will often yield a decade. Supplemented by the Directory and, with luck, a deed, we can usually come fairly close. In what follows, dates preceded by "c" have been documented within three or four years either way.

A-B-C

The Modern Motorways: I 91, I 95, and the Oak Street Connector

A 55-mph overview. Drivers who want to look at the buildings listed may get off onto frontage roads bordering both B and C.

A   I 91, from the North. Opened 1966.

Interstate 91 enters the city along the old route from Hartford and
the north, which came down the Quinnipiac Valley then curved under
East Rock to cross the Mill River at what is now State Street. The
bridge there was the only crossing over the river until the turn of the
19th century. The present bridge crosses at almost exactly the same
spot.

Raised high above the streets, I 91 gives the driver a rare sense of
the topography of the city—the ancient shape of the earth that lies
under the tissue of streets and houses spreading over it. From this
height the basic anatomy reappears. East Rock can once again be
felt as the presiding presence it must have been for centuries before
the plain was built up and the views closed off, and both rock and
waterways briefly reenter the modern consciousness as the great
historic determinants of urban form. Below the bridge, the road
crosses the New Township which was the city's early manufacturing
center, now partly derelict, partly redeveloped. At the intersection

with I 95, swinging to the right, the eye reaches out suddenly over the top of the city to the heights of Allingtown and takes in part of the encircling palisade that forms the bowl in which the town was originally laid. In the 19th century these great headlands made New Haven famous for its majestic scenery.

B I 95, The Connecticut Turnpike. Opened 1958.

I 95 cuts across the bottom of the city along the harbor, on landfill that lies half a mile beyond the original shoreline. The new road, in a sudden brilliant passage of air and light and wind and clouds, has in effect given the harbor back to the people of the city—the once-famous harbor that the 19th century loved so well but which in modern times had been lost behind a barricade of tracks and industry. Today's delight however may be brief, for a new band of fill is planned, a new retreat of the harbor. An island with high- and medium-rise apartments, stores, motel, and marina is proposed.

Here is the new world of Redevelopment: a showcase of industries for the traveler to see as he speeds by New Haven. It is the modern city advertising itself, an imposing lineup of architect-designed factories and commercial buildings in which landscaping and architectural standards have been fostered by the city. This is the Redevelopment Agency's Long Wharf Project, built on made land that covers the wharf which from colonial times down through the 19th century was the center of New Haven's economic life. The site was once the confluence of the East and West Creeks with the harbor, where all the traffic of the town came together. The harbor was dredged in 1949 to make it usable by larger ocean-going tankers and encourage a revival of the port. On the resulting fill, the State Highway Department built the turnpike, and the city brilliantly seized the opportunity to create a motor-age industrial park on its new front doorstep.

B 1 Gant Shirtmakers, 40 Sargent Drive, 1970. Associated Construction and Engineering Company, San Francisco. Landscaped, well groomed, and of inexpensive construction —the model modern, suburban factory.

Next door to the west, **Albie Booth Boys Club** manages the transition from the city to the open road (1970, Davis Cochran Miller Baerman Noyes). The supergraphics are scaled to the highway while the low corner entrance, facing two ways, relates the building to its urban neighborhood (illustrated H 31).

B 2 C. W. Blakeslee & Sons, 90 Sargent Drive, 1966. Orr, deCossy, Winder and Associates. A later addition extended the facade to the south and added a new structure behind it, now being fitted for Southern Connecticut Community College. Symptomatic of the automobile age, the location of the community college is remote from all sectors of the community, identifying itself with the interstate thruway and a parking lot.

B 3 Sargent & Co., 100 Sargent Drive, 1963. Orr, deCossy, Winder and Associates. The Sargent hardware company was established in New Haven in the early 1860s, on a tract covering a large area in the New Township, now partly under I 95. Along with Winchester it became one of the city's biggest industries and today is one of its historic institutions, reaching back to New Haven's heyday as an early manufacturing center.

150 Sargent Drive: **Community Health Care Center,** 1970, Office of Bruce Porter Arneill. 222 Sargent Drive: the **Long Wharf Market,** with the **Long Wharf Theater** by Granbery, Cash and Associates, 1965. Combining a market and a theater was one of Redevelopment's most imaginative and successful ideas. Opposite: the stub of the **Long Wharf** sticks out into the water. The wharf goes back to 1682 when Thomas Trowbridge received permission to build the first dock outside of the creeks. By the time of the Revolution the wharf had been extended but was still short of reaching the channel. Ships anchored offshore and were unloaded by lighter. Not until the Federal period was the wharf finally built out to deep water, a difficult feat that was hailed as one of the great events of the day in New Haven. The hero of the undertaking was a laborer named William Lanson, who scowed the stones down from East Rock; he later said that he had done it to show that a black man could do what a white man could not.

B 4 Armstrong Rubber Co., 500 Sargent Drive, 1968. Marcel Breuer with Robert F. Gatje, New York. Supported on 758 piles in the mud flats of the harbor, this building separates the company's administrative and research functions with an open space, the upper section hung from giant trusses. The deep modeling was designed to create an instantly striking image of light and shadow when seen from a speeding car.

C The Oak Street Connector. Opened 1959.

The West Creek ran under the present road, cutting through salt meadows. Tanneries were built here in the earliest times, and over the next 200 years the area became a leather and shoemaking district, giving its name to Morocco Street, its main thoroughfare. But tanneries do not make good company, and the neighborhood degenerated early and became a poor and troubled place. Although the creek was filled in the 1870s, the declivity continued to act as a barrier, separating the world of Morocco Street from the more elevated society across the cut. The town fathers hopefully changed the name to Oak Street, but its character lived on, and by the 1930s Oak Street was the city's major slum—a dense immigrant neighborhood now nostalgically remembered for its pushcarts, junk shops, and Jewish markets. In 1959 its social ills were ended (or at any rate moved) by burying it under the new highway (for the creekside neighborhood see Itinerary H).

The Connector is the front door to the city, and a massive effort has gone into demolition and redevelopment along it in an attempt to replace decay with an image of prosperity and progress—a program that has been attacked by citizens' groups both for its destruction of ethnic neighborhoods and for its sundering of the urban fabric with barrier roads. As a design matter, the scenery of the Connector shows how difficult it is to achieve urban form when every structure must be surrounded by parking lots. Some of the city's best new buildings have been built here, but as a group they do not coalesce.

The Connector at present is a dead end, but a swathe of demolition stretching to Boulevard marks its future course. Conceived in the first flush days of postwar highway planning, it was designed as a link in a grand ring-road system, its objective being to connect with Derby Avenue. The route beyond Boulevard has not been announced but if it is ever completed it must go through Edgewood Park and thence either along the park or on the still open highlands of the western ridge. The State Highway Department at one time planned 12 lanes but has since come down to 8. Many citizens are questioning the need for any.

The course of the Connector, as it makes its way through the city, is being systematically used by the Redevelopment Agency for such showcase projects as are at its disposal: the overall program shows public schools, housing, and apartments, as well as commercial buildings, located along the banks of the road rather than inland in the more sheltered and central parts of their various neighborhoods. This creates a facade of modernity which, when finished, will stretch the whole way across the city with almost no break. A parking facility utilizing the air rights is to be built over the Connector at York Street, with shops on the lower level (Orr, deCossy, Winder and Associates).

C 1 Tower One, 1969. ML/TW Moore-Turnbull. Using colored air-conditioning units as an ornamental motif is one way of forestalling the ragged facades that result when tenants put them in later. The fenestration pattern articulates the form, a band of windows at the top acting as a cornice.

Many buildings seen from the Connector belong to other tours. Beyond Moore's tower: **Church Street South housing,** also by Moore (H 37). Close to the road, the horizontal brown slabs: **Department of Police Service,** Orr, deCossy, Winder and Associates (H 40). North of the road: the first large building, of pre-rusted steel, is the **Coliseum,** Roche and Dinkeloo (I 23); the brown tower next to it is the **Knights of Columbus Building,** also Roche and Dinkeloo (I 22). **Parking garage** by Paul Rudolph (I 17).

C 2 Yale Laboratory of Epidemiology and Public Health, 1963. Philip Johnson, N.Y., and Office of Douglas Orr. This building suavely dominates the scene, maintaining a sense of urban form and dignity along the brash speedway.

Beyond it the red brick cluster around a patch of green is the **Yale Medical School.** Next, in buff brick and green glass: **Memorial Unit, Yale-New Haven Hospital,** 1951, Office of Douglas Orr (H 15).

C 3 Crawford Manor, 1965. Paul Rudolph. An instance of Rudolph's brilliant sense of site, the powerful bunched verticals of this building (designed as housing for the elderly) control the view from far down the road. The design is subtly scaled for both the long view and the short, and it is rewarding to approach it from afar and come right up under its small balconies.

Across the Connector, the brown tower on Howard Avenue is more **elderly housing** (1973, Herbert S. Newman Associates).

C 4   Carriage House, 19 Howe Street. Remodeled 1971, Environmental Design Group. A derelict barn, probably of the '80s, stunningly given new life as an office.

C 5   Trade Union Plaza, 1968. Victor Christ-Janer, New Canaan. To relieve the bleakness of the basic low-cost housing rectangle and to establish a sympathetic note with the domestic architecture of the neighborhood, Christ-Janer developed a special concrete block with a textured surface like a shingle. Sinking the garages below grade and partly screening them with knolly landscaping makes a tidy solution to this perennial problem.

C 6   Waverly and George Street Housing, 1972. Ahlstrom and Lee. Designed in the image of a village, with its own community facilities at the center, this public housing detaches itself from the neighborhood around it rather than serving as a cohesive element in the urban fabric. Forms are softened by clapboards stained a pleasant natural brown with cream-colored trim and by congenial open spaces, all conspicuously well maintained.

D The Middletown Turnpike: State Street

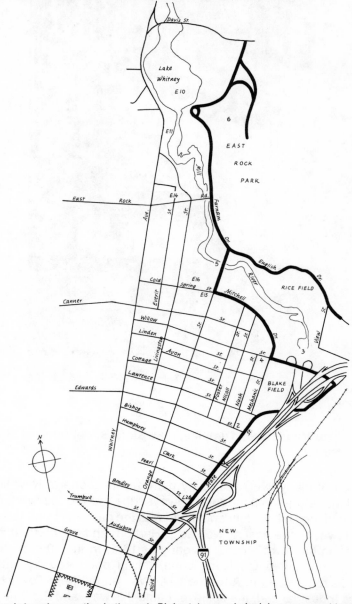

This itinerary is largely an outing in the park. Birdwatchers and picnickers may want to skip the lower part. Those who prefer late Victorian houses to urban waste and subantiques will have more fun taking the northern route up Orange Street (Itinerary L).

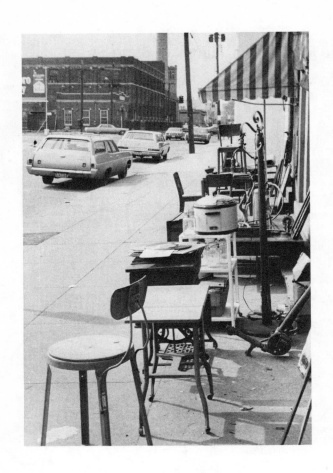

D **The Middletown Turnpike, now State Street north of Grove Street.**

A road of many lives and many names, this is one of New Haven's most ancient and important highways—the road to the Neck Bridge, which in the first century and a half was the gateway to all the shoreline towns of the east as well as to Hartford and the north. It is mentioned in the town records as early as 1641. In the 19th century the road, then called the Neck Lane, lay in open country with poor farms strung along it. After the Civil War, as the New Township became industrialized, the spillover came this way, and the lane began to build up with tenements and the trackside culture that grew along the railroad. In the 20th century, as Route 5, it became the truck route to the north. Today it is a street of minor industries, gas stations, neighborhood shops, small dusty antique stores, and junk dealers.

D 1 The Olive Street Triangle. A reference to the Neck Lane in 1825 gives "Negro" as an alternative name, and this may be a clue to the character of the neighborhood which by then had grown up on the outer edge of town where the lane is joined by Olive Street. Most of the houses here were small and landlord-owned and, from the names of tenants that occasionally turn up in land deeds, a black community—or at any rate a black and white community—can be guessed. Some names are French, implying a West Indian origin, others are surely those of freed American slaves. Some of these men were prominent locally, and it is possible that the Olive Street triangle was a center of the black upper class. Scipio Augustus for example was a leader of the black community, a founder of the African Church, and New Haven representative at a national antislavery convention. He was well enough off to become the owner of the house he was living in, buying it in 1829 from his landlord, Ithiel Town. Similarly, Eli Pierre bought a private lot in the Grove Street Cemetery—surely not the purchase of a poor man—and Alexander and Sarah Dubois have gravestones which may still be seen there. The Dubois's furthermore belonged to a family who owned a farm farther along the lane. This glimpse of land ownership and agriculture somewhat modifies the stereotype of the black man as servant and laborer in this period.

Of the original cluster of houses, only one is still standing—a neat, small house built of brick, dating probably from the 1820s.

On the corner of Humphrey Street: **Mobil Gas Station,** one of several variations on a basic design made for Mobil by Eliot Noyes. Intended for mass use and quick sales identification, the design formula provides considerable differences between models: compare this relatively simple one with the theatrical umbrellas of the highway model on Whalley Avenue (F). This urbane design, enhanced by the addition of a brick wall defining the corner, is a hopeful sign that some-day gas stations may be able to become part of the urban scene without disrupting it.

D 2 Firehouse 19, 19 Edwards Street, 1873; remodeled 1974, John A. Matthews, partner, Gilbert Switzer and Associates. The city has recently been putting old fire houses up for bids for adaptive re-use. Here is a successful example of the marriage of Victorian and modern architecture—welcome proof that old buildings are still important urban assets.

D 3 The Mill River. Pause on the Willow Street causeway, or scramble underneath it to the natural ground level where the river runs, and look north to East Rock. Victorian poets and artists were fond of this spot: a painting by George Durrie shows the meadows at haying time, with the great crag of the rock rising above the winding river. This was one of the city's enchanted places—as early as the 18th century an enraptured young Yale tutor wrote about a picnic here. He described the awesome rock and below it a meadow and a beautiful river. " 'Twas on a plain of about a mile, most beautiful walking. The cool clouds made it more so. Boys were provided to take along the baskets, etc. . . . We took tea, danced to the flute." The riverland became East Rock Park in 1880 (D 6). Little was done to change it—dirt footpaths threaded along the banks, and it remained a neglected refuge for birds, birdwatchers, fishermen, and lovers until after World War I.

In 1921 land at the east end along View Street was filled for Rice Field (compare the sensitive shaping and border landscaping of this early playing field with later models designed by the bulldozer, for example at Beaver Ponds and East Shore Park). In 1933 land below Willow was filled for Blake Field. In 1956 the corner of Orange Street was taken by the city for a high school and parking lot. At about the same time fill was dumped along Mitchell Drive for parking lots for nearby factories. Early in the '60s came I 91, and the Mill River was chosen by the state as the route for the great connector to link I 91 with a projected ring-road system (furious citizens took this one to court and won, but the ramp still remains, pointing up the valley). At present the west bank from Willow to the high school is being filled for an "athletic complex," and a huge graceless structure on Blake Field is being built for a year-round skating rink. In all these respects the Mill River shows what is happening in many of the city parks. Even aside from thefts for schools and highways, it exemplifies the conflict in park planning today between the recreationists and the naturalists, highlighting the harsh fact that modern recreation can be as destructive of the natural environment as modern development. Work so far on the so-called athletic complex consists of one of the biggest blacktop parking areas in the city, an almost continuous desert from Willow to Cold Spring. (For the College Woods see E 16.)

D 4 East Rock Community School, Willow and Nash Streets, 1972. Edward Larrabee Barnes, New York. A symmetrical plan is used to express the fact that this is two schools in one building—a grade school on one side, middle school on the other. Characteristic Barnes shapes, with sharp edges and seamless planes. The paucity of windows may be an aspect of the design or it may be a reflection of the city's growing problem of vandalism and broken glass. Several ranges of fine old sycamores have been saved. These, with grassy yards and a delightful promenade along the back, give a light touch to an austere design.

D 5 Orange Street Bridge, 1920. A piece of open-air sculpture, designed as part of the parkscape. Notice the elegance of the masonry. Upstream, the iron bridge at East Rock Road makes a single slim arc.

On the corner of Orange Street and Mitchell Drive: **Wilbur Cross High School,** 1956, Schilling and Goldbecker. The decade after World War II was one of architectural confusion. The building techniques and the architectural imagery of the past had been knocked out by 20 years of war and depression, but the techniques and the language of a new architecture had not yet replaced them. Modern architecture was neither liked nor understood by most people. The city accepted it because it was cheap and, so it seemed, effortless—you just ordered it by the yard and you laid it out any way you wanted and called it "functionalism." It is against this background that Wilbur Cross and Hillhouse High Schools must be seen—identical plans, both planting a large crude structure in a well-knit residential neighborhood, both cynically taking a big piece of a city park for the purpose. The architects are not to be blamed for the impoverishment of the civic spirit which the buildings express. (For Hillhouse High see F 14).

D 6 East Rock Park, 1880—. Donald Grant Mitchell. The acquisition of East Rock Park was the first step in the creation of a city park system. With its spectacular site it dramatized the idea and caught the imagination both of the public and of potential donors of land, and within the next few years the main outline of the park system had taken shape—a ring of still wild highlands and wetlands (superb as scenery and cheap as real estate) lying around the rim of the city. East Rock Park was designed by Mitchell in 1882 and laid out in the next few years—conceived as a natural landscape with walks and carriage drives designed around a series of long views, now of one side, now of another, and growing in breathtaking expanse as one climbed, interspersed with the nearby charm of woodland scenery. Mitchell furnished it with a scheme of woodland decoration—rustic rails, benches, shelters of bark-covered wood, and walls and curbing of beautifully wrought traprock and fieldstone. Since then the basic layout has had few major changes beyond the widening and paving of the roads, the substitution of a few ugly metal guard rails for rustic posts, and a pervasive shift from the world of the Victorian nature-lover to an automobile environment. At the summit you are met by a radio tower. The **Soldiers' and Sailors' Monument** was designed in 1886 by Moffat and Doyle of New York; a considerable structural feat, it was built by Smith and Sperry. **Picnic shelter,** c1950, by Robert T. Coolidge. East Rock Park has many trails and more points of interest than can be mentioned here. An excellent booklet, prepared by the East Rock Neighborhood Association, is available at the Peabody Museum, the Public Library, and various bookstores and Orange Street shops. (Photograph c1890.)

E The Hartford Turnpike: Whitney Avenue

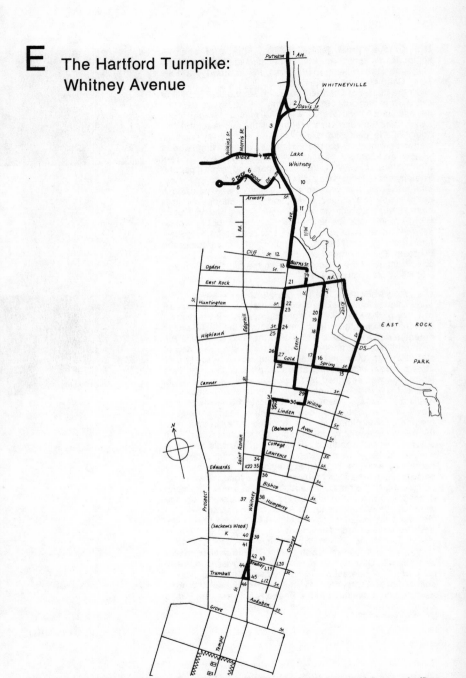

Top-level residential, mostly of the 1890s and 1920s, now going to rented flats and offices. A long tour, best done in a car with occasional stopoffs. Or drive the whole avenue first to get the sweep of it, then go back and walk wherever seems inviting.

E The Hartford Turnpike, now Whitney Avenue.

The Hartford Turnpike, chartered in 1798 by James Hillhouse, followed the route of one of the colonial radial highways. With only
one break, where it crossed the Mill River, it continued this undeviat-
ing line all the way to Hartford, marching over hill and dale like a
Roman road. It was described as "a wonderful and curious work"
because of its high crown, and people came to look at it as they later
went to see the first railroad.

At that time almost the entire northern corridor of the city, from
Grove Street past Whitneyville, belonged to two men—Hillhouse
and his friend Eli Whitney. Aside from profits from tolls, the turnpike
clearly had other uses, opening up an immense tract of their com-

bined real estate as well as providing access to town for Whitney's armory on the falls of the Mill River.

For most of the 19th century these two families held the land, dividing it into great estates and, as time went on, smaller estates: Whitney's opposite the armory and Hillhouse's running down the west side of the Avenue. The east side of the Avenue became the property of a younger Hillhouse's brother-in-law, also confusingly named Whitney—Henry in this case. Near what is now Cottage Street, Henry Whitney built Belmont, a Grecian villa by A. J. Davis and one of New Haven's now legendary houses. Farther down was Sachem's Wood, the estate of Hillhouse's son, another now legendary house (Itinerary K).

The turnpike became in time one of the city's finest streets—an avenue of splendid proportions lined with great trees, forming a processional entrance into the city from the north. It remained parkland until the horsecar arrived in the '90s, when the estates began to break up into building lots and lower Whitney became the town's most fashionable new neighborhood. Its desirability faded after 1900—perhaps when the trolley replaced the horsecar and the best real estate retreated up Prospect Hill (Itinerary K)—and the later houses of the Avenue, from Willow out, became less pretentious. But as a group they maintained the tone. The Avenue should be experienced as an avenue, and is worth a drive.

E 1 Whitneyville. The village grew up early in the 19th century in connection with Eli Whitney's armory and remained a hamlet until the horsecar and the trolley brought the expanding city northward in a rush, transforming it into a middle-class suburb after 1900.

Whitneyville Congregational Church, 1834. This design—recessed porch with two columns *in antis*—was one of the favorites of the American Greek Revival, introduced by Ithiel Town in 1828 in New Haven's Third Congregational Church. Other examples were built in New Haven, but this is the only one remaining—a strong, composed building, with more sophistication than is often found in village churches. The little dome that now tops the steeple does not seem original but is at least as old as 1900. The present dangling effect of the inner pilasters results from the removal of once-broader steps. Enlarged with pulpit recess, 1867, Rufus G. Russell.

At the foot of the lane a **suspension footbridge** crosses the lake. *Demolished 1975.*

E 2 Frederick Grave House, 20 Davis Street, 1906. Brown and VonBeren. Additions 1961, Eero Saarinen and Associates; 1968, Kevin Roche, John Dinkeloo and Associates. Named Lucerne, this was one of the rash of turn-of-the-century castles which took advantage of the superb scenery on the outer edges of the city. The relation of house to grounds and of both to the lake is fortunately still preserved, for, as the romantic name implies, this was central to the design. At one time one of the towers was capped with a pointed roof like a spire, giving a more active skyline. Now the architectural office of Roche and Dinkeloo, the remodeling of the front rooms is deftly understated. Under white wall covering, the original paneling is preserved.

E 3 1108 Whitney Avenue, c1848. The upper part of this curious building was once a separate house standing across the street. It was moved here after World War II, hoisted in the air, and embedded in additions. To see what it looked like before the ascension, there is a near-twin still on terra firma out near Edgewood (F 31). Like E 21, this house was probably once connected with the armory. The porches are much alike, the usual leaves of the Greek Revival capital transformed into extravagant plumes.

E 4 Blake Road. A suburban classic of the 1920s and '30s. Those interested in the scenery of streets will find a comparison with Deepwood Drive interesting. Shown here: **no. 115,** 1931, Jacob Weinstein.

E 5 Deepwood Drive. This is a young street, built up after 1925 on an old estate and today one of New Haven's main enclaves of modern houses. It shows a change in urbanist attitudes between the 19th and 20th centuries—in the conscious effort of the road to appear rural rather than urban, in the departure from building lines. The house now is oriented toward the rear view rather than the street: designed to *see,* not to *be seen.* This would have shocked such an urbanist as James Hillhouse, to whom the function of a house was to create a street. Here every lot is a design unto itself. It is a difficult discipline, for landscaping is required to do some of the work of architecture, and much depends on how driveways and parking lots are handled. The anomaly of Deepwood Drive is that while the modern houses are more striking, the landscaping of the old houses carries the street. Shown here is **no. 129,** 1963, Sidney T. Miller.

E 6   49 Deepwood Drive, 1970. Paul Mitarachi. A disarmingly modest front, scaled to the narrow road. The house should be seen from both sides to appreciate its complex composition and intricate relationship with the great trees and gorge behind.
  40 Deepwood Drive, 1951. Robert T. Coolidge. One of New Haven's earliest modern houses. **45 Bayberry Road, 1956, Vincent Amore.**

E 7   The Connecticut Cottage, Philadelphia Centennial Exposition, 1876. Donald Grant Mitchell & David R. Brown. Whatever became of the Connecticut Cottage? A much-discussed exhibit, it was one of the few state buildings at the Exposition that attempted to evoke America's past, its interior detail and picturesque outline designed in a rustic style vaguely described as Colonial. Since then it was first reputedly rebuilt on the Hudson, later reported at Long Branch, New Jersey; recent word around New Haven is that it is right here on top of Mill Rock—a myth for which no source has yet been discovered. Outbuildings and walls at least suggest that the estate that was laid out here, probably in the 1870s, was designed in Mitchell's rustic style, but the main house (not open to the public) bears no resemblance to the Connecticut Cottage.

E 8   120 Deepwood Drive, 1961. Paul Mitarachi. The south side, hanging on the edge of Mill Rock over a spectacular view of the city, is as sheer and dynamic as the rock itself. Inside, a design of many levels responds to the vertical site.

E 9   121 Deepwood Drive, 1960. Howard Barnstone. The eye is drawn from the street right through the house into the woods beyond—an inviting glimpse of another world.

E 10 Lake Whitney. The dam was built in 1860, creating the lake and New Haven's first water supply. This was a bold and apparently radical project, fathered by Eli Whitney, Jr., James Brewster, and others after the city had refused to have anything to do with it. The lake now covers part of the land of the Whitney armory and of the turnpike, which originally crossed the river here on New England's first covered bridge, designed by Ithiel Town and visible in the picture shown here by William Giles Munson. Also notice the armory and the workers' village.

E 11 Whitney Armory Site, 1798; Shed, pre-1825; Barn, c1810. Eli Whitney made industrial history with his cotton gin and with a revolutionary system of interchangeable parts introduced in his gun factory here on the Mill River. The shed shown in the photograph is the sole survivor of the early buildings, but excavations have recently been made by the National Park Service, and the site has been placed on the National Register. The armory was east of the turnpike, while workers' houses and a store stood along Armory Street. South of Armory Street the frame house that is still standing (much disguised) belonged to Whitney's own estate, which stretched from here to Cliff Street, and probably housed more workers. A bachelor until late in life, Whitney never built the mansion he planned, but his barn survives, neglected but still a superb example of the great ornamental barns of the gentry of the Federal period. Elegantly flush-boarded, with delicate lunette and moldings, it was a noble sight when new, its interior fittings a wondrous display of inventive gadgets; President Monroe, when making a state visit to the armory, was taken to see the barn as well. Connected with the armory was a quarry on East Rock, and the use of traprock as a building stone was promoted by Whitney and Hillhouse. Its sonorous hues of tan, ocher, and rust quickly became a distinguishing feature of New Haven architecture in the Federal and Greek Revival periods, used mainly in foundations. The wing on Whitney's barn is a good example of Federal masonry—sheer as a planed board. Other remains will be found around the site. Paths along the river provide pleasant walks.

E 12 Edgerton Park, formerly the Frederick Brewster Estate, 1910. Stephenson and Wheeler, New York. Mrs. Brewster is said to have told her husband that she would rather have a stone wall than diamonds. Result: the Koh-i-noor of walls. The house was demolished by the owner's orders when the estate was left to the city in 1963, but the grounds are still almost intact. The landscaping is distinguished. Note how ups and downs have been used to give an illusion of distances. The sweep of an English park is suggested by a single open slope, while a miniature ravine evokes a forest, and a little bridge across it, by its very smallness, seems high and giddy. Changes of light and shade, surprises, and a sense of discovery are provided, giving extraordinary range inside the limited world of the walls.

E 13   St. Thomas's Episcopal Church. Parish House, 1930; Church, 1938. Allen, Collens and Willis, Boston. This gray stone building seems a conscious part of the Edgerton landscape. With its square stone tower it looks like the parish church in the village at the foot of the great estate. Wide grounds and big trees still preserve its quality and today make St. Thomas's the gracious keynote of this whole end of the Avenue. (But surely there was some less unsightly way of adding a playground?)

E 14   Burns Street, Everit Street, East Rock Road, and the Mill River. On the border between the Whitney and Hillhouse land ran the old Rock Lane. Whitney's will specified that lots for workers be provided here, and a hamlet soon grew up. Few of the early houses remain, but small lots and a few white fences still give this pocket neighborhood a character distinct from the later blocks around it (shown here: **83 East Rock Road).** Today these quiet streets, though architecturally unassuming, are engaging examples of the semirural quality that was one of New Haven's most noted traits, as Dickens and others remarked. The great Rock looms up behind, and in winter this is one of the most dramatic approaches to it in the city.

The Mill River belongs to Itinerary D, but this is a lovely place to explore. Paths run along both banks, with an old iron footbridge upstream of East Rock Road.

E 15   Cold Spring Street from Orange to Livingston, 1904–07. Turn away from the painful sight of the school (D 5). On Cold Spring Street it is amusing to count the variations that an early developer, Charles T. Coyle, was able to achieve with a kit of interchangeable parts (for those with computer minds, there are more of these houses in surrounding streets —are any two identical?) A contemporary attributed the design to Grosvenor Atterbury. Possibly Atterbury supplied a model, but permits are issued to local men. Houses like this cost $4500–$5000. Well detailed, they are spatially graceful inside, with 12–14 rooms. Toward 1907 owners began adding "automobile houses" out back. The street was higher then than now (look at the park for the natural grade), and the houses sat more comfortably on their lots.

This row brings us to the edge of **Belmont,** the Henry Whitney estate, and from here on the development of the area is the story of Belmont's gradual disappearance. For more about Charles T. Coyle see E 28.

E 16   Livingston Street, north from Cold Spring. One of New Haven's prettiest streets, built mostly between 1910 and 1929. The houses exemplify the restraint of upper-class taste in this period, enhancing the fragile beauty of the park instead of overwhelming it as the '90s might have done. Still nominally Colonial, they show the radical change that took place in the Colonial Revival before World War I, correct historical reproduction taking the place of fantasy, finesse taking the place of size. The image in fact is no longer Colonial at all, but Federal. Shown here: **The College Woods,** once belonging to Yale, today one of the city's more arcadian patches of park, as yet unspoiled by improvements (but see what is now happening at the southeast corner).

E 17 244 Livingston Street, 1909–10. A cottage version of the Hendee house on the Avenue (E 22), lacking its great sweep but better preserved in detail. For another close relation see F 25.

280 Livingston Street, 1914, Aymar Embury II, New York: compare this house with E 19, both unabashed reproductions of the same model.

E 18 294 Livingston Street, 1916. Suave and sophisticated under its sheltering black roof, this house shows a fresh handling of a basically Georgian idea. An opulent door, curving brackets, stucco, and ornamental window treatment are deftly integrated to make a discreet but striking design.

E 19 340 Livingston Street, 1928. Dwight E. Smith. One of New Haven's best houses of the '20s and a climactic statement of the period: meticulously modeled on the Deming house of 1793 in Litchfield, exquisite in detail and reserved in expression. The mansion has been made to look smaller than it really is—a complete reversal of traditional aspiration. Note also how much this effect is achieved by the scale of the setting, the giant oaks in particular. Indeed the role of the oaks in the whole street is crucial. The Deming house was popular in New Haven; besides no. 280, there is a third version at 409 Humphrey Street.

E 20 370 Livingston Street, 1929. J. Frederick Kelly. This is the medium-sized, medium-priced counterpart of no. 340 —the model house of the 20th-century American suburb. Professedly Colonial Revival, it might more accurately be called Colonial Revival-Revival, for it is drawn closely from the Steinert house on Whitney Avenue of 20 years before (E 33).

396 Livingston Street, 1914, Leoni W. Robinson, with an elegant porch.

E 21 749 Whitney Avenue, 1848. Belonging to the hamlet that grew up around the armory (the owner is listed as George Mason, gunsmith), this was one of the few houses on the Avenue before the '90s. A small building with great presence, well kept today even to white paint and dark shutters, it is a perfect specimen of a design made popular by Henry Austin and built in many versions in the '40s—still classical in form but with the wide eaves and brackets that announce the new villa style. The lavishly carved capitals must have been some builder's specialty; compare E 3, F 31, N 39.

E 22 Abner Hendee House, 703 Whitney Avenue, 1900. Richard Williams. This was one of New Haven's most romantic houses and long a landmark of the upper Avenue. It was built in open country, empty fields behind running down to the river and the Rock. Like the classic country houses of the Shingle Style it was designed as part of the land, a design of horizontals. The great shadow of the porch was as mysterious and cool as a cave in the woods, and a porte-cochère carried the long line out into the grounds, holding the house close to the earth and terminating in a low pillar that seemed another part of nature—a tumble of stones. Shutters and diamond sash (a few remain out back) preserved horizontal continuity across the facade. Wood shingles gave the roof the texture of bark, and its color and trim were olive green—a contemporary used the word "moss-covered" to describe the effect. Today wide grounds and trees still recall the setting. The house itself is a lesson in how piecemeal loss of detail can end by losing the meaning of the design. Unscreened parking further breaks the spell. (Photograph 1937.)

E 23 First Church of Christ Scientist, 1950. Office of Douglas Orr. Set back from the street on the site of a Whitney granddaughter's house, the church preserves the memory of the country places that characterized the upper Avenue at the turn of the century. The long raised path is a brilliant device in this setting—formal and ceremonial but still a grassy part of the landscape.

Across the Avenue: **First Presbyterian Church,** 1966, John Dinkeloo.

E 24 Richard Everit House, 641 Whitney Avenue, 1866–67. The Everit family bought the upper promontory of the Belmont land, running back to "a new street" which in time was named Everit Street and sold off in lots. On the Avenue Richard Everit laid out his own estate and built a towered mansion. An old picture shows it standing in open country among fenced fields, a vivid sight with the red rock at its back. Little remains today of the once-celebrated gardens, but the house deserves a look. The filigree delicacy of the ornament and the sprightly finials dancing against the sky are the best examples in New Haven of the fine lacework of the '60s and '70s (compare G 50).

E 25 640 Whitney Avenue, 1912. Tapestry brick with raked joints, a contemporary account says, gives a suggestion of antiquity. Actually, with its clear massing and planar quality, the house seems consciously modern after the hectic design adventures of the preceding decades. In the wake of the Arts and Crafts movement, the tactile feeling for the quality of materials and workmanship is strong. Notice the elegant canopy. Architect, Richard Henry Dana, New York.

E 26   592 Whitney Avenue, 1902. Richard Williams. A contemporary magazine hailed this house as an example of the new trend toward simplicity and unpretentiousness. "It is in fact an English cottage," the writer says, praising it as "a most artistic residence." The cottage effect is best perceived from down the street, where the picturesque curve of the roof and the sloping form of the inglenook around the chimney can be seen. The shingles were originally stained dark red, and the balcony rail was wood.

E 27   591 Whitney Avenue, now the New Haven Woman's Club, c1909. A model statement of the Colonial Revival of the early 20th century. Compared with the '90s the outline is now firm and symmetrical and the whole design more sober, but the detail still plays with many different motifs—the language may be Georgian but the spirit of Queen Anne lingers on. Pilasters and trim were once white: they are the costume jewelry of the house and were painted to *show*.

Next door: Congregational **Church of the Redeemer,** 1949, Office of Douglas Orr.

E 28   Charles T. Coyle House, 569 Whitney Avenue, 1908–09. More turn-of-the-century Colonial—recognizably Georgian but with survivals from an earlier and more whimsical generation, such as the truncated Palladian windows. The side wings were originally open porches, the railing wrapping all around the front of the building, repeated on the balcony above. The grandiose portico deserves to be matched by an equally grand pair of trees.

Here we return to the country of Charles T. Coyle, and this lavish house is a fitting symbol of his career. Coyle began as one of an Irish clan active in the building trades in the old Third Ward—for his early days see H 22. Moving into real estate in the Hill, he made money and soon began to cast a speculative eye uptown. In 1904 he started the row we have already seen on Cold Spring Street (E 15), and in 1907 he plunged into one of the biggest real estate ventures in New Haven, buying from the Whitney estate the entire square from Cold Spring to Canner, running from Whitney Avenue to Livingston Street. Within four years it was solidly filled and Coyle himself was living on the corner, one of the first Irish arrivals on the Avenue (his house a close kin to one of the latest mansions on Newport's Belleview Avenue). Our route here makes a detour through Coyle's development—Cold Spring, Everit, and Livingston Streets: a fine example of an Edwardian neighborhood, tempering dignity with informality, decorum with liveliness.

E 29   Worthington Hooker School, 1899–1900. A statement of civic dignity, this building carries the emotional impact in the community that rightly belongs to public architecture. At the same time gentility of detail respects its residential surroundings. The crude playground at the rear was created by a later generation. (Photograph 1939; note balustrade now removed.)

E 30   Willow Street, West from Livingston, 1895–1905. Willow Street was cut through Belmont shortly after 1890 and built up in a rush. Two-family houses at the lower end of the block, one-family houses near the Avenue—it is an example of cost gradations within the upper social ranks, prices descending as they approach Livingston. Today Willow seems a commonplace street, the sort that people go through without seeing. But look at it as you walk. Though unpretentious, it is well built. Houses like these were the bread and butter of the local architects (for example no. 312, 1905, F. E. Brown; no. 326, 1905, Brown and VonBeren; no. 330, 1906, Allen and Williams; no. 344, 1900, W. H. Allen; no. 350, 1898, Brown and Berger; no. 352, 1897, W. H. Allen). As in Coyle's development, moderate cost ($5000–$7000) and stereotyped images from the magazines nevertheless achieve a high level of livability, warmth, and urban coherence. The noble arch of trees over the road adds the grace of dappled light.

E 31   Lower Whitney Avenue. The '90s were lower Whitney Avenue's great day. Triggered by the coming of the horsecar and the sewer, two big chunks of Belmont went on the market, as did other property. Lower Whitney erupted at once with great brick houses and baronial castles, becoming the patrician showplace of the city. On the west side Sachem's Wood continued to be held by the Hillhouses, on the east Belmont still presided over some ten remaining acres; the Avenue itself was described as "a fine career for generous steeds." It started to lose ground after World War I. As usual, the shift was inconspicuous at first, prestige institutional buildings moving discreetly in among the mansions. Before long they were followed by commercial uses and drab apartments. Today lower Whitney is one of the city's major losses. Twelve of its most impressive houses are gone, leaving a ragged lineup. Individual buildings are interesting, but the Avenue has lost coherence. Shown here: the block from Cottage to Lawrence, a brave show of castles. **389 Whitney Avenue,** 1893. The clerk who issued the building permit noted that the architect was from Boston but failed to catch his name. Originally the south wing was an open porch. Next door, now under aluminum siding: **375 Whitney Avenue,** 1897 (described as "dark red with delicate trimmings"), and **357 Whitney Avenue,** 1897; both by William H. Allen.

E 32   475 Whitney Avenue, 1896. Joseph W. Northrop, Bridgeport. This dazzling building was New Haven's most vivid example of the chateauesque. Though the style was referred to as François Premier and is probably inspired by the New York chateaux of Richard Morris Hunt, here it throws in bits of Romanesque masonry for good measure. The contrast of brownstone, orange brick, green copper, and wine-red tile, which Hunt might have found barbaric, is gorgeously at home in green New Haven. Note the gable over the dormer embossed with fleurs de lis. Beautifully preserved by new owners who have converted the house to offices, this building still triumphantly keeps Whitney Avenue's chin up.

Opposite, the **red sandstone wall** running down from Canner to below Linden is a relic of the Massena Clark estate, carved out of the Hillhouse property in the '60s.

E 33 Rudolph Steinert House, 469 Whitney Avenue, 1908. Albert Gottlieb, New York. One of New Haven's first examples of the later phase of the Colonial Revival—a classic of the style. Houses like this influenced domestic architecture right down to World War II and beyond. Notice the delicate workmanship of the door and central window, and contrast it with the imitation done 20 years later on Livingston Street (E 20), or with the Master's House of Davenport College (G 27). To understand the radical novelty of this design in New Haven, compare it with such contemporaries as E 27 and E 28.

Down the street, the long block from Linden to Cottage is the site of Belmont. The house was demolished in 1926, by which time wealth was leaving the Avenue and the estate was snapped up for apartments.

E 34 Whitney Avenue Fire Station, 1962. Carlin, Pozzi and Millard. A complex design balances the demands of a residential neighborhood and the functional needs of a firehouse. Notice the use of concrete in clapboard-like forms.

Across the Avenue, the block from Lawrence to Edwards, now an office building (1949, Harold H. Davis), was the William Downs estate in the '80s. A studio built for Downs' son remains on Lawrence Street, its charming interior still expressive of the artistic world of the turn of the century. **234 Lawrence Street:** another English cottage, this time by Brown and VonBeren (1894).

E 35 332–34 Whitney Avenue (281 Edwards Street), 1901. Edward T. Hapgood, Hartford. The front of the house originally was on Edwards, overlooking the Hillhouse park. Designed for a corner lot, the Whitney Avenue elevation was given the dignity of a facade, the portico—a deliberate allusion to Belmont up the Avenue—concealing the fact that there was (then) no door. Originally white, it made a striking accent on the Avenue. The elegant Federal fence still gives this corner style.

E 36 Charles Atwater House, 321 Whitney Avenue, 1890. Babb, Cook and Willard, New York. The all-containing gable recalls the famous Low house by McKim, Mead and White (1887). Atwater was William Downs' son-in-law, and his house was a pendant to the Downs house across Edwards Street, repeating its motif of a horizontal banding of windows and paneling. Recently converted to offices (Davis Cochran Miller Baerman Noyes), the remodeling has preserved much of the fine interior. Outside, the front driveway is new. In looking at the house today recall that the lawn once rose to the shingle line and the lot seemed wider. Also remember the companion house, stretching the visual effect along the street front (see E 34).

E

E 37 Yale University Parking Lot, 1968, Zion and Breen, New York; Garage, 1974, design scheme by Edward Larrabee Barnes, New York; Herbert S. Newman, Associate. It all goes to show that a parking lot doesn't have to be an eyesore. A forest of feathery poplars gives a fairyland effect, while levees ingeniously screen the cars from the road. This land belonged to Sachem's Wood; all but the house was transferred to Yale in 1910 and named Pierson-Sage Square (K 20). The earth-structure is the **Nuclear Structures Laboratory**, 1963, Douglas Orr, deCossy, Winder and Associates.

Looking down Humphrey from the entrance to the lot, the sharp needle of the **Humphrey Street Church** closes the view (L 32). Opposite: **315 Whitney Avenue**, 1908, by Murphy and Dana, New York; **Masonic Temple,** 1926, Norton and Townsend; **445 Humphrey Street,** 1901, Cram, Goodhue and Ferguson, Boston.

E 38 271 Whitney Avenue, 1891. One of the few survivors of Whitney Avenue's heyday in the brown decades. The rich interior was typical of the best houses of the time: the hall was finished in sycamore, the drawing room in mahogany; the stair was wainscotted in oak, with splendid carved newels and stained glass on the landing; bedrooms were variously done in birdseye maple, sycamore, and ash, and the billiard room (on the third floor, as was the fashion) was in "light wood." Recently converted to offices, the stylish renovation, while changing many details, is quite in keeping with their spirit. Original front door, which faced the Avenue, now preserved inside. The garden parking lot is a model of how to handle this utilitarian problem in a civil neighborhood.

215 Whitney Avenue, 1893, Leoni Robinson. This quiet Queen Anne house with a soberly handsome Ionic porch epitomizes the more reticent currents of late Victorian taste: well-made and well-detailed, dramatized by its four towering chimneys and ornamental terra cotta and brickwork (notice the fancy stitchery on the front and the relief on the south wall).

E 39 Security Insurance Company of New Haven, now Yale Computer Center, 175 Whitney Avenue, 1924. H. K. Murphy, New York. As the first major intruder in the private sanctuary of the Avenue, the Security Insurance Company took pains to provide an ornament to the neighborhood, placing a palatial building in the midst of generous grounds. The tone is gracious, the scale not overbearing, and it probably worked very well until other less tactful buildings joined it, literally cutting the ground away from it. Inside, an entrance lobby of the utmost elegance is still preserved intact although most of the rest of the building has been altered.

E 40 Peabody Museum of Natural History, Yale University, 1923. Charles Z. Klauder, Philadelphia. Addition 1958, Office of Douglas Orr; second addition 1965. Klauder, a noted builder of Gothic campuses, was also architect of Yale's power plants, and his buildings have much in common —large plain cubic masses veiled with shallow Gothic verticals, the surface characterized by a loving care for the texture and warm colors of brownstone and brown-red bricks (it is ironic that such a color-conscious building should have been given, of all things, a blue glass addition). Inside: a vaulted lobby with new plastic trappings and diagonal shafts of light descending dramatically from the stair tower. A window on the landing, now walled up for a showcase, once added further to the drama of light. The museum was founded in 1876, built around the collection of vertebrate fossils (discovered by the famed early paleontologist Othniel Marsh) now on display in the Dinosaur Hall. The architecture of the great skeletons remains as breathtaking today as when they were first seen a hundred years ago.

Next door to the north, **Kline Geology Laboratory,** part of the Kline Science Center (K 21).

E 41 John North House, now Yale Anthropology Department, 158 Whitney Avenue. In May 1835 North bought the whole lot through to Hillhouse Avenue and the house was soon built, probably in 1836. Both in design and spirit it belongs to the Hillhouse–Whitney development that took place at this time under the aegis of Town and Davis. There is no record of a direct connection with the firm, but a Davis drawing may have existed in the background. Today the North house is one of the few left from New Haven's great architectural flowering in the Greek Revival era, and in some ways it is the most evocative, its light creamy color still conveying the original effect of the classical villa standing on a grassy podium among trees. Changes over the years (a "Tuscan" tower at one time rose on one corner, and the south wing is a later addition) have not impaired it, and it remains a commanding presence on the Avenue. Third floor added after 1909.

E 42 Wayland Cottage, 135 Whitney Avenue, c1855. Gothic was not much favored in New Haven, that stronghold of Congregationalism and the Greek Revival, but the style was considered suitable for ornamental farm cottages. This one stood at the gate of the Wayland estate, which owned the block from Bradley to Humphrey Street. The glass enclosure of the porch now fills in the earlier arcading. Rear addition modern.

E 43 265 Bradley Street, 1936. Carina Eaglesfield Mortimer. A Regency design with a dash of the International Style, this was considered New Haven's first modern house and was known as "the ice box" by shocked neighbors. It shows an inventive rethinking of the traditional relation of house to lot and street, in response to new demands for parking and garaging. For other Bradley Street houses see Itinerary L.

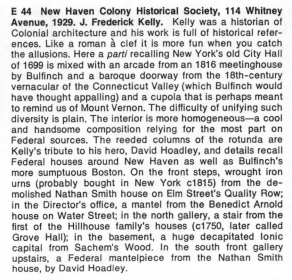

E 44 New Haven Colony Historical Society, 114 Whitney Avenue, 1929. J. Frederick Kelly. Kelly was a historian of Colonial architecture and his work is full of historical references. Like a roman à clef it is more fun when you catch the allusions. Here a *parti* recalling New York's old City Hall of 1699 is mixed with an arcade from an 1816 meetinghouse by Bulfinch and a baroque doorway from the 18th-century vernacular of the Connecticut Valley (which Bulfinch would have thought appalling) and a cupola that is perhaps meant to remind us of Mount Vernon. The difficulty of unifying such diversity is plain. The interior is more homogeneous—a cool and handsome composition relying for the most part on Federal sources. The reeded columns of the rotunda are Kelly's tribute to his hero, David Hoadley, and details recall Federal houses around New Haven as well as Bulfinch's more sumptuous Boston. On the front steps, wrought iron urns (probably bought in New York c1815) from the demolished Nathan Smith house on Elm Street's Quality Row; in the Director's office, a mantel from the Benedict Arnold house on Water Street; in the north gallery, a stair from the first of the Hillhouse family's houses (c1750, later called Grove Hall); in the basement, a huge decapitated Ionic capital from Sachem's Wood. In the south front gallery upstairs, a Federal mantelpiece from the Nathan Smith house, by David Hoadley.

E 45 Arthur Twining Hadley House, 93 Whitney Avenue, 1880. Yale's President Hadley built this house when he was 24. "I go to the architect's office almost every day," he wrote with enthusiasm, but added ruefully: "we are not likely to do anything startling; the money we can spend is so limited . . . The worst of it is that the city fire laws require us to build of brick, and a given amount of money will of course not give nearly as much scope for attempts at architectural effect as if the house were of wood." ("In view of what was achieved even in brick," his son later said, "we must be thankful for the New Haven fire laws.") Family tradition records that the design was modeled on Dürer's house in Nuremberg. The ceilings were so high that Mrs. Hadley said the house would be roomier if it were laid on its side. (Shown here before conversion to shops.)

In the middle of Whitney Avenue the little triangle is **Phelps Park,** given to the city by the Hillhouses and recently redesigned by the Garden Club of New Haven.

E 46 Berzelius, 76 Trumbull Street, 1910. Donn Barber, New York. An austere tomb for a Yale senior society. In a critical location, on a difficult site, the silent facade dominates a complicated intersection and brings the avenue to a close.

F The Litchfield Turnpike:
Whalley Avenue and Broadway

F The Litchfield Turnpike:
Whalley Avenue and Broadway

This tour goes to the city's last frontier—the undeveloped northwest. Along the way: a stretch of honky-tonk, two well-to-do residential quarters, and the village of Westville.

F The Litchfield Turnpike.

The turnpike was chartered in 1797, running west out of the city along Broadway and Whalley Avenue. From early in the 18th century Broadway had been a commercial center and by this time was part of the built-up fabric of the town. Whalley however was in the country. Like most of New Haven's radial highways, it was originally laid out as a boundary between the large parcels of outlots into which the first settlers grouped their fields, and for most of the 17th and 18th centuries it was little used as a road. The way to Westville and the world beyond followed Goffe and Blake Streets (to use their modern names), taking a winding course around the headwaters of the West River and crossing on a bridge upstream. When the turnpike was established, it took the more direct route, and Whalley's role as an artery dates from the building soon after of a new bridge downstream. Whalley then became the main road to the northwest, growing in importance as manufacturing developed in Westville and as the towns of the Naugatuck valley became industrialized.

This northwest quarter of the city was originally the town common, fanning out from the corner of York and Grove to embrace the Beaver Ponds—the cow pasture on "the hither side" of the ponds, the ox pasture on the far side. Perhaps for this reason it developed differently from all the other outlying quarters of the city. It was the last to grow and today is the only one in which there is still open land—much of it even still owned by the city. Consequently, once past Broadway, this is a country with little building history. A scattering of isolated villas remains—a few relics of earlier days, but mostly the story is of late 19th- and 20th-century development. Above, gas station, 1966, Eliot Noyes (New Canaan)—tryout for the Pegasus design now being built throughout the country by Mobil Gas. It will be found at the entrance to the city, at the intersection of the Litchfield Turnpike and Amity Road.

F 1 Broadway. Stand at the corner of York and Broadway. About 90 years ago Henry Howe, New Haven's devoted chronicler, wrote: "One of the most picturesque places in the city is the wide area called Broadway, as seen from the corner of York Street. There, in the course of a few hundred feet, come in from the West four converging highways, viz., Elm Street, Whalley, Goffe and Dixwell avenues. These have at their junction two small gem-like parks, one a little west of the other, but both in full view, where noble elms in the prime of their beauty give a crowning elegance to the whole expanse. One of its main charms is the modest little Episcopal church, in simple Gothic architecture . . . sweetly snuggled in behind the trees, giving a sort of moral aroma to the place." Times have changed.

F 2 Yale Co-op East, 65 Broadway, 1974. Herbert S. Newman Associates. A resourceful remodeling of an old building. Judicious use of paint emphasizes the recessed entrance, creating an effect of planes and shadows and giving style to a plain basic structure. Color adroitly relates the offspring to the parent Co-op next door.

F 3 Yale Co-op, 77 Broadway, 1961. Eero Saarinen. Designed at the same time as Morse and Stiles (J 19), the Co-op is related to them visually and at the rear is part of the internal system of pathways which Saarinen laid out for the main routes of Yale life that flow from York Street to the gym and to the shops on Broadway.

F 4   Christ Church, 1895. Henry Vaughn, Boston. A different image is projected here from the "modest little Episcopal church" that Howe admired. Vaughn had studied with G. F. Bodley, one of the principal ecclesiastical architects of Late Victorian England, and was an eminently suitable choice for a congregation that was both upper class and High Church. Today the building is stranded on a pared-down island in a stream of cars. The great red tower however still asserts itself over the melée.

Three broad streets diverge ahead—**Whalley, Goffe,** and **Dixwell** (named for the three judges who condemned Charles I to death and found shelter in New Haven after the Restoration). They lead on the right to black New Haven, on the left to the dream strip of the automobile showrooms. In 1825 this triangle was a little settlement known as Poverty Square.

F 5   Whalley Avenue. Those who prefer fading Victorian houses to modern commerce may take a parallel route out Elm Street, but connoisseurs of the strip will want to stick with the course.

On the corner of Sperry: **St. Luke's Church,** organized by blacks in 1844 and one of the city's earliest Episcopalian congregations. Originally in the West Village, the present church was built in 1905 by Brown and VonBeren.

F 6   New Haven County Jail, 1857. Behind the little mock castle, the most extensive of later additions is by Antinozzi Associates, Stratford, presently under construction. An Italianate tower originally rose in the center. Sidney Mason Stone, architect.

On County Street: one of a group of architecturally designed playgrounds which the city has recently been putting on vacant lots.

F 7   Beaver Hills (F 7–F 12). Norton Street above Whalley is an example of the urge to ostentation of the later 19th century—an optimistically grand layout lined with modest frame houses unable to support the scale. At Goffe there is an abrupt change. The land here was a 100-acre farm cut out of the old common in an area known since Colonial times as the Beaver Hills, bought in the 1850s, surprisingly, by a Yale student. Around 1910 his heirs laid it out as a development which attracted a certain amount of notice for its attempt to create a social community and to regulate standards of design. Gateposts with beavers may still be seen at the head of Norton, Ellsworth, and Winthrop Avenues; one of the gate cottages is shown here **(389 Norton Parkway, 1908).** This was one of the biggest developments in New Haven and among the first to reflect the arrival of the automobile. It is a good enclave of interbellum suburban building, with examples of the many strains of the time: white Colonial, brick Georgian, California bungalow, Spanish, Elizabethan, and Dutch Colonial; the stucco style, timber style, shingle style, brick cottage style, and others. Architecture in this period seems to become increasingly a matter of "models," and in some of the later blocks north and west you get the feeling that you are riffling through the pages of a magazine. Nevertheless it adds up to an attractive neighborhood, and Ellsworth Avenue today is one of New Haven's handsomer streets under great trees.

F 8 453 Ellsworth Avenue, 1916. The white Colonial house—backbone of the American suburb. This version, with pilasters, pediment, dormers, and hipped roof, perpetuates the popular image of the Georgian mansion. But compared to earlier examples (E 28, F 26), it shows the smoother, thinner, and lighter treatment that would characterize the 1920s. C. F. Townsend, architect.

F 9 460 Ellsworth Avenue, 1912. Porte cochère and veranda make long horizontals and deep shadows that ally this style with contemporary work in California and the Midwest.

F 10 475 Ellsworth Avenue, 1915. R.W. Foote. This house was described as an Italian villa. It is an example of the more general Mediterranean style, emanating out of California, which influenced Eastern fashion at this time. This is one of New Haven's most elaborate examples.

F 11 517 Ellsworth Avenue, 1920. Brown and VonBeren. Houses like this were called Dutch Colonial. This one is nicely designed, distinguished by a big hood over the front door.

F 12 636 Ellsworth Avenue, 1938. The Arts and Crafts movement had focused attention on brickwork, and builders soon learned ways of achieving elaborate handmade effects. Heightened by half-timbering, this example epitomizes the picturesque tendencies of the time. Architect, Lewis Bowman, Bronxville, New York.

F 13 Urban Frontier (F 13–F 19). With the Beaver Hills and Beaver Ponds we enter a part of New Haven that long remained rural and until yesterday kept a feeling of remoteness. This was the old common: it is high, airy country, abruptly heaving up in steep hills. The sheer red face of West Rock is a constant presence at its back, as are long views over the plain—Frederic Church's painting eloquently describes the scene. The headwaters of the West River rise here, making this a place of brooks and ponds. Until World War II a good deal of this land was still almost undeveloped, and much of it belonged to the city. After the war the opportunity to open it up in a way that would utilize and cherish the beauty of the place and make it available to many people was one that modern cities seldom are privileged to enjoy. Our tour will briefly cross this country and some of the results thus far may be seen along the way.

F 14 Beaver Ponds Park. The Beaver Ponds were acquired as a park in 1890, and by 1910 the lower tip had been filled, creating a pleasant playing field at Goffe Street with a wide allée of maples around the edge and benches under the trees—for those interested in neighborhood park design it is well worth a look. Drainage converted the upper swamps into a chain of ponds bordered by a natural landscape making a scenic park, with **Crescent Street** and **Sherman Parkway** curving along the two sides—all in all a distinguished piece of urban planning. After the war came a change. In 1945–47 the section from Munson Street almost to Ellsworth was filled for a stadium. In 1956 the city took the section from Goffe to Munson for a high school, ironically named **Hillhouse High**—see its twin, Wilbur Cross (D 5). By 1950 some of the far end of the park had been transferred to the state for use by a new teachers' college (F 15). Other bites were taken for the Animal Shelter (81 Fournier Street) and a police building (710 Sherman Parkway). At present another piece is being readied for a school at Dorman Street, accompanied by local protest (the design is by Stull Associates, Boston—the city's first school commission to go to a black architect). A sample of the original pond and wetlands scenery remains along Fournier Street. For other city park problems see the Mill River (D 3).

F 15 Southern Connecticut State College, Buley Library, 1967. Antinozzi Associates, Stratford. Southern Connecticut (formerly the State Teachers' College, housed in cramped quarters downtown) moved in 1953 to this magnificent tract of open country. Few colleges can boast a more beautiful site, although the campus plan seems diffuse in view of the potential for protective land use and functional integration which the site suggested. The difficulties resulting from centering the college on a major highway intersection have been hard to overcome. Buley Library comes after the first buildings of the '50s (e.g. Administration Building, Office of Douglas Orr; Fine Arts and Science Buildings, Bradford S. Tilney) and is a good example of the changes taking place in modern architecture in the intervening decade.

F 16 Southern Connecticut State College, Connecticut Hall, 1968. Carl R. Blanchard, Jr. An authoritative building which does a good deal to give a focus to a divided campus. Across Wintergreen Avenue the quarried hill is **Pine Rock.** In 1909 the Gilbert-Olmsted report objected to the injury being done to this feature of the natural scenery. Little did they guess that one day modern technology might remove it altogether.

At **Blake Street** we reenter the 19th century—the change of scale is almost a shock. A few Greek Revival houses **(no. 400, no. 346)** still testify to the growth of the nearby village of Westville in the Canal Age. Blake Street is the old highway out of town, crossing the river upstream where it is divided in three branches. Look sharp as you go along Springside Avenue and you will find the stream going along beside you. On your left, through houses, the rock is suddenly startlingly close. **Springside Avenue** is the approach to West Rock Park and the city's most rural stretch of road. Its conception as a parkway (now only partly preserved) stems from the Gilbert and Olmsted plan.

F 17 Oriental Gardens, Wintergreen Avenue, 1970. Paul Rudolph. A low-and moderate-income co-op, and a much-publicized experiment in prefab housing, using trailer-sized units that were trucked to the site and dropped into place by a crane. Placing units at right angles and making maximum use of projections and recessions, Rudolph creates a characteristic meshed composition of voids and solids.

This slope of the hill is the old town farm, known as Springside. Various city and state buildings are now being sprinkled about here. At Rockview Circle a housing project shows in stark form the planning concepts of the early postwar years.

F 18 Clarence F. Rogers Educational Center, Wilmot Road, 1971. Charles Brewer. Said to be the first open-plan school in the state.

F 19 West Rock Park. West Rock Park dates mainly from 1891; it has been added to until it now covers over 600 acres. It is a lovely and relatively lonely park, more remote than East Rock and less "improved." The road enters off Wintergreen Avenue, just above Oriental Gardens: the left fork leads to the Judges' Cave; the right is Baldwin Drive which in winter must be one of the greatest scenic rides in the state. The road, built during the Depression, is worth more than a casual glance. Compare it with modern road design and note how it rides with the shape of the land; note also the elegant stone curbing and traprock walls. Rustic railings (now being allowed to decay) give a more parklike atmosphere than the usual metal guard rails.

Shown here: **Nature Recreation Center,** 1967, Harold Roth-Edward Saad. Originally sheathed with horizontal siding, shingles have been added recently. Inside: a model shows a projected **Barnyard Nature Recreation Center** to be built down the hill (Davis Cochran Miller Noyes).

F 20 Westville. Westville was inside the town limits but remained a distinct village until the end of the 19th century when the trolley line at last brought New Haven westward and closed the gap. The village had considerable prosperity as a manufacturing center—first paper mills, later the Diamond Match Company and others—and early factories can still be seen along the river as you approach Whalley Avenue. Today the town center seems to have disappeared except as a cluster of stores and a big traffic bottleneck on the road to Woodbridge, but traces of the former village structure are still visible, and a few good 19th-century and Edwardian houses suggest that the center was once pleasant.

512 Blake Street (shown here): an unusually elegant version of the basic Greek Revival house, ornamented with the Greek honeysuckle pattern in the style of Lafever—a unique example in New Haven (see also F 23).

F 21 Masonic Temple, 949 Whalley Avenue, 1926. R.W. Foote. A successful job of siting a large building on a steep bank. In spite of having become an appliance store, it remains Westville's major landmark.

Up the hill, **977 Whalley Avenue.** This pretty mansard house and a few surrounding Italian villas give us a glimpse of Westville in the middle of the 19th century.

F 22 Donald Grant Mitchell Library, Harrison Street, 1964. Gilbert Switzer. An earlier building for the library was designed in a cottagey style considered fitting for the memory of Donald Grant Mitchell. The new building squarely faces up to the challenge of providing greatly enlarged facilities and a modern civic building without shattering the intimacy of the street.

F 23   Westville Congregational Church, now United Church of Westville, 1835.   Somebody in Westville must have owned a copy of one of Minard Lafever's builder's guides, for this neat little flushboarded church with its scrolly ornament over the door is, like no. 512 Blake Street (F 20), based on his drawings—a style not seen elsewhere in New Haven. Wing and other enlargements made in the '70s. Perhaps the sharp spire dates from this time—the Greek Revival did not usually believe in such restless forms, although a spire is shown here as early as 1879.

F 24   Firehouse, Harrison and Fountain Streets, 1915. Brown and VonBeren.   A good example of the domestic scale and the image of pretty, picturesque, old-time village life which the architects and planners of the early 20th century sought to create for the town centers of the new well-to-do suburbs.

F 25   149 Fountain Street, 1906.   This house has a sibling on Livingston Street (E 17), both classic examples of the yearning for nature and rural simplicity (tumbled fieldstones, weathered shingles) that was the other side of the Beaux Arts coin in this decade.

F 26   234 Fountain Street, 1909.   Around the turn of the century the Colonial Revival architects, becoming more archaeological, were fond of making a pastiche of famous Georgian houses—the Hancock House in Boston, the Wentworth-Gardiner House in Portsmouth, and one or two other familiars—and producing a sort of archetype of the 18th-century New England mansion. This is one of the best of many versions in New Haven. Both side wings were originally open porches with balustrades.
   No. 200: Executive House, 1963, Gilbert Switzer.

F 27 Foam House, 137 Laurel Road, 1971. Valerie Batore-wicz. On a wood frame, isocyanurate foam reinforced with fiberglass forms walls and roof: a model house for a system patented by the architect and designed for mass production of factory-made shells (called satellites) which can be assembled at the site to make a variety of spaces and forms.

F 28 Edgewood, 1076 Forest Road, c1870. Donald Grant Mitchell with David R. Brown. Mitchell's role as a landscape architect and author is discussed in the Introduction. He came to New Haven in 1858, choosing this property (after a search through New England) for the beauty of its scenery. The name of Edgewood soon became famous in his books as readers all over the country became familiar with the white village of Westville, the red Rock behind it, and the long view over the city to the harbor and its white lighthouse. The grounds were landscaped and a drive laid out along the ridge which was opened to the public (traces remain in the driveway and woods of the Hopkins Grammar School). As an architect, Mitchell combined features of the early Stick Style with observations of his own made in the English countryside. Edgewood shows both strains in its roofy wooden upper part and its masonry walls below, which mix brick and stone with studied rustic artlessness (notice how the size of the stones becomes smaller as the wall rises). David R. Brown worked with Mitchell on several occasions, Mitchell presumably supplying the designs. Edgewood today is only slightly altered, but its grounds are gone, changing its character altogether.

F 29 Edgewood Farmhouse, 999 Forest Road, c1860. Donald Grant Mitchell and David R. Brown. As the farmer's cottage, this was an example of Mitchell's rustic style, combining features from the stick architecture of the '60s (such as the Swiss boarding in the gable) with his particular brand of picturesque masonry. Note the chimneys. Later the cottage was enlarged for Mitchell's daughter by Brown, under Mitchell's supervision. (Photograph 1930s.)

No. 1031 Forest Road (1929) shows Mitchell's influence as it survived into the '20s (note chimneys): Brown and Von-Beren, architect. At 986 Forest Road: **Hopkins Grammar School,** which traces its history to 1660, now combined with **Day-Prospect Hill.** Main buildings, 1924–, H. K. Murphy, New York.

F 30 2150 Chapel Street, 1935. Brown and VonBeren. Forest Road, as Mitchell left it, must have been one of the most prestigious addresses in the city—notice the houses that were built on the corners of the major avenues.

No. 2141 (1925, Harold H. Davis): first-prize winner in a competition for a small brick house.

F 31   131 Oliver Road. The plain west of the river was almost empty until the end of the century. This rather formal house, which probably dates from the 1840s, must have been very much alone out in the country. A similar design will be found at 26 Trumbull Street. The plumey capitals, like a great bunch of ferns, were probably the specialty of some New Haven artisan—they also turn up on Whitney Avenue (E 3), Lyon Street (N 39), and elsewhere.

F 32   The Edgewood Estate: Alston and McKinley Avenues. The lower part of the Edgewood estate, a tract bounded roughly by Forest, Chapel, Alden, and Woodbridge, went on the market not long after Mitchell's death in 1908. People interested in the World War I period and the '20s will enjoy exploring this area. Comfortably scaled, pleasantly planted, it is a beautifully preserved specimen of an upper-middle-class development in the serene days before the Depression. At its northern border it meets an earlier streetcar suburb which had begun to spread out from Westville in the '90s—hence the change in style. At its southern border there is another change: later and smaller. Alston and McKinley Avenues, with their long alleys of mature trees arched over the road, make the best overall show, but other streets have interesting things. Illustrated: **10 Alston Avenue,** 1928, Lester Julianelle.

F 33   100 Alston Avenue, 1919. With allusions to Colonial, Spanish, and Prairie styles, the long lines of this house are relaxed and graceful.

F 34   140 Alston Avenue, 1932. Jacob Weinstein. More elegant timbering and brickwork of the '30s—compare F 12.

F 35   255 McKinley Avenue, 1921. A stylized version of the ever-popular Tudor style, the simplification of forms intensified by a plain brown and white color scheme. Brown and VonBeren, architect.

F 36 116 McKinley Avenue, 1913. Brown and VonBeren.
Ferdinand VonBeren covered acres of New Haven in the great building years between 1890 and World War I. Here is his own house.

F 37 Edgewood Avenue and Edgewood Park. Donald Grant Mitchell joined with other landowners to open up and beautify the west end. He contributed some of the land as well as the designs for both avenue and park, and both were named in his honor. Keep on the avenue all the way to town to experience the whole progression: first the broad suburban street, then the narrowing at the bridge; next the arcadian expanse of park followed by the formality of the mall (now bare of the row of tall trees designed to give it a processional rhythm). Up ahead Harkness Tower stands in front of you. James Gamble Rogers must have admired Edgewood Avenue —his tower is placed at its head with precision. At Orchard Street the scale changes and you enter the West Village. The avenue becomes a small street, narrower and less bright, and there is a feeling of being in an old part of town. The great tower you have been following is suddenly gone; in its place the village-sized gatehouse of Pierson College appears. It all seems to have been done by some feat of magic.

Edgewood Park was designed probably in 1889 and was long one of the most beautifully laid out of the city parks—a border of wooded drives and walks following the river. Later the river was straightened and various sports facilities and parking lots added. South of the bridge, the river has been designated as the site of an Olympic rowing course, of sports installations, and the extension of the Oak Street Connector. This section is **West River Memorial Park** with **Marginal Drive** on the west (plan, 1925, Frederick Law Olmsted Jr., Boston).

F 38 Augusta Troup School, 1924. Charles Scranton Palmer.
With its large Tudor windows and patterned brick, this is a characteristic example of a widely used model for school design in the '20s. (Photograph 1926.)

At Dwight Street: **Timothy Dwight School,** 1964, Eliot Noyes, New Canaan; Schilling and Goldbecker, associated architects. Opposite: **Dwight Cooperative Town Houses,** 1968, Gilbert Switzer.

G The Derby Turnpike: Chapel Street and Derby Avenue

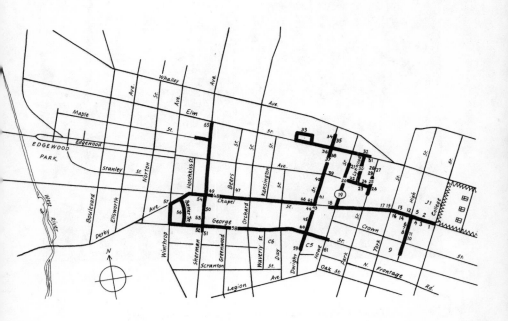

A fading commercial street, an old village complex, a corner of Yale, a late Victorian middle-class development—some wealth, some poverty. Along the way this tour is a good place to observe the development of the apartment house in New Haven.

G The Derby Turnpike: West Chapel Street and Derby Avenue.

Although the western run of Chapel Street existed from the start of the Colony, it stopped at the West River, serving only as an access to fields. As a public way it fell into disuse—indeed 18th-century maps show a house standing in the middle of it. It was not until the Derby Turnpike was chartered in 1798 and a bridge built across the river that West Chapel Street sprang to life, becoming one of the town's main streets—the only one, in fact, that goes straight through from east to west. In the Federal period, as the retail center moved up to the Green, shops began pushing westward along Chapel, blending into the life of Yale up at the corner of College Street. Farther out, a lineup of Victorian mansions was built beyond Howe, becoming at the end of the century the core of a showy, new middle-class neighborhood around Sherman Avenue. Meantime, at the close of the Civil War, Yale built its semipublic art building on the corner of High and for the first time turned its face toward Chapel Street. This stretch became the Gold Coast, a street where affluent students lived in private dormitories and where town and gown mingled for social and intellectual events and for sometimes violent clashes between students and town youths. Prestigious churches, men's clubs, the best hotels, restaurants, ballrooms, and theaters grew up along the street, and from the turn of the century New Haven's main concentration of apartment houses settled here. At its height, the social-commercial wave flowed about as far as Howe Street, then, stopped by the Depression and other ills, it turned and started flowing back. Today the still-withdrawing tide is marked by empty shops and messy little enterprises in once soignée quarters. Beyond Howe, houses are remodeled for apartments or tenements, and the Congregational churches are for sale.

G 1 The Townsend Block, 1000–1006 Chapel Street, c1832. The picture shows the building before fire escapes and neglect had taken over. This was one of a trio of important Greek Revival designs (see I 30, I 49) which brought for the first time an urban style to downtown New Haven. Before this, shops had been little different from houses. Here a long facade, uniform fenestration, an even roof line, a height of four stories, and above all a large expanse of glass on the street between supporting stone piers established a new standard of functionalism and sophistication.

G 2 Yale University, the Old Campus: South Range. On this block in the old days stood one of Yale's most sacred artifacts, The Fence, on which, if tales can be trusted, upperclassmen sat through most of their college years watching girls and picking fights with townies. Now on the corner: **Bingham Hall,** 1926, Walter B. Chambers, New York; in the center, **Vanderbilt Hall,** 1894, Charles C. Haight—both dormitories. Bingham stands on the site of the first Yale building (a relief on the wall suggests what this ancestral building may have looked like). Vanderbilt fills a wide opening through which for over a century the life of the campus poured out into the town. When the new building was dropped into the hole and the campus sealed off, the point of contact was monumentalized, the imagery of a Tudor gatehouse and a welcoming forecourt plainly designed as the university's front door (shown here soon after completion). But nowadays the gate is locked, the bright glimpse of the campus through the arch (seen in the old photograph) is hidden, and the university has turned away from Chapel Street.

G 3   Union League Club, 1032 Chapel Street, 1902. Richard Williams. Another dignified, well-made building standing empty. Its design distinguished by a clean-cut layering of brick planes, this is the sort of undemonstrative but cultivated architecture that gives urbanity to city streets. When it was new it enhanced the whole block; it might still do so if it were cleaned up. Originally there was a grass court, now an alley, on the east, hence the side wall was finished as well as the front.

Up the alley: the shell of the Opera House of 1880 (advertised as one of the biggest theaters in America), later the well-known **Hyperion,** tryout stop for Broadway shows at the turn of the century, now part of Loew's Poli movie theater. Squeezed between opera house and club: the remains of the **Gaius Warner house,** 1860, Henry Austin—originally with a double bow front. Up ahead: one of Yale's best street sequences—the procession of the art buildings.

G 4   Warner Hall, 1044 Chapel Street, 1892. Rufus G. Russell. In the latter part of the 19th century it became the fashion, at Yale as at Harvard, for well-heeled students to live off campus. The Warner was one of several private dormitories built along the Gold Coast of Chapel and surrounding streets. An advertisement offers restaurant, telephones, barber shop, "elegantly fitted throughout, with heat, light, and attendance" for $3 to $15 a week: there was also a bathroom on every floor and a "continuous elevator." This building was a pioneer in the new type of multiple-occupancy structure (expanded both vertically and horizontally from the older urban module) which would become the norm for the 20th-century hotel and apartment house, and its original plan shows the early difficulty of solving problems inherent in the enlarged space: confused circulation, access to one room through another, inadequate fire stairs, and on each floor two or three inside bedrooms.

G 5   Yale School of Fine Arts, now Street Hall, 1864. Peter B. Wight, New York. Street Hall—its pinnacles, tower, and finials never finished—is an example of what a scathing review in the 1870s called the Yale Truncated Style. This was the first college art school in America. It was also one of the country's first examples of High Victorian Gothic and of the new Ruskinian ideal of "truth" in art (Wight, a devout Ruskinian, gathered wildflowers and gave them to his masons, telling them to design the foliage of the capitals themselves as true medieval craftsmen were supposed to do). Today the building has been cheated not only of its pinnacles but of its setting. Founded originally with the hope of fostering contact between Yale and the city, the art school physically embodied this idea, having two faces, one on the campus and one on the street. This duality is now lost, Vanderbilt having covered the campus side. But old views, such as the one shown here, suggest that this was the major front, and when seen in the round with its climax of the projected tower at the back, the design was a good deal more dynamic than it now appears. In its day it made a big stir, and a critic proclaimed that with this building Yale's architectural progress began. A century later Sir Nikolaus Pevsner said, "It is desperately (and loveably) provincial." Northwest corner added 1911, John Ferguson Weir and Leoni Robinson.

G 6   38 High Street, c1840. Half of a onetime two-house row, this little house is fastidious in detail, with correct Doric mutules along the eave corresponding to the Doric porch, and fancy leading in the door lights. **No. 26** down the block is of the same period.

High Street was opened soon after the Revolution and grew up as a place of comfortable houses and student eating clubs (the Gobbl(e)ins, the Pi(e)oneers, and others) and later of apartments. It subsequently fell on hard times—houses lost out to parking lots, a garage, and a dreary taxpayer; a brothel at one time prospered down the block. Today a bit unkempt, there are still nice buildings left and the smallness of the street is engaging.

G 7   The Oxford, 36 High Street, 1910. C. E. Joy. The Oxford was one of the first apartment houses in New Haven and is typical of the early form: a 3- or 4-story block which reflects rising real estate values by making almost total use of the lot, touching the side lines and running back deeply to the rear. As architecture it is pure facadism, the front well designed while the sides are bare, anticipating other apartments on each side to hide them. A problem latent in this type of plan would appear when these later buildings came, namely light.

The block apartment remained popular with downtown developers for the next two decades, facades responding to changing fashions—see **no. 28** for the Georgian model in 1922.

G 8   Cambridge Arms, 32 High Street, 1925. Lester Julianelle. As late as 1919 there were barely a dozen apartment houses in town, but the '20s saw an outburst of them. Tudor was a popular style, partly no doubt because of its informality but also perhaps because turrets and bays provided a useful kit for articulating the difficult expanse of the newly enlarged facades. With picturesque groupings, scale was broken down and fitted into older residential neighborhoods. Notice here that of the seven bays no two are identical; notice also the patterned masonry, carrying out the picturesque effect. The problem of light was halfheartedly faced by giving the building a shallow H shape.

G 9 Crown Tower, 1965. Chloethiel Woodard Smith, Washington. The city's major example of postwar apartment design: the familiar high-rise, low-rise package with balconies and structured parking. Reversing the earlier pattern, outdoor space is generous, indoor space minimal.

G 10 27 High Street, c1870. Originally a double house (the lines of the second door can still be seen), this is a graceful example of the double bow- or octagonal-front so popular in the latter part of the 19th century. The openwork cornice, which leaves the brick showing, was often used at this time.

G 11 31 High Street, c1855. A mid-Victorian villa, perhaps at one time stuccoed and scored with ashlar blocks like no. 35 next door. Originally there were shutters and a balustrade atop the handsome Corinthian porch, relieving the bareness. Remodeled in 1958 by Paul Rudolph, this is an early example of a now popular practice: buying an old city house, preserving the exterior and transforming the interior. Outside, a Victorian villa; inside, a white planar world—the shock of the unexpected is part of the effect. Rudolph's office on the top floor has been altered, but his apartment at the rear is intact—a composition of outdoor–indoor movement at different levels making spectacular use of a white fire escape. **No. 35:** a charming Federal Revival porch, probably c1915, on an older house.

G 12 Yale University, Old Art Gallery, 1927. Egerton Swartwout, New York. Why, one wonders, are bridges not used more often to make one building out of two? Here a picturesque addition to the urban scene houses faculty offices. The Tuscan Romanesque of the Old Gallery follows the Veronese Gothic (so Wight called it) of Street Hall smoothly, its bulk tempered by reliefs, arcading, and huge windows with deftly down-scaling detail. The tawny color of the stone sets a dominant theme for the art buildings complex.

G 13   Yale University, New Art Gallery, 1953. Louis I. Kahn and Office of Douglas Orr.   Begun when he was 50 years old, this was Kahn's first major work and the one that launched his extraordinary, late-flowering career. It was also Yale's first modern building. The reserved, street-respecting exterior attracted little public notice at the time, but the exposed concrete ceiling and round stair tower with the form-work showing were much publicized—the first sign that many had seen of what would soon become familiar as Brutalism. The interior has now been altered—it was said that it "lacked elegance"—and the original floating partitions have been replaced with white walls, partly concealing the concrete frame. Out back a sculpture garden and the court of Weir Hall (J 10) make one of Yale's most idyllic outdoor places.

G 14   Yale Center for British Art and British Studies, 1973. Louis I. Kahn; completed by Pellecchia and Myers, Philadelphia.   Shops line the street, the Center itself is designed around two interior courts, rooms unfolding like leaves from these two main stems. The outside wall is sheer—sheets of stainless steel and sheets of glass almost seamlessly joined. Inside, concrete frame and ducts are exposed and there are floating partitions as originally planned for the New Art Gallery. The concrete work is exceptional for its refinement. Forms made of birch plywood coated with a plastic resin leave a grainless surface with an almost polished finish, spillover between the panels providing fragile moldings. The building is toplighted by skylights covering the roof, the light disseminated by baffles and filters—an experimental design which has been much publicized. Here Kahn reverses the current trend in museum practice, returning to the use of natural light in the daytime and incandescent light after dark. Light in fact is the being and life of the building, feeling out every space, creating luminous volumes. "On a rainy day it will be like a gray moth, on a sunny day a butterfly," said Kahn.

G 15   Yale University Art and Architecture Building, 1961. Paul Rudolph.   This building has probably caused more furor than any other American architectural work of the mid-20th century. After the clear geometry of the Bauhaus era, these dynamic irregular masses, these many levels and recessions and brown textured surfaces came with the shock of a revolution. A storm center from the start—praised as the prophet of a new architecture, damned as willful and egocentric; dogged by misadventure; victim of arson, student vandalism, remodeling, and endless complaints—the A & A Building has had a bitter and embattled career. But despite the storm, what no one disputes is its magnificent presence. A gatepost building at the point where Chapel Street bends and leaves the old inner city, it transfigures a nondescript street and turns the lineup of the art buildings into a procession.

G 16   Calvary Baptist Church, now Yale Repertory Theater, 1871. Rufus G. Russell.   It is too bad that the pious custom of removing the spire from a deconsecrated church ever got started, for it certainly ruins the architecture, as Russell's drawing shows. The church looks a bit dingy today, but it still provides a richness of texture and movement that is a good foil for the modern buildings around it.

G 17 El Dorado Apartments, 1145 Chapel Street, 1922. Brown and VonBeren. With over 40 units, the El Dorado was hailed as the most progressive apartment building in town, its design the result of careful study of "the California style," a style which aside from its popular visual imagery was characterized by economical planning. A typical apartment offered living room, kitchenette, breakfast room, and "library" with In-a-Dor bed. Externally the huge cornice as well as the name provided the California touch. Nicely detailed shop fronts, now covered, set a tone of commercial chic.

No. 1151: **Hotel Duncan,** 1894. Originally "Duncan Hall," the Duncan like the Warner aimed to catch the student dormitory trade. No. 1175: **the Monterey,** 1923—California again. Shopfronts with bronze trim (two obliterated) are memories of former elegance on Chapel Street.

G 18 Far East Restaurant, remodeled 1958, King Lui Wu. The slim impeccable lines of the glass box mate perfectly with the clean facade behind, both graced by the Victorian cornice.

G 19 The West Village (G 19–G 47). The name is modern but describes a separateness that this quarter has long had. Closed off from downtown by the unbroken side of Park Street, it was rural until the 1830s when it was opened up in a rush, and the speculative developments of the Canal Age have left their mark to this day in rows of modest lots and neat Greek Revival houses, advertised as desirable for "merchants and mechanics." Like the other village clusters of the young city, this was a mixed neighborhood of dwellings and small industries—carriage factories for the most part. A few spacious villas appeared, while on Elm Street, which was the trodden path to the Almshouse and was first called Samaritan Street, we hear of emancipated slaves and laborers. The dominant tone was small, tidy, and comfortable. A Congregational church was soon built and also a black Episcopalian church, St. Luke's (F 5). The quarter throve through the 19th century, its social status rising, until in the 20th it began to fade. Today encircled by slums, its intimacy violated by traffic and its fine-grained texture threatened by parking lots and new buildings, the Village is a ragged but still evocative place where students, faculty, old families, and the poor blend. Redevelopment, while extensive, has made few sweeping changes. In contrast to Dixwell and the Hill, the program in the West Village has been to work within the existing fabric and to reinforce it with many dispersed small-scale projects. These make an interesting study of the problem of integrating modern design into old streetscapes, but they are scattered and only a few can be noted on this tour. One-way streets have dictated a winding course. If you have a car you will do well to park it and walk.

G 20 Howe Street. Swinging rehabs and gaping parking lots make up the bedlam of modern Howe Street. **Nos. 88 and 90** typify much that you will find in the West Village: both are Greek Revival but you look twice before you realize it. The oblong window in the gable and the straight side lights of the door are tipoffs; in other cases a traprock foundation will provide a clue. Across Edgewood Avenue another pair typifies the Queen Anne phase of the Village: substantial houses of the '80s patterned with colored brick (**no. 94:** 1886, Rufus G. Russell). This corner was the site of the village church.

G 21   101 Howe Street, 1844.   An unusually crisp example
of the small Italian villa of the '40s and '50s. This is the only
one in the Village that has not been altered or spoiled.
No. 99: a new front, of the '90s, on a mid-century villa.
Spanking white trim and extravagant balconies make this
a bright spot on the street. Note the old monitor, with bravely
painted finial.

G 22   37 Edgewood Avenue, c1835.   On a tiny house this
proper small porch with Doric columns must have been a
powerful symbol of gentility to some rising artisan or tradesman of the canal days.
No. 33: a Queen Anne-Romanesque hybrid from a more
ponderous age surprisingly does not crush its little neighbor—
in fact it upsets the delicate fabric of the block far less than
the vacant lot across the street. **No. 28:** another early one,
with Queen Anne porch and a camouflage of asbestos shingles—see G 31 for what it perhaps once looked like, or
could look like.

G 23   20 and 16 Edgewood Avenue, c1835.   Like so many
others in the neighborhood, these little houses belong to
the borderland between the Federal and Greek Revival
styles. The half-moon in the gable instead of the more
sophisticated oblong of the Greek Revival is one earmark of
diehard vernacular habit. No. 20 has picked up some later
trimmings (Queen Anne porch and side bay, new window
trim and shingles) but retained its original daintiness. So, in
spite of other changes, has no. 16.
Up ahead, the **Pierson College gatehouse** is surely one of
the best pieces of theater in Yale's large repertory of urban
effects. Detached from its long side wings by two lower
sections, it seems to become part of the scenery of the
village street (for the architect's handling of this effect from
the long view see F 37).

G 24 17 Edgewood Avenue, c1835. A full-fledged and impressive Greek Revival doorway on a house that still has a Federal flavor. With two chimneys this was a more deluxe design than its neighbors.

No. 21, today agreeably color-matched to it, belongs to the same long-lingering vernacular tradition. **No. 15:** still another of the company, given a little tonic with a touch of gingerbread on a later door hood.

G 25 Park Street. Park Street, sheltered from the city by the long wall of Yale, always seems a quiet, hidden place (you will sense this more strongly if you are in a car, making your tangled way in from the chaos of Broadway). In the 19th century this was the main manufacturing area of the Village. Carriage factories stood among frame houses (**no. 234–236** is shown here), and the street prospered until it fell into industrial decay in the 20th century. With Yale's acquisition of the east side, an attempt was made to refurbish the upper block. Today it is a place of small shops, apartments, and student rooms.

G 26 Yale University, Pierson College, 1930. James Gamble Rogers, New York. Both Pierson and Davenport are noted elsewhere (J 14, J 15), but if these back gates are open, do go in. Rogers' virtuosity in creating a series of "places" out of a formerly featureless area is dazzling. Notice how he makes you change direction and how he plays on changes of color and changes in the shapes and sizes of courts and passages.

Nos. 211, 215, 217 Park Street are part of Fraternity Row on York Street (J 13): no. 211, 1929, H. Herbert Wheeler; nos. 215 and 217, 1931 and '30, James Gamble Rogers. Rogers, a master of outdoor spaces, was evidently concerned in his whole Park Street plan with connectives through to York and the rest of the campus. Here a crooked path goes past crooked cottages, carrying out the village theme to make one of Yale's most beguiling small walks.

G 27 Yale University, Davenport College, 1930. James Gamble Rogers, New York. Rogers treats the long wall of Pierson and Davenport as a series of historical vignettes: one gatehouse recalls the 17th century while the other alludes to Bulfinch's work of a century later. Between the two in time, the masters' houses (nos. 231 and 271) are Georgian, while over the rooftops peeps a glimpse of Independence Hall. The upper end of the block is treated as a Georgian street, with the back gate to Davenport tucked into one of the seeming houses. Davenport is a year later in execution than Pierson—the imagery even more romantic, the spatial complexity intensified by terraces, stairs, and column screen (main entry J 15).

G 28 St. Thomas More Chapel, 1938. Office of Douglas Orr. The Catholic chapel of the Yale community. A turning point in architectural history takes place here between Rogers' rich fabric, which despite its date belongs essentially to the pre-Depression world, and the spare outline of the chapel. In its time St. Thomas More was a startling building, and it became a rallying point for a Depression generation who were rejecting Rogers' eclecticism as "dishonest" and looking for something which they could identify as "modern." Today we see the chapel less as a manifesto and more as a transition. North addition 1959.

G 29 248–58 Park Street, 1937. Norton and Townsend.
This pleasant block of shops was part of the attempt to
redevelop Park Street in the '30s. Like Rogers, Norton and
Townsend clearly caught the neighborhood's village quality.
Stores, colleges, and chapel are a good piece of urbanist
teamwork (all trim was originally white, relating the buildings
more explicitly to one another). Square lights across the
top of plate glass windows are typical of fashionable shop
design at the time.

G 30 Lynwood Place. An example of the delight of inac-
cessibility in a big city—one always comes upon Lynwood
Place with a sense of discovery and escape. Not opened
until the '80s, by which time the fire district had been established, Lynwood in contrast to the rest of the Village is
a street of brick. Unpretentious houses make a pleasant
background, aided by dark evergreens and ivy against red
walls. Shown here, **no. 34.**

G 31 348 Elm Street, c1835. A model of what much of
the West Village once looked like and of its potential for
restoration. Basically this is the same Greek Revival house
that can still be found all over the Village, the difference
being little more than paint and maintenance.
   No. 344: this sealed masonry building is **Manuscript,** latest
of the Yale senior societies; 1962, King Lui Wu.

G 32 361–63 Elm Street, c1871. Originally a stylish pair
in the lush post-bellum manner, topped by an extravagant
roof (note the telltale cornice which still survives), these
houses were purified by an ardent Colonial Revivalist, probably around 1915–20—the roofline straightened and dainty
Federalist porches substituted for the originals. The attempt
to bowdlerize Victorian architecture is seldom so winning.
   In the next block an inconspicuous small house, **no. 403,**
is probably Elm Street's most publicized building, the house
that Charles Moore remodeled for himself in 1966, restructuring the interior with vertical shafts of space and Pop decoration. 400-06 Elm Street: **Seabury Coop,** 1972, William
Pedersen and Associates.

G 33 University Place. The street was closed off from Whalley Avenue, and houses were moved around it, making this one of Redevelopment's showcase rehabilitation projects. At present still new and not yet settled in, it exposes a problem of scale: Victorian houses accustomed to a full-sized street and full-sized lots look a trifle ill at ease in this cul-de-sac. But mature planting will make a difference. Shown here: **no. 11.**

G 34 276 Dwight Street, c1864. Giddy woodwork of the '60s, topped off with a mock French tower, probably of the '90s, and a porte cochère out of Stanford White's Newport. Carriage house out back.

G 35 267–77 Dwight Street, c1874. Row houses were exceptional in the West Village. This is a medium-priced example. Cornice and top-floor windows make a splashy display, while wooden stoops and brick basements (instead of the fashionable brownstone) give away the economy model. Nos. 271 and 273 still have their iron rails and fences, no. 277 has its original door. The bow-front houses at the end date from about 1890, their full, round, tubular shape characteristic of the period. Residents recall that large corner houses used to give shelter to this block, now open and vulnerable to Whalley Avenue.

G 36 John Richardson House, 424 Elm Street, 1844. This was one of the most elegant villas in the west end—its walls flushboarded (now stuccoed), its roofline ornamented with a carved parapet, its windows trimmed with fine little leafy consoles. The present transformation (1934) is an interesting lesson in how details affect proportions. Eaves have been clipped, wide steps removed, and the one-story porch has been replaced by tall columns: i.e., horizontals have been erased, verticals have been added. Few people would recognize the result as the same building. The delicacy and assurance of the original suggest that the architect may have been Henry Austin, the design perhaps based on A. J. Davis's house down the street (G 60). Inside: a lithe stair with unusual newel post (compare K 6). Granite hitching posts still stand on the curb.

G 37 Dwight Street, Elm to Edgewood. Although the road is now widened, this block still suggests the 19th-century neighborhood. Some of the houses are well preserved (**nos. 235 and 227,** still painted colors the Greek Revival would own to), some are not (**nos. 222 and 232** were once Italian villas probably much like G 21). **No. 223** is an early town house (the clumsy porch indicates conversion to apartments in the 20th century); **no. 236** is a later and larger one (also converted, but more felicitously). **No. 216:** the street kept up with the times—the owners of this lot came back from California in love with Spanish Colonial and told a local architect exactly what they wanted (1919, R. W. Fabian).

G 38 245 Dwight Street, c1840. Originally a routine Greek Revival house much like its neighbors, the building had a dramatic change of life around the turn of the century, acquiring a jaunty little tower, a modish door, and a wrap-around porch imitating in miniature the wide verandas of Whitney Avenue and other fashionable streets. The interior experienced an even greater shock in 1968 when it was remodeled by Charles Moore—a coolly beautiful reworking of inner spaces and an outdoor room at the back.

G 39 61 Edgewood Avenue. Edgewood Avenue was nonexistent until the 1830s, so this one-story, single-chimney cottage of typical Colonial form was either moved here or is an example of a pre-Revolutionary type continuing far into the 19th century. In its present form it exemplifies a building practice of the turn of the century. As the pressure for rental housing rose, it became common landlord practice to raise old houses on brick basements, providing a new ground-floor apartment. Many examples remain in other parts of the city, particularly in the Third Ward where slums were developing (H 6). Photograph 1930s, before loss of clapboards and shutters.

No. 91, off Dwight Street to the west: another of the Greek Revival company, its original appearance well preserved.

G 40 192–94 Dwight Street, c1840. This house and **no. 188** next door are examples of early forms of multiple housing. No. 192–94 is two distinct houses owned by different owners, sharing a party wall and a common porch (this particular porch a later alteration)—a popular model in this period of early urbanization, for it provided a facade of more impressive urban length than either owner could have afforded alone. No. 188 is more intimate, with only one door. Such houses were usually owned by a single owner and half rented out. The blank wall over the door where normally there would be a window indicates the interior partition dividing the two halves. Note the leaf capitals of the porch—a more costly form than was usual in the West Village and a reminder that shared housing of this sort was an accepted custom far up the economic ladder.

G 41   169 Dwight Street, c1875. Here is Victorian Gothic as it made its way into the wood architecture of the back streets. Note the colonnettes of the porch, remote descendants of English forebears, and the shapely window heads. The incised ornament is typical of the Eastlake style which swept America in the '70s. An exceptionally fine Eastlake door, exceptionally well cared for.

G 42   Dwight Place Congregational Church, 1871. David R. Brown. The presence of this enormous Congregational church, which replaced the first village church on Howe Street, tells much about the social complexion of the Village at this time. In less than 30 years it would be joined by a second one, even bigger, only a few blocks away (G 49). The design is unusual, the material even more so. Described as "artificial stone," the building in fact is built of concrete blocks—one of the earliest known examples of this technique. The interior was de-Victorianized in the 20th century. Today the church is vacant and for sale, its appearance much changed by the removal of its three spires of fantastic outline.

G 43   Dwight Place. Crossing Chapel Street the scale changes—lots are bigger, the building line is set back. This end of the street was called Dwight Place, and the blocks between here and Park Street and Legion Avenue were in effect the Wooster Square of the West Village, with the now vanished Maltby mansion providing a park. Too close to the burgeoning slum of Oak Street, the area declined after World War I and today has been largely wiped out by the highway and redevelopment. Dwight Place still offers a few suggestive glimpses. Those who wish may go on down to the end now, where two of the early houses remain (G 59, G 60), or pick them up on the return trip. The photograph shown here was taken in 1896. The house on the right still stands, as shown below.

G 44   128 Dwight Street, 1894. An effective rendering in wood of the brick and stone castles of Whitney Avenue. Well maintained today as a funeral home, this house sustains the declining dignity of Dwight and Chapel Streets.

131 Dwight Street: one of the favorites of the end of the century—partly Queen Anne, partly Colonial Revival. Notice the fine patterning of spindles on the porch—a common mass-produced ornament but seldom done with such sharp delicacy.

G 45 Embassy Apartments, 102–16 Dwight Street, 1924. Lester Julianelle. Land was cheaper away from the center of town, and the low apartment house built in a large U around a court became the norm in New Haven. The expense of an elevator was avoided, the problem of light was solved. Such apartment houses tended to appear in old upper-middle-class streets where the social tone was still a drawing card but where real estate was just beginning to slip. Frequently they were jarring oversized intruders and added further to the slippage. The Embassy is an example of the better sort, pains obviously having been taken to uphold the tone. Although predominantly Georgian, tile roofs and arcade are probably an allusion to the ever-popular California style. (Photograph 1925.)

The tour now leaves the Village. There is a long stretch ahead. If you have parked your car, this is the time to get it.

G 46 1287 Chapel Street, 1877. Rufus G. Russell. After the fleshy moldings of the '60s and before the richly patterned surfaces of the '80s, there was a breathing spell in which a planar, hard-edge style appeared in New Haven—an astringent version of High Victorian Gothic. Except for iron crestings on the roof ridge, flung up like pennants into the sky, little distracts from the geometric facets of cubic and triangular solids or the rectangular pattern of windows and square tiles. Most of the known examples are by Russell (see also G 50). Notice the delicate finial, like a question mark. Up ahead, still far away, the tower of the Plymouth Church already presides over the street (G 49).

G 47 33 Beers Street, c1865. Some inspired builder struck out on his own here.

Beers Street is later in date than the intown streets (1860s and '70s) and a bit more individualistic. **No. 43:** an unusual towered Italian villa in miniature.

G 48 Sherman Avenue and Vicinity. Beyond Beers Street a different community begins, a spacious Victorian development launched in the 1860s and '70s but built chiefly in the 1890s and '00s with big showy frame houses reflecting the euphoria of a suddenly risen new middle class, here in the west end augmented by a strong German element. Broad avenues worthy of Napoleon III's Paris are lined with carpentry palaces. The backbone of the development however is two-family houses and the price range a moderate $4000–$8000. This neighborhood goes on for blocks, telling the story of a social explosion that covered acres of the urban fringe in the '90s, as also seen on Orange Street (L 30) and Howard Avenue (H 17). The architecture reveals the latent excitement. Originally all trim was white or light, and the streets danced with the vibrant outlines of gables, dormers, and prodigies of machine-made ornament. This territory was the special preserve of the hometown architects, chiefly William H. Allen and German-born Ferdinand VonBeren. Sherman Avenue, which was the showplace, marks the beginning, the river is the end. Enthusiasts of the period will enjoy exploring on their own. (The photograph shows Sherman Avenue in 1925, before the loss of the trees.)

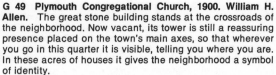

G 49   Plymouth Congregational Church, 1900. William H. Allen.   The great stone building stands at the crossroads of the neighborhood. Now vacant, its tower is still a reassuring presence placed on the town's main axes, so that wherever you go in this quarter it is visible, telling you where you are. In these acres of houses it gives the neighborhood a symbol of identity.

Opposite: **St. Raphael's Hospital.** Older units, built at various times, were detailed with some refinement, making a neighborly civic complex, complementing the church. Additions now under construction: Ellerbe Architects, St. Paul.

G 50   131 Sherman Avenue, 1879. Rufus G. Russell.   In the 1860s and '70s development of the empty Sherman Avenue area was heralded by a row of mansions on Chapel Street where the hospital is today, and these long gave the neighborhood its character. All are now gone, but this close cousin around the corner will serve to remind us of the early High Victorian Gothic style of the west end—of brick and brownstone with slate roofs, fine touches of pierced work on porch and bargeboard, and full, leafy Gothic capitals. Notice also the lintels with polished stone designs and the detail around the eave. The door is much like its contemporary at 169 Dwight Street (G 41) although paint now hides it. Filigree iron crestings once topped the roof ridges like fanciful crowns. Compare G 46, E 24.

G 51   105 Sherman Avenue, c1870.   A standard version of the mansard house, notable in having preserved its iron trim, even on the side wing. This sort of architectural jewelry, breaking up the sharp edge of the roofline with glinting openwork, added height and also a touch of pageantry. It was an important part of the imagery of the period, and it is gratifying to find a well-preserved example.

No. 74   Sherman Avenue, low-moderate income housing, 1970; Louis Sauer Associates, Philadelphia.

G 52   Charles Nicklas and Theresa Weibel Houses, 110 and 114 Sherman Avenue, 1899. Brown and VonBeren.   A tremendous pair, fortunately both still perfectly painted with white trim highlighting every complexity of form as it was obviously intended to do—these were houses of rich effects, and nothing was meant to be missed. Joseph Weibel and Charles Nicklas started a brewing business in the 1850s, and lived near the brewery down on Oak Street. After Joseph's death, his wife Theresa took over, evidently with success, and both families presently migrated up to Sherman Avenue.

G 53 George Alling House, 120 Sherman Avenue, 1867. Rufus G. Russell. This could almost be San Francisco or Texas, although aluminum siding has diminished the chiaroscuro of moldings and window frames. One of Russell's gaudiest commissions, there are several versions of the design among his drawings.

G 54 Two-family house, 1472 Chapel Street, 1906. With the disappearance of the privy, the barn, and the kitchen garden, the traditional deep city lot lost much of its purpose, and the two-family house came in as a way of using this waste space and fitting more dwelling units into narrow city frontages. The two-family house differs from the double houses of the 1830s (G 40) in that it is deep rather than broad and is divided horizontally rather than vertically, giving both families four exposures. Sometimes called a "flat" house, it can be universally recognized by its two-tiered porch. The form first appeared tentatively in the '80s (see L 27 for an early example; also 590 George Street, 1885), then burst into riotous bloom in the '90s, built by the hundreds all over town wherever new middle-class streets were opening up. Prices ranged from about $2000 to $8000 or $9000. Details varied but all had in common a well-designed plan, privacy, and spaciousness: a high standard of livability at moderate cost. The example shown here was unusually lavish. Now used for offices, the living hall with column screen and golden oak can still be seen. The "art glass" window on the landing was a must. (For more about two-family houses see M 6.)

G 55 262 Sherman Avenue, 1893. William H. Allen. Corner castles were special favorites—compare this one with the one above. It has lost some of its festivity with its railings and garlands painted out dark, but none of its authority.

Down the block, **no. 231** (by Allen's partner, Richard Williams, 1902) shows the more sober Edwardian fashion just coming on.

G 56 Edward Malley House, Batter Terrace, 1858. In the west end, as elsewhere, two or three rural estates were built in the mid-century. The Malley house was the biggest and surely the most ornate. Now crowded with apartments, it is still a good example of the Villa style in its ripe, last phase. Arched doorway and opulent brackets are untouched; the stair, though walled up, still has its ornamental window on the landing and the majestic Victorian banister; over the door in the foyer the monogram "EM" still sparkles in frosted glass. Originally the grounds filled the whole block up to what is now 1494 Chapel: the barn (shown below) still stands on George Street, and the driveway is now Batter Terrace. Edward Malley, born in Ireland, founded a dry goods business in the '50s which soon became New Haven's leading department store. Shortly after 1900 the family began cutting up the estate (houses on George Street by Brown and VonBeren) and presently moved uptown. (Photograph 1890.)

At the entrance to Batter Terrace **Bushnell Park** commemorates the man who promoted the *Monitor*. Monument with splendid eagle: 1906, Charles A. Platt architect, Herbert Adams sculptor. The fence seems to be older than the park—sections taken from the Green perhaps? Overlooking the park: **1494 Chapel Street,** a wood version of the Victorian Gothic style we have already seen in brick (G 46, G 50). Cleanly faceted form and high crested roofs remain, but old photographs show how much character has now been lost to aluminum siding.

G 57 First Church of Christ Scientist, now Bikur Cholim Sheveth Achim, 1909. Richard Williams. On a better site and in a better relation to the park, this would have made a handsome visual focus for these rather featureless blocks. Notice the interesting front window.

The tour now turns back to town. For those who want to keep on going: **135 Derby Avenue, Berger Bros. Company,** a factory which settled here in 1914 and became the nucleus of a small industrial quarter (main building 1933 by Douglas Orr, with modernistic lobby). Beyond is the river and Edgewood Park (F 37), and farther out the Yale Bowl (**Bowl** 1913, Charles A. Ferry; **Lapham Field House,** 1924, Day and Klauder, Philadelphia; **Walter Camp Gateway,** 1927, John W. Cross, New York; **Cullman Tennis Courts,** 1973, Herbert S. Newman Associates).

G 58 George Street. An ordinary well-to-do street of the second half of the 19th century. Though it is no longer very prepossessing, the inquiring eye will find things of interest. Notice the moderniza'ion of an Edwardian house at **111 Sherman Avenue** (1971) and the small towered villa at **660 George Street** opposite the hospital; also barns in backyards—a reminder not only that George Street belonged to the carriage trade but that urban barns continued to be part of the city's life right into the 20th century. Shown here: the **Malley barn,** between Winthrop and Sherman Avenues. No. 563 George Street: **St. Michael's Ukrainian Catholic Church,** 1957, J. K. Jastremsky, New York. **Waverly Street housing:** a village inside the Village—see C 6.

G 59 56 Dwight Street, c1862. A survivor of the antebellum villas that once stood on Dwight Place and Howe Street.

Next door: **St. Barbara Greek Orthodox Church,** 1941, C. H. Abramowitz.

G 60 501 George Street. A. J. Davis wrote to James A. Hillhouse in 1836: "Mr. Dean, of Newhaven, has broken in upon me, and I am obliged to 'fit him out' with a double house of considerable pretension." Mr. Dean thereafter lived on this corner, his house facing George Street. But the house here now is a single house facing Dwight Street, the style clearly of the 1860s—this surely is not Davis's house. All the same the porch catches one's eye—such a Greek Revival kind of porch, just what one might find in the 1830s on a villa of considerable pretension. One can only guess that when Mr. Dean's house was remodeled, Davis's porch was saved. The smaller porches on the north and south were evidently the two original entrances (photograph 1939).

95 Dwight Street: **Clarence Blakeslee House,** moved from across the street (1914, R. W. Foote), the last house of "considerable pretension" ever built in this neighborhood. (The housing opposite is noted in C 5.)

G 61 19 Howe Street, 1885. An original variant of Queen Anne, with overblown spindles like Christmas tree ornaments and interesting roof shapes. A vigorous building, enhanced by rich dark colors. The barn is shown in C 4.

H The Milford Turnpike and Boston Post Road: Columbus Avenue, Water Street, and Forbes Avenue

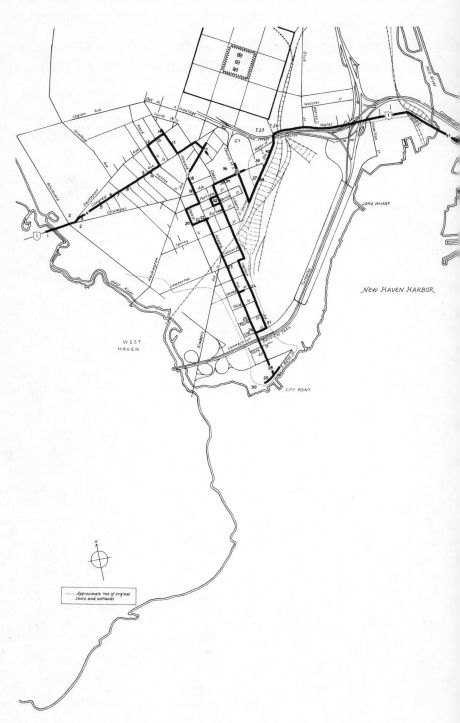

NEW HAVEN HARBOR

WEST HAVEN

LONG WHARF

BAYVIEW PARK

CITY POINT

N

····· Approximate line of original
shore and wetlands

82

H The Milford Turnpike and Boston Post Road (Columbus Avenue, Water Street, and Forbes Avenue)

A long route that crosses the bottom of the city and also surveys the harbor from end to end. This is not a prepossessing tour. It will interest those who are concerned with urban decay and redevelopment, with poverty, industrial waste, and the use of wetlands and waterfront.

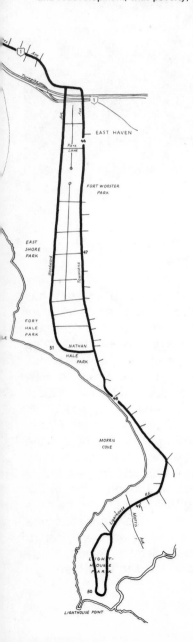

H The Milford Turnpike and Boston Post Road: Columbus Avenue, Water Street, Forbes Avenue.

One of the oldest roads in New Haven, the Milford highway has existed since at least 1639. The first bridge across the West River was here, and from this point the main routes into town diverged: now Davenport, Congress, and Columbus Avenues. At first serving merely as access to fields, Congress was opened to the bridge around 1810. By 1847 Columbus appears as "the Road to New York," and so it remained, linking up eventually with Water Street and Forbes Avenue to become the Boston Post Road and US 1. Those who do not know what motoring was like before the Merritt and Wilbur Cross Parkways or what trucking was like before the Interstates may find it interesting to explore this artifact of the early automobile age. New Haven is typical of every city from Maine to Florida through which US 1 was cut: local and through traffic, trucks and cars and trolley cars together fighting their way across the most congested part of the city, holding closely to the blackened trail of industry, railroad, waterfront, and slums. Our tour will depart somewhat from this historic course because Columbus Avenue today is in the midst of demolition, but those who want to take it straight need only follow the signs—it is still US 1.

H 1   The West River.   Stop on the bridge and look north. If it is late afternoon and West Rock is a glowing rose with purple furrows, you will understand why this spot was once celebrated for its beauty. Along the river still lie the "rich and goodly meadows" that first drew the colonists to Quinnipiac. In the 19th century, as farming declined, the meadows gradually became waste. Their borders however soon found a use as empty land for cemeteries, and with St. Bernard's, Evergreen, Mapledale, St. Lawrence, Westville, Mishkan Israel, and Congregation B'nai Jacob and Beaverdale Memorial Parks, the West River and its headwaters became death valley. Later the meadows found a use as sport fields, and recently they have acquired new value as virgin soil for highways and shopping centers. This may be observed in ripe form today down Boulevard south of US 1. Boulevard itself is a new ring road of the 1890s mostly on landfill in the meadows.

H 2   Cemeteries.   To the north: **Evergreen Cemetery** (1848) with Mapledale added on beyond. Fifty years later than Grove Street (J 24), Evergreen shows the more romantic layout which had become the established style of the American mortuary landscape. A Gothic gate by David R. Brown (1872) was appropriately placed at the head of Sylvan Avenue. Part of the fence remains, but the gate was recently demolished. Chapel (shown here), 1902, Leoni Robinson. To the south: **St. Bernard's** (1851). This was the first Roman Catholic cemetery in New Haven (earlier burials had been in the churchyard), and its presence testifies to the growth of the Catholic community at this time.

H 3   Defenders' Monument, 1910. James E. Kelly.   Commemorating the defense of New Haven against the British in 1779. Kelly was an authority on historical detail: costumes were carefully studied and the cannon copied from a Revolutionary cannon. Here at the entrance to the city we meet one of New Haven's most characteristic shapes: the triangular lot resulting from the diagonals of the radial roads, in this case turned to account as a well-designed small park.

H 4   The Old Third Ward (H4–H40). The Third Ward origin-ally covered the whole southwest quarter of the city south of Davenport Avenue, separated from town by the West Creek. Like the West Village (G 19), it grew up as a more or less cohesive community with its own industry and social pyramid, but its development was slower. By the Federal period a pocket of poverty had settled in the area known as the Hill (H 16), and although more prosperous growth surrounded it, the top crust remained thin. Close to the docks and the rail-road, this became the melting pot. In 1825 the Irish came—first to dig the canal, then to build the railroad; in the '40s came Germans—Lutherans, Catholics, and Jews. Until the Civil War this immigrant community was centered mainly in the neighborhood of the Hill. After the Civil War, as a second generation rose to affluence, solid middle-class houses began to spread over the whole surrounding area until the end of the century when a vast new wave of immigration came—Central European Jews, Italians, and others—changing the face of the Third Ward and producing the tenements that today are its special architectural feature. After World War II another wave of immigration came, with blacks from the South fol-lowed by Puerto Ricans. This represented a displacement, not an expansion, and no new construction resulted. Today the middle class is largely gone, and the old Third Ward—all of it now loosely called the Hill—has become the object of massive redevelopment (H 16, H 20, H 30, H 35).

H 5   890 and 886 Congress Avenue. Matchbox houses like these are hard to date—easily moved, lived in by transients, they seldom leave their history in the city records. No build-ings at all appear in this end of town until the 1850s. No. 886 is probably an example of the minimal working-class house built through the whole middle part of the 19th century. No. 890, with its sharper roof, is later—it does not show up here until after 1888. Both houses have been raised.

Congress Avenue is Main Street. As you go through and look down the side streets at rotting rows of once-painted Victo-rian porches, or shabby factories and now boarded-up tene-ments, or look into backyards and notice an occasional carriage house, the history of the Third Ward gradually comes together.

H 6   Raised House, 827 Congress Avenue. With its full cornice and slim glazing bars in the rectangular gable win-dow, this was once a pure example of the Greek Revival vernacular. It does not appear here until the 1870s or '80s but may have been built as early as the '30s. It was later raised on a high basement to make another apartment, a popular land-lord practice in the developing slums of the Third Ward.

H 7   Philip Fresenius Brewery, 820 Congress Avenue, 1874 and 1878. By the 1870s the Third Ward had a strong German element, and fortunes were being made in beer. Character-istically the breweries and the houses of the beer barons were flamboyant affairs. Little is left today of this once exuberant architecture, but the Fresenius Brewery comes closest to preserving the spirit. Old photographs show a tower, central cornice, and a beer barrel chimney pot which are all now gone, but the heroic beer drinker on the gable remains. Across the avenue a Fresenius mansion appeared in 1889—the **stable** can be still seen fronting on West Street. Architect of the stable was Clarence H. Stilson, and it was apparently considered interesting enough to have been pub-lished in 1890 in the *Inland Architect and News Record.*

H 8 744 Congress Avenue, 1883. One of the few early tenements of the '70s and '80s. Built specifically for multiple occupancy on the "flat" principle, these buildings were an advance over older frame structures, which had been simply big single houses in which many families lived together. In the Third Ward the builders of tenements were apt to be earlier immigrants who had prospered and gone into neighborhood real estate. Note J. Miller's name on the facade. Miller had a meat market on the ground floor; he and his wife Katarina lived in part of the building and rented the rest.

H 9 625 Congress Avenue, 1897. Brown and VonBeren· These were among the most deluxe apartments of the Third Ward, costing about $1500 a unit. A comparison with the Oxford on High Street (G 7) shows a difference in style between Congress Avenue and uptown, but basically both designs are facades only, and both are nearly lightless inside. VonBeren designed many apartments in the Third Ward.

H 10 86 Hallock Street, c1875. An architectural oddity, this little mansarded octagon plainly belongs to a time when the street was occupied by people sufficiently well off to be style-conscious but not enough so to be inhibited.

H 11 Welch Training School, 1883. Leoni Robinson. Before turning north on Ward Street, observe the school up ahead. A sheer high-shouldered pile of gables and bays looms like a crag over the playground beside it—one of the few echoes in New Haven of Norman Shaw's London. This was the most ambitious school building, outside of Hillhouse High, that New Haven had yet built. It still provides a rousing bit of drama to enliven a dreary street.

Ward Street is an ordinary middle-class street, mainly of the '70s—a helpful reminder of the character of much of the neighborhood before the huge migrations and new tenements of the end of the century. The east side is scheduled for demolition for an eventual public school, to replace Welch on four acres of land. At the corner of Davenport: **Zion Lutheran Church,** 1969, Granbery, Cash and Associates.

H 12   145 Davenport Avenue, 1860.   A Swiss cottage in the manner of A. J. Downing. New Haven tended to be cautious about such styles. Here a clipped gable, scalloped eaves, and vertical boards produced an unusually whole-hearted specimen. A porch similar to no. 122's has been replaced with a two-decker of the 1910s.

Davenport Avenue began to develop in the '60s as a good residential neighborhood, and these blocks by the hospital long kept their character. Until recently, St. John's Catholic Church, with its mid-Victorian rectory and shade trees, stood where the parking lot is, forming a green island around which the whole intersection turned. Part of the fence remains.

H 13   122 Davenport Avenue, 1864.   Another of the stylish early houses on the block. By 1910 the avenue was a well-to-do mixed neighborhood of Irish, Yankees, and Germans.

H 14   836 Howard Avenue, 1886.   A nice example of the bricklayer's craft, this house belonged to George Treat, mason and builder. Notice the paneling of the facade, terra cotta tiles in relief, floral stained glass window, and elaborate window trim. **No. 840** next door (built probably in 1873) belonged to Treat's father, Lyman, head of the firm—another advertisement of the mason's skill. This pair is a pat illustration of the different brick styles of these two decades.

H 15   Yale-New Haven Hospital.   On Davenport and South Street: Memorial Unit, 1951, Office of Douglas Orr. On Howard Avenue: north corner (shown here), 1964, E. Todd Wheeler and Perkins & Will with the Office of Douglas Orr, deCossy, Winder and Associates; middle section, 1963, E. Todd Wheeler and Perkins & Will; south corner, at Howard and Congress Avenues, 1973, Douglas Orr, deCossy, Winder and Associates. Of the 19th-century hospital complex, founded on this site in 1826, one wing remains, buried in additions: Tompkins East, 1873, Frederick C. Withers. The **Yale Medical School** is behind the hospital on Cedar Street.

H 16 The Hill. Around 1800 the section south of the West Creek was called Sodom Hill and described as a place of poverty and crime. That name long ago disappeared but it is still commemorated in the name of the area today: The Hill. This is a tract of high ground rising steeply from the creek bed, comprising a dense small knot of streets between the hospital and a secondary creek near Columbus Avenue, now a railroad. After the West Creek was filled in the 1870s the neighborhood spread down over the flats along Oak Street. Oak Street became mainly the home of Central European Jews, while Italians took the place of departing Irish and Germans on the Hill, founding St. Anthony's church before they in turn moved on to be followed by blacks and Puerto Ricans. Today all memory of the neighborhood's checkered past is in the process of being erased. The Connector now covers Oak Street, and redevelopment is obliterating the rest (see map, H 35). Only a glimpse remains of the old narrow streets, the somber dirty buildings—most of them already empty and waiting for the wrecker. Above all this **St. Anthony's Roman Catholic Church** still presides, like the church of the Italian village that it was lovingly designed to recall (1903, Richard Williams).

H 17 Howard Avenue, City Point, and the West Side of the Harbor. The tour here makes a long detour down Howard Avenue and back. Those who want to skip it can turn off on Carlisle Street and pick up the route at Spireworth Square (H 32). Howard Avenue is the spine of a promontory that lies between the harbor and the West River, now losing its onetime water-girt character as landfill increasingly packs it in on both sides. The street may owe its noble width to James Hillhouse, who early in the 19th century tried to open up this area. Little came of his plans until the 1860s when the horse-car came and a slow build-up began. Toward the end of the century Howard Avenue had its heyday as the fashionable center of this end of town—an eruption of ornate frame houses which, like Orange Street and Sherman Avenue, represented the new money and the new style of a swiftly rising middle class. By World War I the bloom was over: tenements began moving down from Congress Avenue, industry and poverty inched in from the railroads too close by. This building history can still be plainly read along the street and only a few examples need be mentioned. But the grand sweep of the avenue itself should be noticed.

At the tip of the promontory is an older hamlet, an oystering community originally called Oyster Point which grew up before the Civil War as an offshoot of the oystering port of Fair Haven (Itinerary O). The shape of the waterfront has changed drastically in the last 25 years. The dredging of the harbor in 1949 resulted in an extension of made land to the east, and ten years later the turnpike created another on the west. The map at the head of this itinerary shows the original shoreline.

H 18   657 Howard Avenue, 1911. Rocco Davino. The triple-decker was a favorite type of tenement around World War I. Responding to the great demand for rental housing resulting from the boom in New Haven's munitions, these buildings went up in enormous numbers in all the poorer parts of town. Most were cheap frame structures with little pretension. The one shown here is the better sort, aiming for a vaguely Georgian stylishness in the design of the porch. Traditionally in tenement architecture, prestige is expressed by the cornice. This one is so exuberant the building seems about to take flight.

H 19   Nicholas Countryman House, 622 Howard Avenue, 1866. Rufus G. Russell. The solid square shape perpetuates the traditional Italian Villa, but sharp dormers, ornamental bracing and a big roof pulled down over the walls like a bonnet are early signs of the Gothic Stick Style of the '70s. Countryman, one of the town's leading builders, also built the church next door: **Howard Avenue Congregational Church** (1867, Rufus G. Russell), founded by abolitionists from the South Church (H 33), now shorn of its spires. In the next block: **Grace Methodist Church,** 1888, now Wesley United Methodist Church. *(Congregational Church demolished summer 1975.)*

H 20   Hill Central K-4 School, 1971. Carlin, Pozzi and Associates. Clusters of hexagonal classrooms along the rear can be converted from closed to open plan in many combinations: an inventive solution to the problem of changing methods of teaching.

No. 267–281 Portsea Street: a row of the 1880s handsomely renovated in red and black by the Redevelopment Agency. Opposite: a **pocket playground** (in-house design by the Agency) makes an architectural abstraction in a landscape of rubble. This whole area is the site of the Hill's major redevelopment thrust, covering the large tract of demolition which can now be seen and more yet to come, lying roughly between Columbus, Washington, Spring, and DeWitt Streets. A 5–8 school is to be built (William Pedersen and Associates, architects), and new housing (Edward E. Cherry, architect). Demolition when completed will include over 50 acres, extending east to join the Church Street South Redevelopment area: see map, H 35.

H 21   181 Putnam Street, c1855. A fresh version of the Italian Villa, prim lines loosened up with ornamental moldings, arched doorway, and sprightly monitor on the roof. You come upon this house with sudden pleasure, surprised to find such a piece of work on such a street. The answer is that it has not been here long. It was built up at the corner, on Howard Avenue. This section was then the avenue's best (traces of elegance survive in the wreckage of **no. 552** which was the next-door property, and in **no. 559** with its carriage house behind on Carlisle Street). In 1899 a developer moved the villa to the rear of its lot facing the back street, where it now continues to queen it over the neighborhood, missing only its cast-iron fence, which got left behind (H 22).

H 22   Charles T. Coyle House, 530 Howard Avenue, 1899.
Behind the iron fence belonging to the Putnam Street villa
are the three usurpers who took its place, built by an Irish
entrepreneur named Charles T. Coyle. The first generation of
Coyles had come to New Haven in the 1850s and settled near
the Hill, producing a close-knit clan working mostly in the
building trades. Young Charles learned his way around City
Hall, in time became a lawyer, and went into real estate, using
his family connections to build and sell houses in the Third
Ward. He himself moved into the fashionable section of
Howard Avenue, but only briefly. His affairs evidently pros-
pering, he soon moved onward and upward to Whitney
Avenue—for his activities there see E 28. It is interesting to
compare this trio of rather unsophisticated Howard Avenue
houses with the row he built a few years later on Cold Spring
Street (E 15).

**H 23   All Saints Episcopal Church, now Church of the As-
cension, 1887.**   An effective design for a corner lot, the tower
anchoring the building from whichever angle it is seen. Leoni
Robinson, architect.

**H 24   Seamless Rubber Company, 253 Hallock Avenue,
1919.**   Good showcase industrial architecture of the '20s;
loft construction with brick and glass infill, ornamented with
Doric pilasters at the entrances and plain globe lights. Note
the airy effect of the two open sections on the second floor.
The parking lot in the foreground may be a crude assault on
Howard Avenue, but for the first time it is now possible to see
the factory.

**H 25   Howard Avenue Methodist Church, now New Light
Holy Church, 1875. Forepart and Tower 1890. Luzerne I.
Thomas.**   A pleasant country church. The older part, first
built on Sixth Street, made a stately three weeks' progress to
its present site—service one Sunday was held in the middle
of Howard Avenue. Thomas, a builder and carpenter living
down at the Point, was noted in the trade for his knowledge
of drawing and design. This church is also called the Oyster
Point Church. It marks the beginning of the old oystering
community.

H 26 164 Howard Avenue, 1885. This house, which belonged to a prosperous oyster cultivator, brings us to the oystering village at the end of the point. With red and black brick, brownstone, terra cotta, shingles, and paneling, it is a good example of the local builder's Queen Anne style. On the corner, **no. 154:** a vernacular castle of the '90s, with French tower and "art glass" window. **No. 142,** slightly later, shows an image of relaxed American living replacing romantic castles.

The Connecticut Turnpike crosses the Avenue here, raising a point about highway design. Here is one of New England's biggest throughways cut right across a suburban street, and yet it causes less rupture than might have been expected. Compare this with the total sundering of the urban fabric made by the Oak Street Connector (Itinerary C). What makes the difference?

Under the turnpike lies part of **Bay View Park** (1890, Donald Grant Mitchell). Originally a drive lined with windswept trees ran along the harbor (part of the drive remains, but the harbor has gone). In the interior was a lake where children sailed toy boats, with an island reached by a rustic bridge. Though small, Bay View was considered one of the city's most enchanting public places.

H 27 76–78 Howard Avenue, c1865. A decorous villa dressed up with fancy carpentry. It does not appear to have been built for two families, and the upper part of the porch may be later.

Other villas and Greek Revival houses nearby indicate that the oyster business was flourishing by the 1850s. **No. 19** is probably the oldest, a plain Greek Revival house sporting a porch in the A. J. Davis manner (G 60); in the '90s Luzerne Thomas lived here. **No. 36–38** is a happy marriage between a straightlaced villa of the '50s and some later Saratoga frippery; the house has been raised and a new story set under it. **No. 45,** a pleasant example of the '70s. **No. 32** is one of the Point's last houses, a bungalow in the California style popular around 1915.

H 28 Oyster Point, now City Point. This is the river's mouth. Oystermen's shacks are known to have existed on the estuary as far back as the 18th century. In the 19th, as New Haven oysters became a major local industry, an oystering village grew up at Fair Haven and a hamlet settled here. Although oystering declined in the 1930s (victim of the Depression, hurricanes, starfish, and pollution), boats have continued to be the life of the tiny community. Off season it keeps a feeling of remoteness from the city and a sense of the past. The presence of the sea is still felt here.

A few oyster docks remain. At the end of one (shown here) a sea-gray **restaurant** fits into the scene (1974, William L. Pereira Associates, Los Angeles.)

H 29 111 South Water Street, c1849. This oysterman's house was designed with style (the central section is the original part), with flushboarded walls and nicely paired narrow windows under a flattened gable. Porch and traprock terracing provided a base for the dainty superstructure. One section of the Victorian railing that formerly bordered the porch may still be seen on the steps.

South Water Street is an unusual example of the old architecture of the waterfront, the houses built against the bank and raised on high cellars where oysters were unloaded and stored. The tide used to rise to a few feet from the cellars, and boats floated almost to the door. This is an ancient building form which the colonists seem to have brought with them from Europe and which persisted here and on the Quinnipiac into the 19th century. It is an interesting facet of New Haven architectural history, described more fully in O 10.

H 30 Point West. Walk down to the end of South Water Street where it fades into the great salt meadows of the estuary. Among bedsprings and old tires you will see tons of urban rubble. This is the beginning of the platform for Point West, an 800-unit housing project to consist of three towers and surrounding row houses (Don Mott and Emil Steo, architects, Melville, N.Y.). The wetlands will be filled and land pushed somewhat farther into the river. Sea Street will be closed so that all access will go through South Water Street. This whole riverland area is to be a major center of development. To people approaching New Haven on the turnpike the towers will serve as a herald of the modern city, while for the section north of the road new industry is planned. On the point itself, on the east end of South Water Street, apartments and a marina are projected.

H 31 Hallock Avenue. At the foot of the avenue a modern building mediates between the old world of Oyster Point and the new world of the turnpike (**Albie Booth Boys Club,** 1970, Davis Cochran Miller Baerman Noyes—see B 1). Hallock Avenue provides an opportunity to observe the receding waterfront. On Third Street there was once a yacht club, and the embankment on Cedar Street was a bluff along the shore with a swimming beach below. The avenue is named for Gerard Hallock, one of several who tried unsuccessfully to develop this section. Around 1840 he built a Tudor manor on the harbor at Cassius Street, and the area became known as the Hallock Quarter. In 1866 the railroad (New York line) bought the estate and filled the flats below for yards. Lying under the Hill, the railroad intensified the working-class character of the Third Ward and settled the destiny of the west side of the harbor. More fill and more tracks followed around 1910, and in 1949 spoil from the dredging of the harbor finished filling in the whole triangle between the Long Wharf and Oyster Point. Today these lonely flats with their desolate railroad shops are a strange faceless country, a back door to the forgotten heights of the Hallock Quarter.

H 32 Spireworth Square, now Trowbridge Square. It is hard as you now stand in this disheveled little place to perceive its spatial order, but the map will show you that Spireworth is the central square of a miniature nine squares whose outer dimension is the same as one of the nine squares of New Haven. The first tentative layout goes back to 1800 and to New Haven's great exponent of urban order, James Hillhouse. After the failure of his project, the area fell on hard times—a poor community which by the 1830s was named Mt. Pleasant and described as a "plague spot." It was then acquired by Nathaniel and Simeon Jocelyn—artists, social reformers, crusaders for black rights, and among the biggest real estate speculators in the city's history (see also N 43). It was the Jocelyns who designed the model layout and its tiny green, reflecting the formal grace of the wealthier center of the city (the name Spireworth alluded to "a slender spindling sort of grass" that grows only in poor soil). But like Hillhouse, the Jocelyns were too hopeful, and by 1850 only three houses had been built (169 Cedar Street survives). Gerard Hallock next entered the scene, along with the Trowbridge family, a merchant dynasty who had owned land in this part of town since the first Colonial grants. It was they who built the church (the tower can be seen just beyond the rooftops—H 33) and probably the cast iron fence, imitating the one on the Green; and in the end the Trowbridges did much developing around the area. The south side of the square was built in the '50s (the southeast corner house remains); the north side in the '60s (all houses remain except the west corner); the west side in the '70s (all remain except the north corner); and the east side was finished off in the '80s with four houses on the upper end (all remain). Modernizations have since disrupted this small well-knit place, principally the school (1925, Brown and VonBeren, now the Trowbridge Recreation Center), whose gaping corner demolished the enclosure of the square. The damage was completed by the removal of part of the fence and some of the shapely border of trees outlining the green. Spireworth Square nevertheless remains a place of unusual interest. An unverified tradition persists that one range of houses was built by the Jocelyns for fugitive blacks from the South. In any case the square is a rare example of working-class housing over a sequence of four decades. It is also a contribution to American 19th-century urbanism of a rare sort.

H 33 South Congregational Church, now Sacred Heart Church, 1851. Sidney Mason Stone. Donated by Gerard Hallock and Thomas Trowbridge, the church was designed, in Hallock's words, to "please the eye with beautiful proportions and a simplicity that never tires, rather than tickle it with ornament for a time, to be disgusted in the end." Hallock's pro-slavery sympathies in the Civil War caused many of the congregation to leave (see H 19), and in 1875 the church was bought by the Catholics. This is one of Stone's few surviving works. The present entablature covers original Romanesque arcading under the cornice, and the cupola and belfry replace a Gothic tower.

H 34 Katherine Harvey Terrace, 81–95 Liberty Street, 1961. Office of Carleton Granbery. With private gardens behind walls and an inviting little central court, this unpretentious elderly housing looks snug and cosy. The grass is green, shrubs in the court are flourishing and cared for, and vines grow over the garden walls. Down the street: **Liberty Square Homes,** 1962, Carl Koch, Cambridge, Mass.

H 35 Redevelopment: Church Street South. Standing in front of the church you are on the edge of the Hill: below you is a panorama of redevelopment. Pause a moment to reconstruct what was here before. This is the place where the East and West Creeks met the harbor—energizing center of the city for 300 years. At the foot of the hill Columbus Avenue crossed the West Creek. Beyond was the Long Wharf, with the East Creek, later the canal, and finally a web of railroads converging from New York, Boston, the Naugatuck Valley, and the north. Docks, coal yards, and factories surrounded them. In these few acres of land and water lay the fertile triangle from which the city grew outward like a fan. By the 1940s this old center had fallen into decay. When the state cut through it in the 1950s with the Oak Street Connector, the Redevelopment Agency joined in, and Church Street South (shown on the map along with contiguous redevelopment in the Hill) became one of its most sweeping programs of demolition and reconstruction. Louis Kahn was briefly retained to plan the Hill section, and Mies van der Rohe was initially engaged to plan Church Street South, later succeeded by Charles Moore.

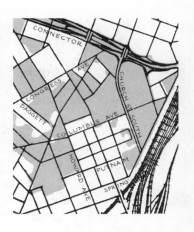

H 36 Lee High School, 1964. Kevin Roche, John Dinkeloo and Associates. Recognizing the importance of public symbols, New Haven's redevelopment program sought to bring to the city a high standard of public architecture. Lee High, fittingly named for Mayor Lee, is the most monumental statement of this effort. Lying in a shallow, modeled bowl of earth and approached by bridges that tie it only lightly to the passing street, it creates a static space in which the huge form lies at rest. Administered educationally as four "houses," the symmetry of the design expresses this fact, joint athletic facilities projecting at the rear.

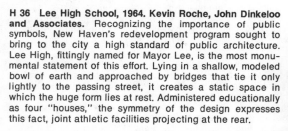

H 37 Church Street South Housing, 1969. ML/TW Charles Moore Associates. Moore's housing attempts to rethink current planning stereotypes with their strong suburban bias and to provide a civilized urban environment, preserving some of the traditional qualities of the urban context—permanence, dignity, festivity, interaction, variety. Georgian terraces face the outer world with impeccable urbanity, while along the spine of the pedestrian street an inner world unfolds of inventive and exciting effects: manholes form a circle defining a plaza, arcaded screens give de Chirico perspectives ("low-moderate baroque" *Progressive Architecture* has called it). Built to minimum standards, the buildings are simple, the spaces between them exploited for maximum effect. Although the project has not been completed as planned, there is much to study and enjoy.

H 38 Union Station, 1918. Cass Gilbert. Addition, 1954, Yamasaki, Leinweber and Associates, Detroit. The Gilbert-Olmsted plan sought to refit New Haven with symbols of the American 20th century. Central to the plan was the creation of a formal railroad entrance—a new station with a grand plaza and an avenue lined with trees leading to the Green. The station was realized but nothing else was, and in the end Union Station was left a forlorn palace in a decaying part of town. The design, like the Library (I 9), shows Gilbert's effort to create a specifically New Haven idiom, mixing Colonial motifs with the new grandeur of the Beaux-Arts movement. Barbarously treated in recent years, the station is now threatened with demolition. Citizens and the city are seeking to restore it for use as a transportation center.

H 39   Restaurant, 5 Columbus Avenue, 1967. Paul Mitarachi.
A dramatic but formal design which effectively advertises
its function amid a confused street pattern.

**H 40   Department of Police Service, 1973. Douglas Orr,
deCossy, Winder and Associates.**   The streets in this part of
town were oriented toward the creeks. When the creeks
disappeared, what was left was a curious lozenge pattern
which has long made a coherent street architecture difficult. The Police Building, although some have found it
menacing with its narrow window slits, is a restorer of architectural order, giving itself affirmatively to the odd shape
of the lot and defining the streets around it. Compare it with
the doggedly square shape of the older building beside it.
  As you go under the Connector, you are crossing the head
of the Long Wharf; the railroad bridge beyond takes you
over the East Creek and the canal. **Water Street,** as its name
plainly says, was the waterfront—in New Haven's maritime
heyday a forest of masts, later a highly charged stream of
energy connecting wharves, railroads, rivers, and creeks.
Today it is far from the shore, a nondescript place under
the hulk of the turnpike. **No. 119:** office building, 1968, Leo
F. Caproni Associates. The apartment building in back of
Water Street is elderly housing, **60 Warren Street,** 1963,
Office of Carleton Granbery.

H 41   Tomlinson's Bridge.   Twenty years ago a solid mass
of traffic, often compounded by a freight train going down
the middle, the bridge today lies nearly idle under the shadow
of the turnpike. The drawbridge was hit by a ship, and one
lane has been left in the up position for years. The river
mouth is wide here where the Mill and the Quinnipiac come
together, and it was not bridged until 1796 when a toll bridge
was built, bringing the east side of the harbor at last in
easy reach.
  South down Hamilton Street, the sere expanse of rubble
was **Waterside Park.** Bought in 1890 and designed by Donald
Grant Mitchell for playgrounds, with a bathing pier and
allées of lindens and willows, some of it is now under I 95, the
rest has been sold to the telephone company for development.

**H 42   Boathouse, 74 Forbes Avenue, 1909. Peabody and
Stearns, Boston.**   Built by Yale as the Adee Boathouse, this
piece of architectural finery with its elegant brickwork and
well-finished interior detail is an amazing reminder of the
days when universities could spend such money. Sold in
1958, it has been remodeled for commercial use with verve,
preserving the lofty spaces and great windows (1969, James
Collins). The result is a building filled with the shimmer of
light. Built, as a boathouse should be, right out in the stream,
it is plunged in moving water, almost at sea.

H 43   Waterside.   An enraptured Victorian wrote: "The
beauty of the scene cannot be described. The light hangs
in a lovely radiance over the long reaches of the salt meadows, terminated by the noble crag of East Rock. There is a
neat hamlet with some respectable houses." The hamlet,
named Waterside, had grown up before the Revolution
around the Jehiel Forbes shipyard. Even after the opening
of the bridge it long remained rural—old photographs show
it as a tree-lined lane leading to the bridge between white
fences. It was transformed swiftly around 1900 when Standard Oil and American Steel and Wire built big installations
on the river.

H 44   Jehiel Forbes House, 153 Forbes Avenue, 1767.   One of a handful of Colonial houses left in New Haven and the only one known to have been built of stone. The house was shelled by the British in the Revolution, the household goods having providentially been rushed to safety first, including a baby in a brass kettle. A cannon ball lodged in the wall, which is said to have been removed not long ago, leaving the hole visible in the gable. When the church was built next door with a Forbes bequest, the house became the rectory, acquiring the Gothic porch, triple windows, and slate roof (an earlier roof was shingled).

H 45   Church of the Epiphany, now Eastern Plumbing and Heating Company, 1904. Mantle Fielding, Philadelphia.   Built as an Episcopal chapel by the Forbes family, this small but well-wrought building, with its fine Colonial rectory, was designed to grace the pretty hamlet of Waterside but was almost immediately engulfed by its new community. Today the inside deserves a compassionate look.

Ahead, the red stone retaining wall that follows the road up the hill belonged to **Kenmore,** one of the baronial castles built at the end of the 19th century on the highlands that rim the city—sold in 1944 to a restaurant, later to Sweet Daddy Grace, and later again to a utility company which tore it down.

H 46   Townsend Avenue, Lighthouse Point, and the East Side of the Harbor.   The tour of US 1 breaks off here to make a long salient down the east side of the harbor. Cut off from the city by the river mouth and high bridge tolls, the east side was slower to become industrialized than the west. Townsend Avenue goes through country developed as farms in the Colonial period (two or three Colonial houses remain—**no. 1138** is an example, much disguised). The terrain is a splendid highland, running along the shore, and in the 19th century it attracted country estates overlooking the harbor. Toward the end of the century the trolley brought a few new houses, but major growth waited for the day of the automobile, when a middle-class suburb sprang up after World War I. With the dredging of the harbor in 1949 and the arrival of the turnpike, increased industrial use has appeared at the northern end. The east side of the harbor was taken over by New Haven from East Haven and is known as **The Annex.**

On the heights just past Park Lane: **Fort Wooster,** which saw action in the British invasion and is now a park. Bought in 1890, the winding road was soon laid out. Since then there has been beneficent neglect—no blacktop, no metal railings, no aluminum lights. Next door to the south, one of the big 19th-century estates was recently added to the park. The High Victorian mansion burned soon after. This territory along the shore was the reservation of the Quinnipiac Indians, set aside by treaty with the first English settlers. The northeastern slope of the hill was the Indian burying ground.

H 47 Raynham, 709 Townsend Avenue, 1804 and 1856.
Built by the Townsend family, merchants in the city, Raynham
was one of New Haven's earliest country estates. Surrounded
by more than a hundred acres, the house was placed on a
height well back from the water, its fields sloping down to
the shore in front of it. The original design, with a barrel-
vaulted portico of wood, was a flight of Federalist fancy—
probably an ambitious local builder's response to the new
fashions which Peter Banner was then introducing to New
Haven. In 1856 a transformation took place, so thorough
that few would guess today's Gothic villa did not come out
of the pages of A. J. Downing (one Federal door with fan-
light still remains). Gazebo and cast iron fountain, rescued
from a family house on Wooster Square, complete the setting.
Still in the possession of the family and meticulously preserved inside and out, Raynham is probably the best remaining specimen of its period in New Haven—with its red roofs
and "stone-colored" walls the only one that still conveys
some sense of the colors of the period. Originally called
Bayridge, the name was changed to Raynham around 1875,
after Raynham Hall in Norfolk, seat of the Marquis of Townshend.

H 48 Morris Cove. A country estate in the mid-19th century,
Morris Cove was developed as a summer resort in the 1870s
—a typical seaside cottage city of gingerbread houses on
small lots. In the housing shortage during World War I the
cottages began to be converted to year-round use. Since
then all but two or three have been modernized and have
lost their flavor. **No. 187** suggests the original Victorian holi-
day air. The site is still superbly unspoiled, most of the beach
now a city park.

**H 49 Thomas Morris House, 325 Lighthouse Road, c1680
and Later.** After blighted urban neighborhoods, the pure
white lucidity of these calm forms is astringent. This is a
valuable 17th-century survival—a rare example of the stone-
ender in Connecticut. The house was begun around 1680
and the ell with stone wall added to the west in 1767, perhaps
in stages. On the night of July 5, 1779, the house was burned
by the British. Chimneys, stone walls, and some timbers
survived and were used in rebuilding—charring on the beams
may still be seen. Extensive restoration in the early 20th
century makes it hard to judge how much detail is now
original. Given to the New Haven Colony Historical Society,
the house today is a museum called the Pardee–Morris
House in honor of the donor. Open May to October.

H 50 Lighthouse Point Park, 1924. An incomparable site
crudely handled. The lighthouse, second on this spot, was
built in 1840.

H 51 Fort Hale Park. Designed by Donald Grant Mitchell in 1892, the plan was never completed. This is another case of a place of extraordinary beauty poorly treated. Woodward Avenue has been put through the middle, the boat ramp is raw. Worst blot is the U.S. Government's contribution. Land that had been given to the park was later taken back and given to the Naval Reserve for a crude and messy installation (1948) with no pretense of landscaping or of harmony with its neighbors. To the north, the Coast Guard station by contrast is well maintained and planted (1970). The Navy now plans more construction.

Fort Nathan Hale dates from the Civil War (1863)—an early use of concrete for fortifications. Plans are under way to restore it, also to build a replica of the first 17th-century fort on the far end of the point. All told, four forts have stood on this site, originally called Black Rock.

East Shore Park, to the north, at present can hardly be called a park at all. Although one refreshingly well-designed building has been provided for skating (1970, Charles Brewer; shown here) and some playing fields have been made, it would be hard to make a glorious site less attractive. Originally this was Raynham's shore, sold to the city for a park in 1924. A plan made by Frederick Law Olmsted Jr. was obviously not used. At the end of the tract the mysterious towering structure with its cold winking light belongs to the United Illuminating Company: **New Haven Harbor Station, Unit No. 1,** 1973; Carleton Granbery Associates, consulting architect.

The Green and Downtown

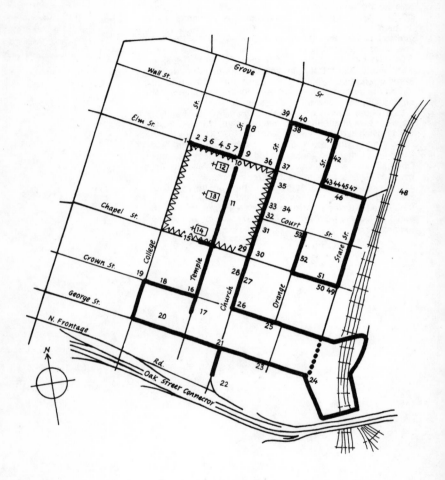

This area has long been the heart of the city's civic and business life. It is all of a piece and so has been put in a single tour, though some may want to take it in smaller bites. The route conforms to one-way streets as far as possible, but walking is recommended as some buildings may be entered and traffic is heavy.

The Green.

The Green is a square of roughly 17 acres, 850 feet to a side. Laid out on a slope, most of the eastern, or lower, half was once a swamp.

In the original town plan this square was held as common land and used as a place for military drill, the burying ground, and other public necessities. As in most New England towns, it was called the Market Place, and the first meeting house was built somewhere on it: its exact location, contrary to popular tradition which insists on putting it in the middle, is not known.

For the next 150 years town life centered on the waterfront, and the Market Place was remote. By 1740 only about 14 houses had been built around it, along with the new Yale College, standing among cornfields. The square itself was a ragged lot—rutted and dotted with a motley group of buildings, some dilapidated—the meeting house, courthouse, school, jail, and others. The graveyard, over-crowded and untended, was described as an offense to public taste.

In the new prosperity of the mid-18th century efforts at improvement began: a state house and new meeting houses were built, and the offensive graveyard was finally hidden by a board fence painted red. But the Revolution halted this dawning urbanism, and it was not until after the war that the Market Place was legally designated a public space and The Green as we know it today was created. Even then it was only the lower half. The upper half, as the city charter of 1784 plainly said, might be sold and the proceeds used for highways or another green.

The Federal period is the decisive moment in the Green's history. In one of the most important urbanist programs in America at the time, the field was graded, fenced, cleared of old buildings and roads, and transformed into a public square and civic center. The graveyard was moved away, and elm trees were planted all around the edge. The climactic event was the building of three churches as a monumental composition down the center (I 11). A generation later, the old state house, which spoiled the symmetry, was replaced by Ithiel Town's great Doric temple on the College Street side. As the elms came to maturity, the New Haven Green became one of the most celebrated public squares in the country.

In a burst of ecumenicism in 1821, the Methodist church was allowed to build on the northwest corner. But this decision was soon regretted, and by 1849 the Methodists had been persuaded, with the help of $8000, to move across the street (I 2). Since then no buildings have been allowed on the Green.

Town life meantime had moved up from the waterfront. Retail shops spread along Chapel Street, residences rose on Elm. With the building of The Exchange (I 30), the corner of Church and Chapel became the hub of downtown, as it still is. A new County House established the town government on Church Street, where it remains, and Yale bought the whole College Street frontage, which it still occupies. The Green's strategic position as the psychological center of town life was set.

Throughout the rest of the century, the basic scheme received only a few changes. The churches were painted buff, the white fence was replaced by black cast iron; a Gothic City Hall and a Gothic college (I 33, J 4) supplanted red brick with white trim, and in the '80s the now unstylish Doric temple was torn down. But although density and height gradually increased around it, as late as 1910 the aspect of the Green was still on the whole that of a New England town.

It was not until around World War I, with the Taft Hotel (I 15), the library (I 9), post office (I 31), and courthouse (I 36), that the Green acquired an urban 20th-century look, and soon thereafter a building boom totally changed the east and south sides. At the same time, in a wave of nostalgia, a move to preserve and restore the north side arose. White trim reappeared, and the paint was sandblasted off the churches. A "pure Colonial skyscraper" on the corner of Elm and Church perfectly symbolized the mood (I 37).

A new wave of change came in the 1960s with Mayor Richard C. Lee's redevelopment program, today still in the process of completion. On the south a shopping mall has been built (I 28), reorienting the retail center toward parking and links with the suburbs, and away from the Green. At the same time, a projected Government Center along Church Street (I 34) and the sale of the library for a juvenile court indicate new directions for the east and north sides. It is too early yet to tell what impact these changes will have.

Today the New Haven Green is almost unique among old New England cities. It differs from the historic centers of other towns in two important ways: it is still physically intact and it is still functionally alive. Many towns long ago made real estate out of their market places; others saw them bloom in the 18th and 19th centuries as centers of business or fashion only to die of blight in the 20th. What has distinguished the New Haven Green is that it never became any one thing—never just downtown, never just a government center, never just a residential park, never just a grove of academe. It has continued to be many things and so has held its place as *the center.* Along with this, consciously or unconsciously, an urbanist discipline created an architectural fabric around the perimeter that for many years was directed toward increasing the definition and enclosure of the space, dramatizing the concept of centrality. It is these two remarkable balancing acts—a balance of social functions, a balance of architectural scale and rhythms—that have hitherto given the Green its special visual quality. How long such a delicate balance can be held in an age of great urban and technological change remains to be seen.

I

I 1 Elm Street. Elm Street after the Revolution became Quality Row. Today its character is largely the creation of the Colonial Revival of the 20th century, which restored some of the old buildings and added new ones in the Revival style, making the north side of the Green a symbolic image of Old New Haven. This image, combining with the other symbolic images around it—churches, university, government and business—plays a critical part in making the Green the mythic-psychological center of the city today.

Around the Green: **the fence,** "set" c1846 by Nahum Hayward. **Streetlights,** 1968, Sasaki, Dawson, DeMay Associates, Watertown, Mass.—an effort to reduce the clutter of modern street furniture by combining parking meter, sign, and light in a single fixture. The globes were intended to make a "necklace of lights" around the Green at night, a pleasant idea now somewhat swamped by other city and commercial lighting.

I 2 First Methodist Church, 1849. Henry Austin. Portico and Steeple, 1904, Charles C. Haight, New York. In its original form the building pointedly identified itself with Center Church across the way—a surprising throwback to the Federal period with its blind arcades and Georgian tracery. Its later history charts 19th-century taste. For 50 years it was systematically de-Federalized; urns and balustrade removed, the double tier of windows changed to a single tier, Georgian tracery changed to Italianate (still visible on the facade), and finally even the steeple was gone. Then, *volte face,* in 1905 it was all re-Federalized—at least in a manner of speaking. Portico and cupola were vaguely of the period, and the handsome interior—although the chairman of the Building Committee said it was Byzantine—recalls the Federal interiors of Bulfinch or Latrobe (the new vaults cut across the windows, so the window heads had to be blanked up, which explains the curious discs now on the outside). In the lobby original doors remain and traces of original wall decoration (plaster scored like ashlar—one of the few known examples of this once popular interior finish) and of original windows; also a pair of the most beautifully sinuous stairs in town (neither intact). In the gallery: four giant deacon's chairs matching the choir stalls—an impressive set.

I 3 Nicholas Callahan House, now Elihu (a Yale Senior Society), 175 Elm Street, Dated Variously 1762 to 1776. The Callahan, Mix, and Pierpont houses together form a striking group in the middle of downtown New Haven. Individually they are perhaps not remarkable, each being a stock production of its day. What *is* remarkable is that they are all still here. Together they give a valuable glimpse of the character of the Green in the early 19th century. They also give a handy guide to the change from the Colonial to the Federal style: note the greater depth of the later Mix house, the more generously spaced windows, the higher foundation, and the lower pitch of the roof. But *caveat visitor:* all three have been much restored, and how much detail is original would be hard to say. The Callahan house originally had a level roof line. In Victorian times a two-story porch was added over the front door, and with it the little pediment. In the modern restoration the upper half of this porch was removed and replaced with what seems to be a Federal entrance porch perched in the air (perhaps salvaged from an old house—a popular early 20th-century practice). East wing a later addition, subsequently Colonialized. The house was acquired by Elihu in 1911 and remodeled by Everett V. Meeks.

I 4   Jonathan Mix House, now the Graduate Club, 155 Elm Street, 1799. Fine Federal detail contrasts with the plainness of its neighbors—note window heads and cornice. However there is some question whether the Palladian window is original—possibly it is a piece of salvage added by the restorer. Some apparently original interior work remains. Addition, 1902, by R. Clipston Sturgis, Boston.

I 5   John Pierpont House, now the Yale Faculty Club, 149 Elm Street, 1767. Built for the gentry, this house shows how simply New Haven lived before the Revolution. Like the Mix house, it received a little pediment and a two-story porch in Victorian times, duly removed by the modern restorer. A pair of symmetrical rear wings was added after 1900 by Delano and Aldrich, copying a Federal house then in the next block. Metal roof replaced shingles after 1870. Inside, fireplaces and some paneling remain—how much is original is not known, for the house was remodeled in 1929 by the architect and antiquarian J. Frederick Kelly, an expert at salvage and reproduction. Further additions on the rear, 1950, Robert T. Coolidge, and on the east side, 1963, Office of Carleton Granbery.

I 6   Hendrie Hall, Built as the Yale Law School, 1894 and 1900. Cady, Berg and See, New York. Cady, Yale's chief architect at the end of the century, built 14 buildings of which 5 survive. Here he lightens the simple stone block with a facade from a Venetian palazzo. The building seems out of scale with its neighbors, but in 1894 who could have guessed that all those unimportant little wooden houses were going to last? Hendrie was apparently seen as the first step of a grand new development of Elm Street (the unfinished side walls are the tip-off). But as it turned out, it has stood alone for 75 years. Hendrie is best observed from a distance; from the sidewalk its showpiece, the great *piano nobile,* is little seen.

I 7   Ralph Ingersoll House, now Yale Offices, 143 Elm Street, 1829. Town and Davis. Ingersoll wrote to Town and Davis in May complaining that the drawings had arrived without the specifications. Presumably the omission was remedied, and the house was put up by its builder, Nahum Hayward, without further interference from the architects, as was often the practice. This is an impressive example of the early Greek Revival; the 5-bay facade is still transitional, but the high basement of dressed stone, the great flight of steps, and the simplicity of the Doric porch make a noble statement on the street. Originally the walls were stuccoed or painted, and a white parapet, simply detailed with Greek ornament, concealed the roof and dormers. The basement windows and the pigeon-repeller that spoils the classic cut of the porch are modern (Davis would have wept!). The interior was finely restored for Yale in 1919 by Delano and Aldrich—unfortunately not all of this has been preserved. Stair, door casings, two black marble mantles, and some hardware remain. In the hall, photographs show the original interiors, and in the Historical Society the Ingersoll Room is set up with some of the furniture shown in the photographs.

Pause at the corner and notice the pleasant historic medley of brick running up the other side of Temple Street: Federal Revival library, Victorian villa, modern parish house, and Colonial Revival college.

I 8 Ezekiel Trowbridge House, now Center Church Parish House, 311 Temple Street, 1852. Sidney Mason Stone. A newspaper account at the time indicates that this house was the architectural event of the day, and a glance at the porch, monitor, and brownstone window heads shows why. Today it suffers from parking lots and the loss of its lawn and fence, but with a little imagination it is easy to guess its onetime quiet splendor. The walls were painted a pale tone—probably sand color—to give a smooth background against which the ornamental richness of the trim stood out. Open balustrades around the roof and the top of the porch gave finish and lightness, and a cast iron fence completed the foursquare symmetry of the composition. This house, which was evidently the model for the Perit house on Hillhouse Avenue (K 17), is one of Stone's principal surviving works. The intricately carved porch is unique in New Haven.

No. 323: **United Church Parish House,** 1961, Pedersen and Tilney.

I 9 New Haven Free Public Library, 1908. Cass Gilbert, New York. The building of the library belongs to the upsurge of civic spirit that took place at the start of the century in New Haven, leading to the formation of the Civic Improvement Committee, with which Gilbert worked closely. In the library as in the railroad station, Gilbert sought to create an architectural image that would express the new spirit of the city, celebrating its colonial past while at the same time adding a spacious grandeur that proclaims the wealth and power of the 20th century (note the setback from the street, the podium, steps, and marble rails). Colonial Revival sentiment by this time was in full bloom, and the library, in contrast to Hendrie Hall, was a delicate exercise in scaling, achieving monumentality without overwhelming the churches or the domestic character of the street around it. The interior is exceptionally handsome, particularly the oval vestibule. It deserves to have been better appreciated by its owners, but the building has now been sold and is slated to become a juvenile court and detention center, a role for which it scarcely seems appropriate.

I 10 Temple Street. This was the street that made New Haven famous, a place of quiet and enchantment in the middle of the city, with the churches secluded under the celebrated "cathedral vault" of elms. Today the old trees are gone; on the west they have not been replanted. Their place is taken by formidable pylons hung with lights, and the grass in front of the churches is black-topped for parking spaces. Bus shelters, 1971. (Photograph 1863; notice the closed gates.)

I 11 The Churches on the Green. The importance of the churches as an urbanist composition has already been mentioned: such a coordinated design undertaken by three separate congregations as part of the creation of a monumental city center is unmatched in Federal America.

On the lower Green: **flagpole,** 1928, Douglas Orr, winning entry in a competition for a memorial to the dead of World War I.

**I 12 United Congregational Church (the North Church),
1812–15, Ebenezer Johnson. David Hoadley, Builder.** A
German architect published a design of an English church
in a French book which found its way into the hands of a
New York architect and ended up on the New Haven Green.
This in a nutshell is the design history of the United Church.
The German was C. L. Stieglitz, the English church was All
Saints in Southampton, and the New York architect was
John McComb, Jr., one of the well-known architects of the
Federal period. Events are unclear, but it seems likely that
the church sent off to McComb for a mail-order plan, which
was later redrawn by Johnson, a member of the committee.
To make matters more complicated, a comparison with
Center Church next door suggests that borrowings from
Asher Benjamin were also thrown in. By rights all this should
have resulted in a muddle. On the contrary, the United
Church emerged as a first-rate example of Federal design—
its steeple one of the masterpieces of the period. Perhaps
this is due to Hoadley, who may have determined the proportions. The exterior today is barely altered. The interior was
remodeled in 1849 by Sidney Mason Stone, re-Federalized
in 1966 by Gerald Watland. Shallow dome and ceiling
ornament are original, as is the glorious chandelier. The
North Church was an influential design in its time, and
borrowings from it can be found as far as North Carolina and
Ohio.

**I 13 First Congregational Church (Center Church), 1812–
15, Asher Benjamin. Ithiel Town, Builder.** Another knotty
design history. It starts with a mail-order plan from Asher
Benjamin of Boston. Next, a protégé of Benjamin's was
hired as builder, but he, being apparently occupied with
other work, quietly slipped a fellow-Benjamin apprentice
into his place, one Ithiel Town—a man about whom, the in-
dignant Building Committee said, they knew nothing. Nevertheless Town held onto his job, and thus inadvertently began
one of the most important chapters in New Haven's architectural history. Thus also began one of New Haven's favorite
arguments: Who designed Center Church—Asher Benjamin
or Ithiel Town? The records leave little doubt that Benjamin's
plan was used, but Town supporters feel sure that he changed
them in some significant way. The design is one of many
American derivatives from St. Martin-in-the-Fields in London,
here given a Boston flavor with Benjaminesque blind arcades
and interior dome (a technological innovation then still new
in America). An odd touch is the leafy scroll, and also the ox
skulls on the frieze—a "heathen" ornament severely criticized at the time. Today the exterior is unchanged except
for the addition of the marble panel on the facade. The
interior was remodeled in 1842 by Henry Austin: the windows
of the pulpit wall were bricked up and the wall painted with an
illusionistic recess (replaced in 1894 with the present window), galleries were lowered, and the high Federal pulpit
replaced by a low marble table (it too in time fell out of style
and became known as "the soda fountain"). In the crypt:
remains of the old Colonial burying ground, over which
the church was in part built.

I 14 Trinity Church, 1813-14. Ithiel Town. Trinity Church seems mild enough today, but in its own time it was a radical building, fitting symbol of the insurgent Episcopalians who were at last challenging the Congregationalists' long control of the state. As one of the first three or four Gothic Revival churches in America, Trinity was also a revelation of a legendary kind of beauty to a country that had never seen a medieval building in all its history, and for many years it was Trinity, not the meeting houses next door, that visitors to New Haven wrote about. To later more sophisticated generations, it lost its magic. Plaster vaults and wooden battlements began to seem false, and alteration commenced. In 1870 the present upper part of the tower replaced the earlier wooden superstructure (E. T. Littell, New York; this was topped by a short red pyramid with gilded crockets, removed in 1930). In 1883 came new pews and gallery breasts, in 1884 the chancel (Henry Congdon, New York), in 1893 a new pulpit, in 1894 the altar, in 1911 the reredos (Charles C. Haight, New York), and stained glass windows at various dates, two probably by LaFarge. In 1906 most of the interior structure was cut out and replaced with the present stone columns and new plaster vaults (Leoni Robinson), and in 1961 wings for stairs were added on each side of the chancel (Douglas Orr). Today it is hard to realize that as it came from the hands of Ithiel Town, the interior was all white, with tall wandlike piers and sun pouring in through 1400 panes of clear glass in the great west window. About the only sign of Town now is the clock on the east gallery, his gift to the church.

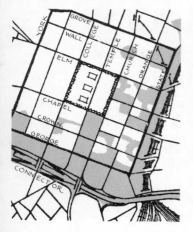

I 15 Chapel Street and Downtown. Long the Fifth Avenue of New Haven, Chapel Street has been often rebuilt. On the east block now is Chapel Square (I 28). The west block belongs mainly to the interbellum and once had considerable chic. The eye still picks out **Hamilton's** (1923, Brown and VonBeren) and the **Bohan-Landorf Building** with finely carved stone arches (facade 1915, Shape and Bready, New York). Lately Redevelopment has been shifting shopping from Chapel to Church Street where it can be tied to parking and the lifeline from the suburbs, and this, along with other forces of urban change, is affecting Chapel Street's style. On the corner of College Street, the **Taft Hotel** (1911, F. M. Andrews, New York). Symbol of the social renascence of New Haven in the era of the City Beautiful, the Taft's great arched windows and well-bred Adamesque detail once touched New Haven with a glow of Ritz-Carlton elegance. Today the hotel is vacant, and plans have been proposed for its conversion to low-moderate elderly housing (1975, Charles Moore and Edward Johnson).

Downtown (I 15–I 53). The south and east blocks around the Green are downtown, or, in the language of redevelopment the CBD—the Central Business District. The CBD has been the target of a giant renewal program in the last 15 years, its aim to replace the past with the image of an all-new, up-to-the-minute business community. Shown on the map: sites demolished and rebuilt, or scheduled to be demolished and rebuilt—a staggering accomplishment which, when completed, will have purged downtown of almost all of its 19th-century buildings.

I 16 124 Temple Street, 1909. R. W. Foote. Another of the city's collection of Venetian palazzi, here in creamy colors and delicately faceted brick, marble, and terra cotta; until recently with bronze arched glazing bars in the windows and handsome bronze lights in front. Built as the United Illuminating Company Building.

No. 80: present **United Illuminating Company Building,** 1938, R. W. Foote. **144 Temple Street,** 1973, Hirsch, Kaestle, and Boos; New Britain.

I 17 Temple Street Parking Garage, 1961. Paul Rudolph. Despite immense length, these subtly rounded surfaces, broken lines, and matte shadows give the building a suppleness and rhythm that fit it to the city street. It is rewarding to go in and climb up through shadowy ramps to observe the ingenious plan, the form work, and at the top a wonderful airy world of roof-buildings and concrete lights suggesting fantastic flora. Note also from here the startling eye-level view of the steeples on the Green. Capacity, 1280 cars.

I 18 Crown Street Parking Garage, 1970. Granbery, Cash and Associates. Black and white shadows make a checker pattern in contrast to the long fluid lines of the Rudolph garage: an alternate solution to the problem of fitting parking facilities into the urban fabric. Capacity, 750 cars. On the street level: **Harold's Restaurant** (1973, John Fowler).

I 19 Ira Atwater House, 222 College Street. Ira Atwater belonged to New Haven's leading building dynasty in the 18th and 19th centuries. He bought this lot in 1817 and probably built not long thereafter. The photograph used here was taken c1900. Today the building is a lesson in how little it takes to spoil a good house.

I 20   Trinity Church Home, 303 George Street, 1868. Henry Austin. One of Austin's most interesting projects. Commissioned by Joseph Sheffield, the Church Home was a group of seven units forming a little court off George Street. Up front were two pairs of town houses, one of which Sheffield gave to each of his four daughters. Set back from the street between them was a chapel, flanked by a home for aged women and a school. All that is left today is the chapel and the home (spire and towers gone). Both have recently been cleaned, and the orangy-red brick and its banding of tan stone have emerged in resplendent color.
297 George Street, 1965, Simeone and Wendler.

I 21   Church Street. An early center of business, Church Street has been restructured as the city's grand entrance from the Connector to midtown. Fifteen years ago a shabby place cluttered with cheap signs, today it is a handsome avenue, one of Redevelopment's most successful transformations. In order to shift the retail center to this new lifeline, Malley's, New Haven's leading department store, was moved here from the Green and other stores were settled around it. The whole west side has been rebuilt. On the east, a few older buildings have been allowed to remain: note how they give interest and vivacity to the street. **Park:** 1972, Kevin Roche, John Dinkeloo and Associates—a charming urban space with a Parisian air. Benches are a reproduction of the benches at the New York World's Fair of 1939. **First New Haven National Bank,** seen through the trees (1960, Office of Douglas Orr).

I 22   Knights of Columbus, 1967. Kevin Roche, John Dinkeloo and Associates. This is a signpost building. One of the highest points on the New Haven skyline, it has an instantly apprehensible shape which can be seen for miles on all the suburban approaches to the city, marking the Coliseum and the entrance to downtown. Brown tile covers heavy cylindrical corner towers housing stairs and utility stacks. Between them a gossamer web of steel and glass is suspended.

I 23   Coliseum, 1969. Kevin Roche, John Dinkeloo and Associates. The arena is below, parking is on top, thus freeing the street for pedestrian approaches. Over the arena the exposed roof truss makes a clear span of 184 feet; cars are layered inside it. The scale is gigantic. For an experience of sheer spatial intoxication, go through the Orange Street underpass. Or take a ride on the escalators. Capacity, 2400 cars.

I 24   Community Services Building, 1965. Douglas Orr, deCossy, Winder and Associates. From George Street, this building is framed by the menacing lid of the Coliseum, looking inviting at the end of the tunnel. In a formerly blasted location, with the railroad at its back and the oblique angle of State Street at its front, it handles a tough site well, outwardly defining the intersection while turning inward to its secret garden. The parking garage transforms the usual basement into a visual delight by the use of lightwells, curving spaces, planting, and color.
From here pedestrians can go direct to the next entry; motorists must follow the one-way streets as drawn on the map.

I 25 New Haven Gas Company, 80 Crown Street, 1872. Rufus G. Russell. The old 18th-century heart of downtown, near State and Meadow Streets, was extensively rebuilt in the 1870s and '80s. Today these buildings are being demolished wholesale for reconstruction of the entire area. The Gas Company so far still remains, symbol of an era. Fortunately it is one of the most distinguished commercial buildings of its time, with its handsomely shaped stone lintels and forceful rhythms. Amid the visual trivia of a shabby street, it gives dignity and stability. *Demolished, summer 1975.*

No. 100: **the New Haven Water Company,** 1902, Leoni Robinson.

I 26 Connecticut Savings Bank, 1906. Gordon, Tracy and Swartwout, New York. Banking had an architectural golden age in the Edwardian era. Riding the tide of the Beaux Arts movement and prosperity, banks blossomed with a new classical image (typically a one-story building of temple-like form), becoming a potent force in giving style to the American downtown. This example, especially noted by the Gilbert–Olmsted report for its importance to the quality of the street, was New Haven's best—a piece of luck, for it is the only one that has not been destroyed or spoiled. Crudely remodeled not long ago, the interior has recently been restored by a public-spirited management. **Annex,** 55 Church Street, 1972, Shreve, Lamb and Harmon Associates, New York.

I 27 Simons Building, facade 1909; Johnson Building, facade 1914, Brown and VonBeren. Recently restored with modern black and white decor, this striking pair joins the bank in livening up the street. White terra cotta was an Edwardian specialty.

I 28 Chapel Square, 1965. Lathrop Douglass, New York. Key piece in the Redevelopment Agency's strategy to shift retail trade from Chapel to Church Street and link it to the Connector, this shopping mall acts as a pivot, facing both ways. A complex scheme, the exterior respects the urbanist need for street frontage, while the interior is hollowed out in a cave of stores. Shops open both inward and outward, making the ground floor porous, the shops themselves becoming corridors. Via bridges, an indoor path goes from the Green through Macy's and Malley's to the parking garage and the Connector. The concourse is spatially effective, achieving the mix of excitement and intimacy considered conducive to buying. A subtler question is one of identity: Is this psychologically indoors or outdoors?—public or private? Compare it with older European arcades, where the sense of *public street* is never lost.

I 29 Bennett Drinking Fountain, 1907. John Ferguson Weir. The Athenian monument of Lysicrates has been one of the most fertile inventions in the history of architecture—spawning lanterns, tombs, finials for skyscrapers, and here the old town pump.

I 30 The Exchange, 1832. Above the visual disorder of the street, the even rhythm and level sills of this Greek Revival building are strong and clean. One of an important trio—with the Street Building (I 49) and the Townsend Block (G 1)—it is a landmark in New Haven building history, the first functional statement of a truly commercial architecture. The ground floor, which was opened up between stone piers to form a row of wide shopfronts, was a dramatic innovation after the small shop windows of the past, while the long uniform facade gave a new urbanity to the street. As the public symbol of the city's business life, the Exchange was crowned with a domed cupola, marking the corner of Church and Chapel as the hub of downtown. Today the cupola has been replaced by a billboard. The building itself, under dirt and signs, still retains its integrity. The architect is not known, but such a cosmopolitan design suggests Ithiel Town, who was already familiar with this commercial style in London, Boston, and New York. The builder was Atwater Treat. The Palladian window on the south side is modern. For an example of the original pier system, see the Street Building. An example of the older Federal type of commercial structure still stands in Fair Haven—essentially an overgrown house (O 14).

I 31 Post Office and Federal District Court, 1913. James Gamble Rogers, New York. The Post Office was built soon after the County Courthouse (I 36), and together they brought 20th-century magnificence to the Green. Both used the classical temple front, the standard American image of civic dignity, but Rogers had to accommodate his version to a long frontage on a built-up city street. He accordingly flattened his portico against the wall and stretched it to the unclassical length of ten columns, deftly turning the temple image into street architecture. Beautifully finished side and rear elevations make this building one of downtown's best sights from many directions. Inside: balanced spaces, filtered light, and the utmost elegance of bronze detail (superb screens over the windows, desks, stair rails, etc.); much of it recently concealed with sheetrock, acoustic tile, and plastic counters. The second floor, however, remains one of New Haven's most majestic interiors. The Post Office is now scheduled to move out, and plans for restoration have been announced (William F. Pedersen and Associates). In 1966 the New Haven Preservation Trust averted an attempt to demolish the building.

I 32 Powell Building, 157 Church Street, 1921. R. W. Foote. Tudor arches are combined with stone, bronze, and glass to form an arcade on which the tall shaft of the building rests. Compare this with the earlier Taft Hotel (I 15) or with the Second National Bank down the block: the Powell Building marks the stage in the developmental process where the skyscraper stops being merely a stretched-up palazzo and begins to be realized as a tower. Note that the shaft is finished on all sides, recognizing that it is going to soar above the rooftops. A design of grace and elegant detail, this was New Haven's finest skyscraper before the Kline Tower. Today owned by the city, it is scheduled for demolition.

I 33 City Hall, 1861. Henry Austin. City Hall was in the vanguard of the High Victorian Gothic movement—a surprisingly early example of the dynamic massing and rich surfaces that would characterize the next quarter century of American architecture. Even the lofty critic of the *Architectural Record,* on a visit to Yale, took note of City Hall, remarking, "I should like to celebrate the architect if I knew his name." Today the building looks deformed with the top of the tower gone (compare it with the old photograph shown here), but plans for its restoration have been announced. Inside, Austin creates a wonderfully clear volume of vertical space occupied by a stair which the late Carroll L. V. Meeks called one of the finest High Victorian iron stairs in the country. Originally a skylight, now blacked up, sent light cascading down it, while in the surrounding halls oak woodwork and rich colors made contrasting shadows—a stair for municipal pageantry and magisterial mayors. Next door, the **Old Courthouse** (1871, David R. Brown) was added by Austin's former associate and conceived as part of the earlier building, making an extended composition. Inside, another rousing Victorian stair. Both buildings are scheduled by the city for demolition for the Government Center, although the tower and facade of City Hall are to be retained in an ornamental capacity (I 34).

I 34 Proposed Government Center. Paul Rudolph. This has been a bone of contention for a decade. In 1965 the city announced plans for a Government Center designed by I. M. Pei. Most of the east side of the Green was to be demolished, Court Street was to be absorbed, and a tower was to rise from a big plaza. The front wall of City Hall was to be left standing alone against the new buildings. Citizens, led by the Preservation Trust, objected (a) to the height of the tower, (b) to the redundant plaza alongside the Green, destroying its enclosure and centrality, and (c) to the demolition of City Hall and the Post Office. The plans were eventually dropped, and since then the job, in modified form, has been assigned to Paul Rudolph. But although the Post Office is now to be kept and the plaza has been eliminated, objection continues to the demolition of City Hall and to what some regard as an overbearing architectural scheme that threatens the traditional composure of the Green. An early sketch is shown here.

I 35 New Haven Savings Bank, 195 Church Street, 1972. William F. Pedersen and Associates. A suave tower that solves a complicated corner problem with a complicated response. Normally on this site a strong, clean right angle would have been expected, defining the shape of the Green and containing it, but the bevel on the existing building across the street made this awkward and led to counter-beveling. When plans for the bank were first announced, the Preservation Trust protested against such height on the Green and against the proposed use of reflecting glass. The management cooperatively modified its plans.

I 36 New Haven County Courthouse, now State Circuit Court, 1909. William H. Allen and Richard Williams. America's age of Neo-Classicism found appropriate expression in New Haven in a mixed Greco-Roman building of immense solidity and whiteness—its sheer weight deliberately expressed by the thickening of detail and the absence of flutes on the columns. Inside: an astonishing spatial fantasy —under the vast vault of a Roman bath, a floating three-dimensional composition of bridges and mezzanines. With diagonal vistas, changes of height, and sudden shafts of light, it is far more Piranesian than classical—an exciting place. The library is fine. The rich reds and greens still on the wall probably show the tonality that the other rooms originally had—no doubt there was a bit of gold somewhere too. Outside, sculpture by J. Massey Rhind.

I 37 Union and New Haven Trust Company, now Union Trust Company, 205 Church Street, 1927. Cross and Cross, New York. Colonial Revivalism to the nth degree. Allusions to the churches on the Green are applied to a commercial skyscraper, and the Federal vocabulary is stretched upward through 13 stories. Nevertheless this is a building of urban gentility, and the banking room today is one of the best remaining interiors of the Golden Twenties—it is a handsome gesture on the bank's part to maintain it so well. Cross and Cross intended their design as a tribute to New Haven's Federal Green, creating what they called a tower "of pure Colonial design" and other "refinements of appropriateness." But is it a refinement of appropriateness to steal the cupola of the United Church and upstage it with a higher one?

I 38 Southern New England Telephone Company, 227 Church Street, 1937. R. W. Foote and Douglas Orr. New Haven's best example of Modernistic. The Art Deco lobby, in granite, muted metal, and geometric frescoes is a beautifully preserved specimen, even to the ecru and smoky rose and blue-green colors so characteristic of the style.
No. 221: the **Quinnipiack Club, 1930,** also by Orr. **No. 234:** the gold mirror building, 1971, Bonsignore Brignati Goldstein and Mazzotta, New York.

I 39 Trinity Church Parish House, 53 Wall Street, 1923. Charles Scranton Palmer. An informal building of fine brick and modestly elegant detail. This is a retiring design, easily overlooked. But recently while the lot opposite was empty pending construction of the gold mirror, it had a moment in the limelight, and the part it plays in the quality of the neighborhood became apparent. On Church Street, a graceful court, now a parking lot. (Photograph 1925.)

I 40 New Haven County Courthouse, 1971. William F. Pedersen and Associates. Deep shadows emphasize the thickness of the wall, while window openings increase in height as they rise, giving the block an effect of verticality. Compare this design with the Savings Bank (I 35), built by the same architect at almost the same time.

No. 258: the **Abby Salisbury House;** wrongly attributed to Town and Davis (theirs was *another* Abby Salisbury house, now demolished).

I 41 Congregational Church of the Redeemer, now Trinity Lutheran Church, 1870. David R. Brown. The outline of the steeple, dark and fantastic at the end of the narrow street, is the result of accident: the pinnacles which originally stood at the base of the spire, giving it a conventionally graduated silhouette, were long ago removed, leaving a great hollow. The architect would no doubt be pained, but the result is a haunting landmark at this end of town. Brown, who had worked on City Hall nine years before, here shows a mastery of High Victorian Gothic, producing New Haven's most important church of the later 19th century. A richly ornamented building, handsomely maintained by its present congregation.

Across the street, **no. 291:** souvenir of a once-stylish Victorian neighborhood. Eli Whitney earlier owned the west block, his house (finished after his death) facing Elm Street. **No. 284** is thought to be New Haven's first apartment house, though how completely it has been rebuilt is not known. Built c1875, it was called the Kensington Flat, obviously inspired by the great Queen Anne apartments then going up in London's Kensington. The innovation turned out to be too much for New Haven, and apartment houses did not take hold until after World War I (see Itinerary G).

I 42 William Pinto House, 275 Orange Street, c1810. In the later 19th century the street was widened and lowered, requiring the steps to be moved to the side of the porch and the columns to be cut off and replaced with consoles—the new foundation tells the story. With its Palladian window in the gable, this is another charming example of a favorite New Haven model (J 39), now attractively converted to commercial use (bay window and rear wing are modern). Legend has it that Eli Whitney was living here when he died, his own house not yet built across the street; but all that is certain is that Whitney once held a mortgage on the house. William Pinto and his brother Jacob are the first Jews known to have settled in New Haven, although as Ezra Stiles records, they "renounced Judaism and all religion." They were men of means and probably came from the West Indies. They and other members of their family settled in this quarter. Later in the century an upper-class Jewish neighborhood built Temple Mishkan Israel here (L 5).

I 43 53 Elm Street, c1875. Many buildings like this were built downtown in the '70s and '80s, with big cornices, polychromed surfaces of brick and stone, and the hairline incised ornament of the Eastlake style. Not too many are left. This is one of the best, its strong horizontal banding carrying the line around the corner. Today these buildings are often considered eyesores and torn down, when in fact it was not the building but the tenant that was the eyesore.

No. 5: another example, at the corner of State Street (1878).

I 44 Imperial Granum Building, 1877. Rufus G. Russell. The great era of the cast-iron front largely passed New Haven by. This is the only known example today—a dainty little building to bear such a resounding name (Imperial Granum was a medicinal food "for all diseases of the stomach"). Russell's drawing survives among his papers in the Historical Society, and along with it a few photographs of iron fronts which he had evidently bought in New York, one of which appears to be the parent of Imperial Granum. The building today is shown in the photograph above.

I 45 John Cook House, 35 Elm Street, c1807. This is an interesting house, preserving a conservative late-Colonial outline but making use of a then novel material—today it is the earliest stucco building known in New Haven. The most striking feature of the house is the ballroom on the top floor, using the ridge of the roof to create an arched ceiling. We know that such rooms became fashionable in New Haven at this time under the influence of the English architect Peter Banner, but this is the only one left. It has been suggested that it was added after 1814 when David Hoadley had arrived in town and when the house changed hands. Unfortunately there are no grounds for this hopeful theory—in style the room could as well belong to 1807 as 1814. Originally a balustrade dressed up the bare roof. Dormers and Greek Revival porch are obviously later.

I 46 Timothy Bishop House, 32 Elm Street. One of the great houses built in New Haven in the Federal Period, this is a precious survival. No precise date is known beyond the fact that the lot was bought in February, 1815, but it is likely that the house was built soon afterward. The design has often been attributed to David Hoadley, but there are no grounds except the similarity of the portico to that of the United Church (I 12). Inside, much original work remains, restored (and perhaps somewhat supplemented) after World War I. The stair rail, it is said, came from the Eli Whitney house. A ballroom on the top floor was built in the 1930s, emulating the Cook House. The street has been lowered and widened, causing the removal of the front steps and the addition of the high basement. Now used as an office building, the house has been well cared for by its present owner.

I 47 Caroline Nicoll House, 27 Elm Street. At one time the entire block belonged to Abraham Bishop, and this house was built near his own for his daughter Caroline. The date cannot be ascertained now that the city tax records have been thrown away, but it is between 1828 and 1838. The Nicoll, Cook, and Timothy Bishop houses are three survivors of what was long New Haven's most elegant street.

I 48 Central Fire Headquarters, 952 Grand Avenue, 1961. Earl P. Carlin. The building was planned as a gateway to the newly rehabilitated Wooster Square neighborhood, and the view from this corner shows how well it fulfills its function. Peter Millard, Design Associate; Paul Pozzi, Associate.

State Street, bordering the East Creek and later the Farmington Canal, was Main Street all through the 17th and 18th centuries—lined with wharves, shops, and well-to-do merchants' houses. When the canal became the railroad in the 1840s, residential and retail functions moved away, and State Street became first the wholesale district and finally, in the 20th century, a place of sooty buildings, second-hand furniture stores, and a paradise of Italian markets. Now mostly demolished, it is due to be rebuilt with a parking garage nearly half a mile long, from Grove Street to George.

I 49 Street Building, 1832. The Street Building has already been mentioned as one of the city's first three important commercial buildings—the others are the Exchange (I 30) and the Townsend Block (G 1). The Street Building is of particular value as the only one that retains the original monolithic granite piers with Doric capitals, between which the shopfronts were opened to the street. These may be seen on the State Street side. The two-story stone front on the Chapel Street side is a later addition. Builder, Elihu Atwater.

I 50 Monson Building, 760 Chapel Street, 1891. One of New Haven's best stores in its day, the Charles Monson Company was proudly described as being comparable to Altman's in New York. The building caused quite a stir, the newspaper reporting that it was "of a handsome style of architecture with all the modern conveniences including Otis Bros.' electric safety elevator; the arc and incandescent light, pneumatic cash carriers, etc." Today, above the strident sign, warm orange brick and a striking pattern of windows make this one of the street's outstanding facades. Photograph c1925.

I 51 Tradesman's Bank, 1856. Henry Austin. "One of the few remaining examples of a mid 19th century banking building," the Historic American Buildings Survey wrote in 1964; with a banking room "of monumental scale" and rich trim. The building was demolished while this book was being written, but since its memory is still alive, its picture has been allowed to remain.

I 52 Young Men's Institute, 139 Orange Street, later the Palladium Building, 1855. Now that Austin's bank is gone, this is the next best example of the antebellum era left downtown. It is so similar in handling to the vanished bank that it is hard to resist the assumption that here is another example of Austin's style, marked by his always slightly wayward fancy.

818 Chapel Street: the **Phoenix Building,** 1840, a fascinating bit of commercial show-off—Greek Revival outside and Egyptian Revival inside.

I 53 New Haven Savings Bank, 1900. Brite and Bacon, New York. Designed by the architect of the Lincoln Memorial in Washington, this is another of New Haven's good Edwardian banks, another monumental banking room. On the street, melon-colored brick and a pair of sumptuous green copper lampstands with globe lights make this Orange Street's most memorable corner. The bank is scheduled to be replaced by a federal office building (William F. Pedersen and Associates). *Demolished, summer 1975.*

200 Orange Street, **Hall of Records,** 1929, Egerton Swartwout, New York: a well-proportioned colonnade by the architect of the Connecticut Savings Bank (I 26) and the Yale Art Gallery (G 12). This monumental piece of street architecture merits better neighbors.

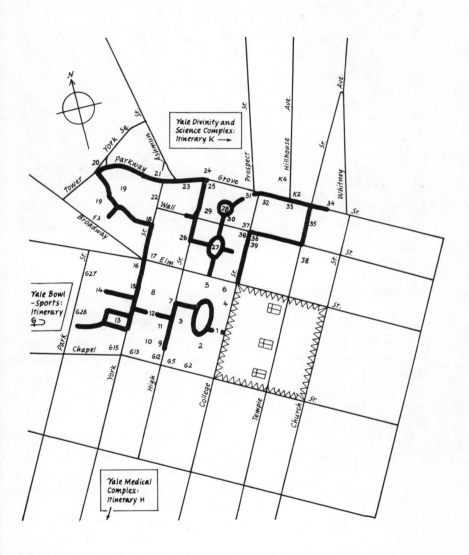

J Yale University: The Central Complex.

Yale architecture is city architecture. It holds to the building line and creates its open spaces inside the resulting hollow blocks. Through archways, glimpses are revealed of green courts, and these glimpses are one of the special delights of the streets that thread through the university, as are the courts themselves. Yale's outdoor spaces in fact are as carefully designed as its buildings, and Yale's landscaping is an important part of its architecture.

This brief guide cannot begin to catalogue Yale's wealth of artistry and craftsmanship. Tourists will have to sharpen their eyes and notice for themselves such things as the color of stones, the elegance of lead gutters, stained glass, carving, and a whole fantasy world of pinnacles, domes, and turrets along the rooftops.

Yale's first building was built in 1717 facing the Green (G 2), and the second—Connecticut Hall, which still stands (J 2)—was built in 1750. After the Revolution, in a wave of expansion, Yale undertook the formal creation of a campus—probably the first designed campus in America. Planned by John Trumbull and James Hillhouse, this became the Brick Row, a straight row in line with Connecticut Hall, facing outward to the Green. The Green itself at this time was being redesigned as the monumental center of the city, and the college buildings were part of the larger urban composition.

In 1814 Hillhouse sold Yale a building north of Grove Street for a medical school, and around this outpost, along Hillhouse Avenue and Prospect Street, Yale's scientific center began to grow up (Itinerary K), remote and distinct from the academic center.

After the Civil War came a new expansion of the main campus, for the first time a turning away from the Green, replacing the Brick Row with an outer row built close to the street and facing inward to create a green of its own.

During the rest of the century the college fanned out planlessly along the city streets, the academic and scientific centers remaining remote, until in 1901 with the creation of University Quadrangle (J 28) the gap suddenly began to close, and the need for unification became urgent. In a master plan finally commissioned in 1919, John Russell Pope proposed a grand Beaux Arts design of axes and cross-axes pulling everything together from Chapel Street as far north as Edwards.

But it was too late—too much already stood in the way. In the end it was James Gamble Rogers who designed the Yale of the 1920s and '30s. Freshened by enormous gifts of Sterling and Harkness money, this was the third of Yale's great building periods—a restructuring of the undergraduate body into ten (later twelve) "colleges" modeled on the English universities.

The timing was fortunate. The rhetoric of the Beaux Arts era was waning, and Rogers could conceive of the university in more human terms, seeing architecture as experience as well as symbol. He took his cue, as Yale itself had, from Oxford and Cambridge, and his aim was to reproduce the individuality—the irregularities, even the idiosyncracies—that centuries of building had given the English universities. By mixing styles, he sought to contrive a metaphor of history. This can be seen in both his Gothic and Georgian ensembles: while historical vignettes abound, there are no period pieces.

Using the ground thriftily, respecting the city fabric, Rogers created urbane streetscapes and spaces that are human-sized, personal, and poetic. Monumentality he reserved for the air, giving Yale a skyscape of towers. These are the banners and the fanfare for high moments—on the ground they do not tyrannize over everyday places. Pope's concept of unity in the grand manner had been abandoned, but in its place Yale was knit together with a continuum of intermeshed spaces and buildings, and with an unfolding of visual experiences designed for pedestrians in motion.

After this brilliant period, Yale relaxed, coasting through the '50s without much apparent thought until, first, Douglas Orr and Eero Saarinen (c1956) and next Edward Larrabee Barnes (c1964) were retained as planning consultants. Currently, planning emphasis has shifted from expansion to concentration and to a less aggressive approach toward invading city real estate. It is also concerned with questions of movement—parking, jitneying, and pedestrian connectives; and with the problem of preserving a well-knit fabric while building on the scale demanded by modern needs and technology. In place of the grand designs of the past, Yale's planning today is described as a "flexible low-profile attitude."

J 1 The Old Campus. Phelps Gate (1895, Charles C. Haight, New York) leads into the Old Campus and is Yale's front door (in the Information Office, maps and booklets about Yale buildings are available). Phelps was dropped neatly into the last remaining hole on College Street, a hulk of a building scaled down to look like a Tudor gatehouse. Today the Old Campus, which is where Yale began, is devoted mainly to freshman dormitories but it still remains the psychological center of the university. Commencement is held here, and the academic procession, in vestigial commemoration of the historic tie between town and gown, still crosses the Green and enters through Phelps Gate. Next door to the south: **Welch Hall,** 1891, Bruce Price, New York.

J 2 Connecticut Hall, 1750. Builders (Francis Letort and Thomas Bills) were imported from out of state, and the design was based on Harvard's Massachusetts Hall. To John Trumbull, later designing the Brick Row in a modish Adam manner, Connecticut Hall was hopelessly dowdy. He damned its gambrel roof as "Gothic" and expensively rebuilt it. Later still, as Adam fell from grace and Gothicism triumphed, the building was damned again, described as "scabby and malodorous," and slated for destruction with the rest of the Brick Row. But before demolition actually began, the pendulum swung once more, and a wave of Colonial Revival sentiment arose just on time to save Connecticut Hall. In 1905 Trumbull's modish roof was expensively removed and the Gothic gambrel recreated (Grosvenor Atterbury, New York). In 1952 the interior was entirely rebuilt (Office of Douglas Orr and Richard A. Kimball).

The unexpected preservation of Connecticut Hall created a problem of campus design, solved by providing **McClellan Hall** as a partner (1925, Walter B. Chambers, New York). At the cornerstone laying, unsympathetic students put on a sarcastic Pageant of Symmetry.

J 3 The Old Library, now Dwight Chapel, 1842. Henry Austin. Yale's second oldest remaining building and first Gothic Revival design. Although later generations, raised on Ruskinian ideas about true medieval construction, scorned these plaster vaults and wooden pinnacles, in its day the library was an exciting herald of a new Yale—still elegant and dainty in the Federal manner but with its classical outline tempered by romantic brown shadows and Tudor towers, slim and agile as minarets. John Russell Pope called it a building of distinction and to him goes the credit for saving it and suggesting its use as a chapel: the interior, taut and tall and dim, might have been made for this purpose (adaptation, 1931, Charles Z. Klauder, Philadelphia). West window, 1931, Nicola d'Ascenzo; east window, 1961, Vincent Filipone. On the roof of the south wing a lantern, encircled with finials like a crown, lets light into the hall below; originally matched by one on the north. This was Austin's first major work, based apparently on a drawing of St. Katharine's Hospital in London.

Next door: **Linsly-Chittenden Hall.** Chittenden (1888, J. Cleveland Cady, New York) was built as an annex to the library; Linsly (1906, Charles C. Haight, New York) was later slipped in between them. "Blessed is the peacemaker," said Montgomery Schuyler, pointing out the value of Haight's work in unifying the campus. (In Chittenden, window by Louis Tiffany, 1890.)

J 4 Farnam Hall, 1869. Russell Sturgis, New York. Farnam, Durfee, and Battell Chapel were the cornerstones of the new campus. All three were by Sturgis and together formed an influential example of the High Victorian Gothic style which put Yale on the forefront of American architecture in the 1870s. In contrast to the delicate fantasy of the Old Library, Farnam, with its vigorous gables, sheer planes, and scrupulous masonry shows the earnestness and manliness of the new style.

Next door: **Lawrance Hall,** 1885, also by Sturgis. All these buildings need cleaning. Try to visualize hot earthy colors: the red of bricks set off by tans and blacks, and the sea green of copper roofs.

J 5 Durfee Hall, 1870. Russell Sturgis, New York. Durfee, Yale's first dormitory of stone, was regarded as a high point in the serious architecture of the '70s. "It will be a long time," said *The American Architect and Building News* in 1878, "before the quiet dignity of its roof and chimneys will be surpassed anywhere."

Next door to the west: **Wright Memorial Hall,** 1911, William Adams Delano, New York.

J 6 Battell Chapel, 1874. Russell Sturgis, New York. The siting seems odd—"pushed off to the corner, and suffocated before it is born" Montomery Schuyler said. The exterior was more striking before it got dirty, carved capitals and vine leaves and the appliqué of the arcade making a tapestried surface (southwest corner, 1893, Cady, Berg and See, New York; ugly doors later). But it was the interior, designed by George Fletcher Babb, that was the chapel's real distinction: "One of the most beautiful interiors to be found in the whole range of modern American church architecture," Schuyler said. He praised the "symphonic" colors of frescoed walls, the painted and gilded woodwork, the glass—true "mosaic work" without paint or enamel. Most of this has now been removed (present altar and reredos, 1947, Andrew Euston). Around the apse a section of painting remains, with Morris-like floral banding; also the gallery breasts and windows. Major loss is the great organ screen, pulpit, and choir.

J 7 Harkness Memorial Tower, 1917. James Gamble Rogers, New York. As you leave the Old Campus, the tower is in front of you, built of a warm yellow stone chosen to stand out lightly amid the browns around it. Its upward flight has been likened to the jet of a fountain, dissolved at the top in a foam of turrets and pinnacles. This familiar silhouette on the skyline of New Haven has long been the symbol of Yale and its particular architectural treasure—as nearly as possible a medieval building built in the 20th century. In medieval fashion, an elaborate decorative program clothes it with carving—leaves and flowers, allegorical figures, whimsies, and portraits of everyone from donor to stone-mason (Lee Lawrie, sculptor). In the archway, on the vaulted ceiling, James Gamble Rogers on the east boss.

J 8 Memorial Quadrangle: Branford and Saybrook Colleges, 1917 and 1933. James Gamble Rogers, New York. Built as dormitories, the buildings were remodeled when the College Plan was adopted, becoming Saybrook (entrance on Elm Street) and Branford. The Memorial Quadrangle was Rogers' first work for Yale and shows his early use of long ranges of street buildings set close to the sidewalk, enclosing courts of varying sizes, imagery, and color. The central court is formal, the smaller courts more intimate, like outdoor living rooms. Rogers' imaginative variations can be followed through his whole subsequent series of outdoor spaces. **Wrexham Tower,** at the far end, modeled on St. Giles in Wrexham, Wales, where Elihu Yale is buried, stands above a huddling of roofs, in contrast to Harkness, rising sheer from the ground.

J 9 Skull and Bones, 1856 and 1903. A Greek Revival form in dark brown stone gives this senior society a proper air of solemnity and mystery. As the oldest of the Yale societies, Skull and Bones exhibited a new architectural type: the small sealed structure, residential in scale but awe-inspiring in manner. The original building consisted only of the south wing. Confronted with the need for expansion, the architect produced a Rorschach image without loss of character.

J 10 Weir Hall and Court. Begun c1910, Tracy and Swartwout, New York; finished 1924, E. V. Meeks; altered 1932,
James Gamble Rogers, New York; library 1965, Charles
Brewer; towers 1851, A. J. Davis. A romantic alumnus
dreamed of building a dormitory that would be a replica of
Oxford and a cloister of serenity "amid the city's jar." He
raised a great mound of earth and surrounded Skull and
Bones with an immense wall for secrecy. In 1911 he acquired
the stone from A. J. Davis's Alumni Hall which was then
being demolished, and reerected the towers on his plateau.
Soon after he went broke, and his unfinished hall lay empty
until Yale took it over and another architect completed it.
Despite this mixed-up past, Weir Court is one of Yale's
loveliest places (one suspects the hand of Rogers in shaping
these unexpected terraces), and the hall itself now makes a
handsome library for Jonathan Edwards College. (Weir
Court is temporarily closed pending construction of an
underground auditorium: 1975, Herbert S. Newman Associates. Trees are being preserved and the court is to be
restored as before.)

**J 11 Jonathan Edwards College, 1925 and 1932. James
Gamble Rogers, New York.** J. E. was remodeled as a college
from Rogers' earlier dormitories, which bequeathed it a narrow site and diverse surroundings, which Rogers deftly turned
to advantage. With a few brilliant touches, the south side
of the court, made by the looming pile of Weir Hall, has
been made a dramatic contrast to the lighter scale of the
rest (notice the towers and the small fantastic lead turret).
The result is one of the most picturesque of the college
courts.

J 12 Library Street. Originally a street, now a pedestrian
path. Rogers was constantly concerned with connectives
in the fast-growing university, and this walkway was plainly
designed to bring the newly annexed territory of York and
Park Streets into contact with the Old Campus. The street
was originally so named because the Old Library stood at its
head. The **University Theater** now balances the other end
(1925, Blackall, Clapp and Whittemore, Boston; facade redesigned by Rogers, 1931).

J 13 Fraternity Row. As planner for the group, Rogers
seized the opportunity to create a patch of village scenery
in the midst of the urban grid—a tumble of slate roofs and
chimneys that is both sentimental and enchanting. Again
his concern for through-walks is apparent, and it is worth
ducking under the arch in the south corner where a beckon-
ing path wanders off to Park Street. **204** York, rear (1926), and
no. 224, the Fence Club (1928), both by Rogers. **No. 212**
(1929), Everett V. Meeks. In the center, **Wolf's Head,** a senior
society (1924) by Bertram Goodhue, New York, incorporates
the dining room from an earlier building by McKim, Mead and
White (K 9). **No. 202,** with magnificent carved grapevine, is
the **Yale Daily News** (1932, Adams and Prentice, Hartford).
The apartment beyond is (or was) known as **"Mrs. Cooney's"**
(1905, Brown and VonBeren), one of the private dormitories
of the Gold Coast days (see G 4). All but one of Yale's
fraternities (the Fence Club) have now been converted to
university use. For the Park Street end of the row see G 26.

J 14 Pierson College, 1930. James Gamble Rogers, New York. With Pierson, Rogers made a change, driving a long formal entrance straight through the block like a shaft, breaking out into a court whose expanse is suddenly breathtaking. Make the circuit, as Rogers meant you to. At the end: the Slaves' Quarters, an unexpected bit of old Charleston. The superb tower, modeled on Philadelphia's Independence Hall, gives Pierson a Georgian counterpart to the Gothic towers around it. For the Park Street entrance see G 26.

232 York Street: another former fraternity, 1930, James Gamble Rogers.

J 15 Davenport College, 1930. James Gamble Rogers, New York. One of Rogers' virtuoso performances—Georgian formality mixed with picturesqueness, capped by the pageantry of a mimic Boston State House presiding over the court. People used to ridicule Davenport for using both Gothic and Georgian in the same building. Today we are more appreciative. For the Park Street side see G 27.

254 York Street, formerly the **Yale Record,** 1928, Lorenzo Hamilton, Meriden.

J 16 Langrock Building, 268 York Street, 1927. Jacob Weinstein. In the palmy days of the '20s, elegant shops grew up around Yale, and York Street bloomed as New Haven's Savile Row. An ad in 1928 says: "Mr. Langrock first began to create clothing styles for Yale men 31 years ago with the conception that university men should dress in a style fitting their station in life." David Langrock also thought that his new building should fit Yale's architecture, and he had his plans checked by Rogers. Today his shop is no more, nor are his well-dressed young men, but they have left the city a good building that mediates between the gentility of York Street and the motley world of Broadway.

No. 262: J. Press, the most celebrated fixture of the Row. Above the shopfront, the remains of a particularly racy mansard house.

J 17 Trumbull College, 1929. James Gamble Rogers, New York. Under the immense shadow of the Sterling Library, on a cramped lot, Trumbull, like J.E., turns poverty to riches. The style is more individual than in the other colleges, attuned to the modern Gothic of the library. Note the strong rhythm of massed windows, particularly along the dining hall.

J 18 Mory's, 306 York Street. In a modest Federal house, an institution almost as renowned as Yale itself.

J 19 Morse and Stiles Colleges, 1960. Eero Saarinen.
Walls are made of a poured aggregate—"masonry without masons," Saarinen said—harmonizing with the texture of the older university buildings, as pleated planes and narrow windows harmonize with their verticality. Notice the relationship of the towers with the Gym, and notice the supple way Morse gives itself up to the shape of the Graduate School. Saarinen, like Rogers, was concerned with connectives, and his solution follows Rogers' precedents: a crooked route channeled between buildings, with changes of level and direction, with near and far views to catch the eye. The scale, however, is bigger, the drama harsher. Abstract forms take the place of historic allusion and poetic metaphor, light and shadow replace costly materials. Saarinen spoke of Flemish villages and of the towers of San Gimignano, suggesting picturesqueness, but his stony passageways have a more haunting, disturbing quality, intensified by the planting—the druid circle of gingko trees, the single magnolia springing from the stone. Sculpture by Costantino Nivola. In the Morse Court: *Lipstick* by Claes Oldenburg.

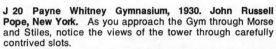

J 20 Payne Whitney Gymnasium, 1930. John Russell Pope, New York. As you approach the Gym through Morse and Stiles, notice the views of the tower through carefully contrived slots.

Tower Parkway is a characteristic urbanist creation of the '20s, planned, as its name says, as a *parklike way* and originally planted with trees and grass—now little more than a speedway. Designed by Frederick A. Davis, Jr., landscape architect.

J 21 University Heating and Power Plant, 1917. Day and Klauder, Philadelphia. A power plant suavely designed as part of a residential neighborhood that is now gone. Red louvered panel on the facade and penthouses added later. The parking lot commemorates **York Square,** one of New Haven's fine urbanist creations of the Greek Revival period, demolished gradually by the city and Yale from 1894 on.

J 22 Hall of Graduate Studies, 1930. James Gamble Rogers, New York. Notice the stamped bricks as you walk along Tower Parkway, also the carving on the main front on York Street.

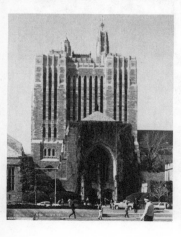

J 23 Sterling Law Buildings, 1930. James Gamble Rogers, New York. The Law School is one of Rogers' most ornamented buildings—watch the walls and windows as you walk along the street. There are medallions in the windows and small carvings (foliage, prisoners' chains, portraits, and a sprightly group of legal humoresques around the Wall Street portal) all tucked here and there—you have to look for them. Aloft on the southeast corner, riding the rooftops like a ship, is the library—with its four towers, a fragile and airy evocation of a Gothic chapel and of a long 19th-century American tradition of college libraries. Underground addition, 1962, Skidmore, Owings and Merrill, Chicago.

J 24 Grove Street Cemetery, 1796. Gate, 1845. Henry Austin. One of James Hillhouse's most interesting contributions to the city. Owned corporately, divided into family plots, and laid out, planted, and maintained as a "garden for the dead," Grove Street, as far as has yet been ascertained, was the first such cemetery in America, indeed perhaps anywhere. It was one of the famous sights of New Haven until eclipsed by the more romantic landscapes of later cemeteries at Cambridge, Brooklyn, and Philadelphia. The original entrance was east of the present one, and "Maple Avenue" was then the central aisle: Hillhouse's grave is here, in the middle. Fences originally surrounded the plots—white painted wood at first, later cast iron. Most ended up on the scrap heaps of World War II. The Townsend family's still survives as a stalwart example. Inside the gate the little building with the gold butterfly was built as a chapel, 1872; now shorn of its turret and spire.

J 25 Book and Snake, 1900. R. H. Robertson, New York. A Greek temple houses a senior society, fittingly designed as a part of Yale's only classical quadrangle. Notice the fence.

J 26 Sterling Memorial Library, 1927. James Gamble Rogers, New York. Above the low building rises the great stack tower—a majestic composition inventively handled. The style, said Rogers, "is as near to modern Gothic as we dared to make it." By this time Yale's "medieval orgy" was coming under attack in circles where Gropius and Wright were beginning to be talked about. "Yale has denied the present," said the undergraduate *Harkness Hoot*, describing the library as "the merest, cheapest copy-work." But cheap it was not. It was sumptuously, exquisitely made—a fact which today, in an age which can no longer produce such things, would make it a treasure regardless of ideology. Inside, Rogers provides a progression of spatial experiences and splendid rooms: the processional nave drama'ized by low cave-like aisles; the Reading Room with huge traceried windows; the Art of the Book Room with fine carving and metalwork; the dim cloistered walk to the Wall Street door along an enchanting green court; the tall elegance of the old Rare Book Room (now Manuscripts and Archives) with its magical small apse glowing with splintered light where once the Gutenberg Bible was displayed in solitary state. The building is richly ornamented: sculpture planned by Lee Lawrie, executed with alterations by Rene Chambellon; glass, G. Owen Bonawit; iron, Samuel Yellin. In the nave a stair descends to the **Cross Campus Library**, 1968, Edward Larrabee Barnes, New York.

J 27   The Cross Campus, 1933, and University Avenue, 1902.
Created to provide a setting for the library, the Cross Campus
(which runs from High to College Street) was one of the few
grand, space-consuming gestures that Rogers allowed himself. It soon became sacred ground, and one of the most
massive student protests of the '60s occurred when the
architect of the underground Cross Campus Library proposed
to dot the lawn with skylights. Four walled light courts rep-
resent the compromise. The cross-walk from Elm to Wall is
University Avenue (now Blount Avenue). It dates from the
opening of University Quadrangle (J 28) and was designed
to connect the old campus with the new one. At the south
end: **Noah Porter Gateway,** 1912, Howells and Stokes, New
York.

Along High Street: **Berkeley College** (shown here), 1933,
James Gamble Rogers, New York. The college is in two
pieces, connected by a tunnel. On College Street, on the
north, **William L. Harkness Hall,** 1926, William Adams Delano,
New York; on the south, **Calhoun College,** 1931, John Russell
Pope, New York.

**J 28   University Quadrangle (now Hewitt Quadrangle) and
the Bicentennial Buildings, 1901.**   Yale celebrated its bicentennial with giant pomp, opening a new quadrangle and
three buildings: Woodbridge, Commons, and Woolsey Hall.
Bridging the gap between the scientific and academic centers, the group symbolized the new Yale—a *university* in the
full sense, as the names University Quadrangle and University
Avenue made clear. From the start the eventual form of the
completed quadrangle was implicit: University Avenue would
be continued through from Wall Street to end in a court in
front of Commons (the plan shown here is as Rogers inter-
preted it in the '20s). Temporarily, the west end of Commons,
due to be concealed, was left bobtailed, and the shapes of
avenue and court were indicated by paving and trees. For
60 years succeeding architects held to this plan: Harkness
Hall and Berkeley were sited to define the avenue, and the
Commons colonnade was placed on axis. Then in 1961 the
plan was dropped. The Beinecke Library was given the
whole remaining vacancy for a centripetal counterplan, cutting down the trees and erasing the paving in order to possess
the whole space with its own granite floor. The result was a
battle of giants for the center of the stage, and nobody won.
Today the west end of Commons remains bobtailed, the
hole in the corner gapes, the colonnade is off-center, Woodbridge looks like a mistake—it is all a monument to the
pitfalls of long-range planning.

J 29 Beinecke Rare Book and Manuscript Library, 1961. Gordon Bunshaft of Skidmore, Owings, and Merrill, New York. A marble box floats above a granite plaza. The architect describes it for us: the only visible supports are four granite columns curving up from the granite paving. The facades are large trusses, spanning from corner column to corner column. Individual truss members are four-pointed stars, clad in granite, whose ends are connected, forming octagons in between, filled with marble. Inside, translucent marble walls dimly illumine a vast, hushed space. In the marble court, marble sculpture by Isamu Noguchi.

The aim of the design was "to dramatize the fact that the building contains great treasures," and it has emphatically succeeded—partly by the use of precious materials, partly by the use of precious land, withdrawn from use at the heart of the university. This huge empty plaza is a major break in Yale's integrated fabric and its tradition of street architecture.

J 30 Woodbridge Hall, 1901. John Mead Howells and Isaac Newton Phelps Stokes, New York. Proclaiming a new era for Yale, the Bicentennial Buildings made a spectacular break with the past, replacing the Gothic tradition with Beaux Arts classicism. Woodbridge Hall, the first to be finished, shocked oldtimers with its whiteness. Some doors and mantles were taken from demolished New York houses.

J 31 Woolsey Hall, Commons, and Memorial Hall, 1901; Flagstaff, 1908: Carrère and Hastings, New York. Colonnade and Cenotaph, 1927: Thomas Hastings with Everett V. Meeks. On the right is Woolsey Hall, on the left is Commons—the noblest room in the university, at present a bit cluttered. Pass through the rotunda of Memorial Hall. On the street, the circular portico effectively masters a splayed corner that is not quite a right angle. The hall was designed as a key link in the Bicentennial plan to connect the scientific and academic campuses. Pointed straight at the science complex, it was an indoor path intended to lead across the street and on to Hillhouse Avenue whenever its partner on the opposite corner should be built. But when the new building at last came (**Strathcona Hall**, 1931, Zantzinger, Borie and Medary, Philadelphia) it failed to get the message. Instead of becoming the gate to Hillhouse Avenue, Strathcona became a monumental obstacle.

J 32 Byers Hall, 1902. Hiss and Weekes, New York. Modeled on the Petit Trianon, Byers (now part of Silliman College and shorn of its front steps) was designed to complement the Bicentennial Buildings. With this group, Yale's foray into Beaux Arts classicism began and ended.

J 33 Silliman College, 1940. Eggers and Higgins, New York. The last of Yale's prewar architecture, the end of an era. Notice the elegance of materials—the sensuous surface of the brick, the faultlessly profiled stone trim. On Grove Street the gatehouse makes a visual terminus for Hillhouse Avenue. Otto Eggers, successor to John Russell Pope, had worked with Pope on earlier Yale projects.

370 Temple Street, formerly **Vernon Hall** (1906, Satterlee and Boyd, New York), and 111 Grove Street, formerly **St. Elmo** (1912, Kenneth M. Murchison, New York), built as fraternity dormitories. Good urban background, with dark Edwardian brick and white stone.

J 34 William Kingsley House, 105 Grove Street, c1845. A plain Greek Revival house prettily dressed up in the 1930s with an iron trellis—testimony to a sympathetic meeting between two periods. In 1971 this demure building set off a major battle when Yale proposed to tear it down to make way for two new colleges (Mitchell/Giurgola Associates, Philadelphia). A compromise was finally reached and Yale agreed to move the house (in the heat of the fray few noticed how much its present charm depends on the green oasis where it is now); but in the end Yale had a falling out with the city over taxes and the whole plan was dropped.

J 35 Timothy Dwight College, 1933. James Gamble Rogers, New York. Contrast the pictorial and mobile quality of Rogers' style with the formality and repose of Silliman.

John Lynde house, 66–68 Wall Street, 1806. Originally the door was on Temple Street (the lattice now marks the spot) and the house looked much like the Elizabethan Club (J 39), as the telltale traces of a Palladian window in the gable reveal. An errant truck one day stove in the front, occasioning the removal of the entry to the side (1921, J. Frederick Kelly). No. 320, now **Alumni House:** a Federal house disguised with mid-Victorian bays, mansard roof, and a particularly dashing little porch. Down Wall Street, no. 82: **Rosey's Cleaners and Tailors.** J. Press and Langrock may have supplied the clothes, but for two generations Rosey has been holding them together. In 1928 the senior Mr. Rosenberg reminisced: "I used to sleep on the doorstep of Durfee Hall and wake up students at five in the morning to collect their bills, so I got to know the Campus pretty well." He felt that student interior decoration was declining. "It's nicer, of course, and more comfortable. Cleaner perhaps. But when you've said a big sofa and a jazz phonograph, you've said it all. I can remember rooms that were better than a side show." Yale's future plans anticipate replacing this row of buildings with a **music center** (Cesar Pelli of Gruen Associates, Los Angeles).

J 36 York Hall, now Stoeckel Hall, 1897. Grosvenor Atterbury, New York. This corner is a heady place. Gothic, Venetian, Byzantine, and Federal—a kaleidoscope that by rights should be absurd but for some reason is wonderful. York Hall (now a music building) stems from the era when fraternities built large private dormitories, and it has the theatricality of fraternity architecture. Recently cleaned, its colors have emerged in all their Venetian gorgeousness—melon-colored brick with golden lace. The ghostly outline of a former house remains on the south wall.

On the north corner: **St. Anthony Hall,** a senior society (1913) and Van-Sheff on both sides of it (Vanderbilt-Scientific Halls, 1903), by Charles C. Haight, New York—called by Montgomery Schuyler the most agreeable buildings at Yale.

J 37 Scroll and Key, 1869. Richard Morris Hunt, New York. A small exotic gem of a building for a senior society—the only remaining example of Hunt's work in New Haven. Notice the cast iron fence, and the colors of the polished granite columns with bone white capitals.

J 38   Sprague Hall, 1916. Coolidge and Shattuck, Boston.
A delightful rendition of a Federal theater such as might
have been built in New York or Boston in the 1790s—even
such details as the lamps are carefully carried out.

**J 39   Leverett Griswold House, now the Elizabethan Club,
459 College Street, c1810.**   One of New Haven's best examples of the small, prosperous house of the Federal era. The
Palladian window in the gable was a favorite fancy of the
day. It gives height to the design, and slims its lines.
   451 College Street: formerly **Franklin Hall**, another fraternity dormitory (1910, Chapman and Frazer, Boston). 435
College Street, formerly the **Department of University Health,**
now offices (1929, Cross and Cross, New York).

K The Hillhouse Quarter

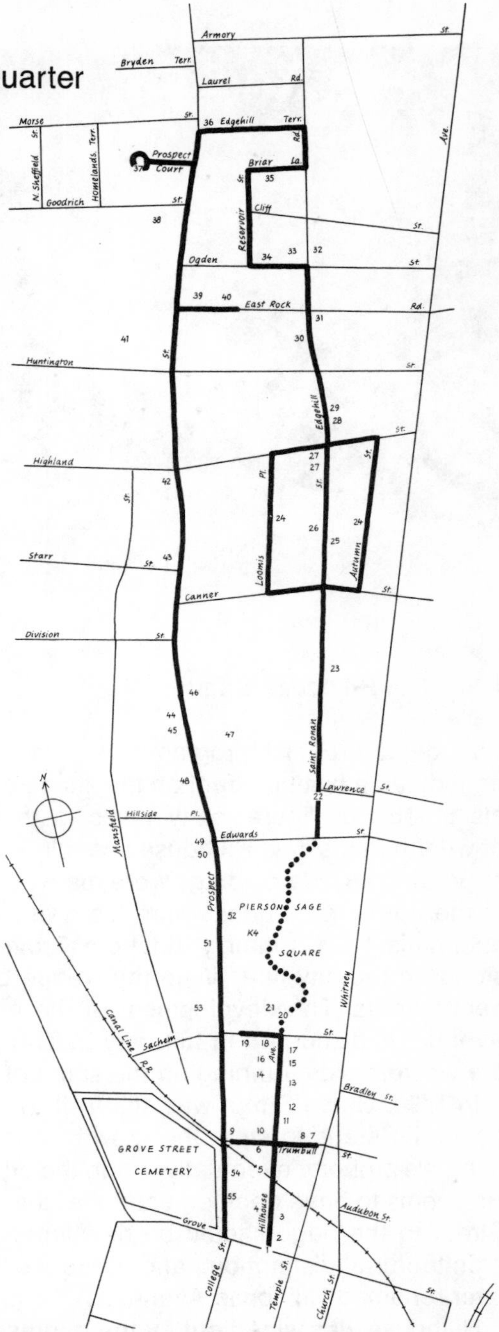

Armory   St.
Bryden Terr.
Laurel   Rd.

Morse   St.   36 Edgehill   Terr.
N. Sheffield St.   Homelands Terr.
Prospect
Court
33
Briar   La.
35
Goodrich
Cliff
38   St.   Reservoir
Ogden   34   33   32   St.

39   40   East Rock
31
41   30   Rd.

Huntington   St.   St.

Edgehill
29
28
Highland   St.
42   27
PL.   27
St.
24
26   24
26   25
Starr   St.   43   Loomis   Auburn
Canner   St.

Division   St.

23
46
44
45   47
SAINT RONAN
48
N   Lawrence   St.
22
Hillside   Pl.
Mansfield
49   Edwards   St.
50

Prospect
PIERSON SAGE
52
K4
51   SQUARE

Whitney
53   21
20
Canal Line R.R.   Sachem
19 18   St.
16   17
14   15
13
Bradley St.
12
9   10   11
8 7   St.
GROVE STREET   6 Trumbull
CEMETERY   54   5
55   Audubon St.
Grove   3
Hillhouse   2

College St.   Temple St.   Church St.   St.

Yale's Science Complex and Divinity School, Albertus Magnus College, and 150 years of the
city's top domestic architecture.

133

K The Hillhouse Quarter.

The great urbanist programs of James Hillhouse in the Federal period had a lasting effect on the shape of the city, and we have met his ubiquitous figure many times in these pages. Like most men of wealth in his day, Hillhouse speculated extensively in land on the edge of town. His holdings were many, but his greatest interest was in the northern corridor where his own farm lay. Here he owned an enormous tract, running out from Grove Street, where the house stood, to the city line, filling the wedge between Orange and Prospect Streets. The development of the eastern side, along Whitney Avenue, is discussed in Itinerary E. The present tour is confined to the western side, running up the spine of Prospect Hill.

In 1790, Grove Street was still in the country, and Hillhouse took energetic steps to steer the growth of the city in his direction and bring his property eventually within the orbit of the real estate market. He seems to have decided early that the high land rising from Grove Street to the ridge should be developed as a place of beauty and architectural distinction, and there he laid out Temple Avenue, later renamed Hillhouse Avenue.

Hillhouse was wiped out by the depression following the Embargo in 1807, and development came to a standstill until the 1820s, when two providential events occured: the Farmington Canal laid its course across the Hillhouse land, and Hillhouse's son, James Abraham Hillhouse, married a New York heiress. For a wedding present young Hillhouse was given the northern corridor of New Haven, and he revived its development. Factories grew up along the canal on Audubon and Church Streets, houses rose on Trumbull and Whitney, and a number of mansions appeared on Hillhouse Avenue. Backed by his father-in-law's money, young Hillhouse became an enthusiastic patron of architecture, and under his leadership and that of his friends Ithiel Town and Alexander Jackson Davis, the Hillhouse Quarter blossomed forth as New Haven's most beautiful and prestigious neighborhood. At the head of the avenue James Abraham built his own house, Sachem's Wood (shown above—razed in 1942 by the will of his daughter Isaphene), and in the country around it other estates settled. By the time the boom inspired by the canal collapsed in 1837, the lower portion of the Hillhouse property was established.

But the city's expansion to the north was slow, and it was not until the turn of the century that the ridge to the north had its day, becoming all in one swift movement, between about 1895 and World War I, the garden suburb of the upper class.

Today the Hillhouse Quarter is outwardly not much changed, but most of its larger properties are now owned by institutions, principally Yale and Albertus Magnus College. Yale in particular is entrenched in the Hillhouse Avenue–Prospect Street area. This connection goes back to Hillhouse himself, and to his sale to Yale in 1814 of a building for a "medical institution." Later acquired by Joseph Sheffield, financier and philanthropist, this was returned to Yale as the Sheffield Scientific School and, with the addition of Sheffield's own house (bequeathed to Yale in 1889), became the nucleus of the Yale science complex. Yale's physical and social sciences now fill most of the lower part of the Hillhouse Quarter.

K 1 Hillhouse Avenue. New Haveners will tell you that Dickens called Hillhouse Avenue the most beautiful street in America. Possibly he did, although no one now seems able to find just where he said it. In any case the claim is an indication of the spell the street has cast over its own town. Its projected layout by James Hillhouse has been described above. Its realization by his son, influenced by the ideas of Ithiel Town (whose own house was built here) and A. J. Davis, created one of the urbanist masterpieces of the Greek Revival: an avenue of majestic width, with houses set back 50 feet from the right of way, the intervening strip planted with trees and called "the Grove." The overall effect, despite the strict initial Federal layout, was parklike, recalling with its white temples and villas glimpsed through trees such prototypes as Regent's Park in London; even the canal played its part.

Throughout the whole of the 19th century the avenue maintained its style, but early in the 1900s Yale and St. Mary's suddenly filled the lower block with large buildings, changing its character from residential to institutional—and, alas, not to very good institutional, for by bad luck on this most beautiful of streets Yale put up a row that is one of the low points of its architectural history. With the acquisition of Pierson–Sage Square soon after, Yale realized the need to make Hillhouse Avenue a Yale street, and systematically set about acquiring the upper block in the 1920s. Today the avenue still maintains prestige as the home of Yale's president, but behind stately facades most of the upper block is now cut up into offices. Only the Skinner house remains in private hands.

Although Yale has tried to become a conscientious custodian of the city's treasure, the avenue today is a sad place. The elms are long since dead, young trees have not yet grown to take their place—the light is now too bright, the houses seem exposed. The cast iron fences and the planting of the Grove are gone—parking meters are a poor substitute—and the roadway has been widened, losing its scale and suppleness.

And finally a word should be said about color, the most conspicuous change of all. Greek Revival colors had been pale and luminous—the colors of marble. Italian villas were gentle tans and grays—the colors of stone. Trim, which in the language of architecture is expressive of a different material and a different function from the wall, was of a slightly different hue, neither a strong contrast (as now in K 6) nor a monochrome (as now in K 16 or K 17).

It was in the Brown Decades at the end of the century that a change occurred. As brownstone increasingly became the fashionable material of the big cities, and as city smoke increasingly darkened its color, the popular spectrum deepened, and the style-conscious residents of Hillhouse Avenue, following the trend, began to paint their classical temples brown. This happened in many other places. What is surprising about Hillhouse Avenue is that it is still hanging on. Today the street seems to be in mourning.

K 2 Cloister Hall, 1887. H. Edwards Ficken, New York.
Addition, 1915. Originally a fraternity, this building is an
example of the partly whimsical, partly domestic style that
fraternity architecture affected. Yale publications list the
architect as Clarence H. Stilson, a local man, but the design
was by Ficken, a well-known "architect's artist," or renderer,
of the time. Possibly Stilson was supervisory architect. (The
attribution has also sometimes been made to R. H. Robertson,
for whom Ficken at one time worked.) Originally the building
consisted only of the south half, with its entrance on Grove
Street and with what appears to be a super-stable and
stableyard planned for the north end where the later addition
is now, designed by Metcalfe and Ballantyne, New York.

K 3 St. Mary's Church, 1870. James Murphy, Providence.
Direct descendant of the first Roman Catholic church
founded by the immigrant Irish who came to New Haven
in the 1820s, this building was a challenging assertion of
the new wealth and power of the once-poor community.
Precluded from the possibility of building on the Green,
the Catholics did the next best thing and moved right into
the patrician stronghold of old New Haven. Their neighbors
did not accept them willingly, but the church won and has
ever since made itself at home on the avenue. A
magnificent spire was originally planned for the tower. There
is an impressive interior with clustered piers and leafy Gothic
capitals.

No. 5: **St. Mary's Rectory,** 1907. No. 9: **Mason Laboratory
of Mechanical Engineering,** 1910, Charles C. Haight, New
York. No. 15: formerly a fraternity, now **Yale Collection of
Musical Instruments,** 1894 (attributed to J. Cleveland Cady).
This Richardsonian stone block balanced the Cloister in
the design of the street until the Mason Lab was stuffed in
beside it. No. 17: **University Health Building** (1969, Wester-
mann and Miller, New York). The avenue here crosses the
Farmington Canal, converted to a railroad in the 1840s by
Joseph Sheffield. Sunk deep below grade, the line seems
never to have been considered a drawback to the avenue's
style.

**K 4 Joseph Sheffield House, 1836, Ithiel Town; 1859, Henry
Austin.** Demolished 1957. Although it is not the role of a
guide book to dwell on vanished buildings, this house, like
Sachem's Wood, was so powerful a presence that its disappearance is still felt. The central section was Ithiel Town's
own house, built to hold his famous library; the enlargement
was by his New Haven pupil and successor—each in its
own way a climactic work of its architect's career.

No. 2: **Kirtland Hall,** 1902, Kirtland K. Cutter, Spokane.
The odd siting, leaving the cornerstone of the avenue
adrift, is without explanation (Strathcona came along later
and made things worse). No. 10: **Dunham Laboratory,** 1912,
Henry G. Morse, New York; and beside it, **Dunham Laboratory
Addition,** 1958, Office of Douglas Orr. It is hard to look at
the Dunham Addition without pain—it was for this the Sheffield house was demolished. No. 12: **Leet Oliver Memorial
Hall,** 1908, Charles C. Haight, New York.

K 5 Competition for Proposed Mathematics Building, 1969. Winning Design, Venturi and Rauch, Philadelphia. The Yale Math Building competition was a sensational and vitriolic architectural event, won from among 468 contestants by the iconoclast who had shocked the country as the apostle of the "ugly and ordinary." The competition marks a turning point in Yale's architectural development, a reaction against the design heroes and monumental statements of the previous decade and a search for a new kind of order— for livability, usability, and even that most elusive of architectural qualities, modesty. As a document of the times, the program is as interesting as the entries: "The architecture of Louis Kahn, Eero Saarinen, Philip Johnson, Paul Rudolph, Gordon Bunshaft and others, which has focused international attention on the campus, mostly stands in strong contrast to the buildings and courts of the years around 1930 . . . which form a superbly integrated fabric unifying the central part of the campus. Not surprisingly, Yale proud as it is of its modern monuments, now finds itself looking again toward the integration of new buildings into the strong existing fabric and to the provision of workable, economical, generally non-monumental space." The site is the lot between Leet Oliver (to which the Math Building is connected) and the railroad. Plans for building are now uncertain.

K 6 James Dwight Dana House, 24 Hillhouse Avenue, 1849. Henry Austin. A mature example of Austin's Villa Style— a prim cube relieved by exotic trim. Both the plantlike columns and the cornice imitating the fringe of some lavish oriental canopy traveled a long journey to Hillhouse Avenue, coming from India via English picture books which Austin may have found in Ithiel Town's library. The vegetable columns with square, turned-down capitals became one of his favorite motifs. Austin's drawing for the house survives. It shows a more delicate color scheme—pale sand color with trim slightly accentuated. The color was meant to suggest stone, as was the "penciling" of ashlar blocks on the stucco, a standard feature of the Villa Style which will be seen on other houses up the avenue. Wings have been added, otherwise the house is little changed. Inside some of the Dana furniture remains, as well as ruby glass, mantels, and a remarkable newel post (see G 36 for another). Adjoining the house is the cut for the Farmington Canal, later the railroad. Until modern times it was crossed by a narrow bridge, providing a picturesque ornament for the avenue.

K 7 83 Trumbull Street, c1882. Out-of-town architects bestowed a number of individualized Queen Anne designs on New Haven in the '70s and '80s, but this house is a classic of the local style. Notice the complexity of forms, the variety of windows (there are at least ten different sizes and shapes), and the elaboration of the surface with colors, materials, and textures—painted wood, brownstone, red tile, terra cotta, and three kinds of brick. All this is held together by a tight vertical movement and by modulation of tones. Inside, stair and fireplace of glazed blue brick remain, also the characteristic tiling of the entry floor.

No. 84. an extreme case of Colonialitis. A group of three row houses of the 1870s, whose stoops and porches have left their shadowy marks in the brick, have been turned into an apartment and camouflaged with an improbable portico and other bits from the historical grab-bag.

K 8 Maple Cottage ("A house for Mrs. Lent"), 85 Trumbull Street, 1836. Alexander J. Davis. Mrs. Lent (who in the end never lived here) was a family connection of young Hillhouse's, and he threw himself into planning her house, partly, we may assume, from kindliness, and partly with a view to promoting the development of his empty street by planting a charming decoy on it. Pains were not spared to make this a little gem: "a beautiful cottage residence" with "verandah front" and rafter ends exposed under the eaves in the new Tuscan style. Davis supplied the elevations, but Hillhouse, himself an amateur designer, kept butting in, until at one point, after he had said that the windows looked too close to the frieze, Davis replied stiffly: "As to the 'looks,' suffice it that you have my *dictum,* and when I place windows close to the friese, be sure it is no *ordinary vulgarity.*" After this there were no more arguments. Today the house has been much changed. Walls, originally flushboarded, have been stuccoed, and the Tuscan rafters along the eaves are gone (one section remains on the porch). Possibly the third floor is an addition—what other changes may have occurred we can only guess. Nahum Hayward was the contractor. (Photograph 1905.)

K 9 Wolf's Head, now University Offices, 77 Prospect Street, 1884. McKim, Mead and White, New York. Less outré than some, this senior society building nevertheless makes an instant impression with its stepped Dutch gable, round arch, and Richardsonian impregnability. Note the fineness of the detailing: the stonework around the arch, the slim windows and spiky gate. The building was sold to the university when Wolf's Head moved to new quarters, taking the dining room with them (J 13).

89 Trumbull Street: in the wake of Russell Sturgis's mansion for Henry Farnam, Victorian Gothic turrets appeared in fashionable quarters in the '80s. **No. 87,** a house with a chameleon past. It is called the Benjamin Silliman house after Yale's famed pioneer scientist, but that is stretching a point, for only the frame was ever Silliman's. The house first stood on Hillhouse Avenue. It was built by James Hillhouse shortly before 1807, employing a new building technique, the wood frame being filled with traprock walls and stuccoed. In 1871 the masonry walls were removed, the frame was disassembled and one section dispatched to Davenport Avenue, while the rest was rebuilt here. It was covered with clapboards following the original lines, but the trimmings were new: arched gable windows, window heads, and porch. Around the turn of the century, brick wings and perhaps the room over the porch were added; at the same time, the front door of the historic Roger Sherman house downtown was saved from the wrecker and installed here. This was later carried off to another house on Prospect Street and the present door installed.

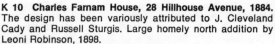

K 10 Charles Farnam House, 28 Hillhouse Avenue, 1884. The design has been variously attributed to J. Cleveland Cady and Russell Sturgis. Large homely north addition by Leoni Robinson, 1898.

Edwin Wheeler House, 30 Hillhouse Avenue, 1884: an example of the catastrophic result of blindly modernizing a good Victorian house. Originally a lively and interesting design, it was stripped and stuccoed sometime after 1908 and is now a nonentity. **George P. Fisher House,** 27 Hillhouse Avenue, 1865. A surprisingly gawky version of the late-late Villa Style. Drabness used at least to be relieved by contrasting color tones that highlighted the classical porch with Corinthian columns and the handsome window hoods.

K 11 Abigail Whelpley House, 31 Hillhouse Avenue, c1800(?) or c1827(?). Remodeled 1860s, Henry Austin. Mrs. Whelpley was a widowed relative of the Hillhouses who came with her half-sister, Mrs. Apthorp, to live in New Haven. Young Hillhouse eagerly took charge, ever glad of a chance to pump-prime on the avenue. It happened that a house he owned on Whitney Avenue stood in the way of a new link planned for the turnpike; it also happened that his friend Samuel F. B. Morse, who had been renting this house, had left for New York, grieving over the death of his wife and abandoning one of his promising inventions in the garden, his "portable painting room." Young Hillhouse ingeniously wrapped everything up: Morse's house was moved across the avenue for Mrs. Apthorp (its further adventures are told in L 14), and the portable painting room was moved here for Mrs. Whelpley (evidently as a wing or an outhouse). The main part of Mrs. Whelpley's house James Abraham thriftily designed himself then asked Ithiel Town for a facade. But plans may have changed, for the house that presently appeared on the avenue in 1827 or soon thereafter is certainly no work of Ithiel Town's. It is a stock vernacular design much like Mrs. Apthorp's, and like hers it may have been moved here. Austin's remodeling, done for Yale's President Noah Porter, added the mansard roof and corner boards with filled angles, also two Victorian porches, duly removed when the house was re-Federalized in the 20th century.

No. 37: 1866. The '60s were not a brilliant moment in New Haven. Here the old Villa formula has been tarted up with a small pediment, broken segments of arches for window heads, and pretty bits of ornament that you now have to strain to see under brown paint.

K 12 Mary Prichard House, 35 Hillhouse Avenue, 1836. Alexander J. Davis. Another widow of means, another chance for pump-priming. Again young Hillhouse took over all the arrangements, and again his friend Davis made the plans while he himself supervised. In December he paid for the painting and papering and built the fence—this gives us the date when the house was finished. In later years when Davis visited at Sachem's Wood he used to enjoy dropping down the street for a game of chess with "Madam Prichard." With its tall Corinthian porch this is one of his most stately houses. Until recently it was painted a delicate lemony cream with classical white trim, perfectly recalling the onetime character of the Greek Revival avenue with its pale villas and white columns. Originally a parapet surrounded the main roof and antefixes bordered the roof of the porch, giving the house a lift now missing. Bay windows and wing are later additions. Ira Atwater and Nelson Hotchkiss were the builders.

K 13   Henry Farnam House, 43 Hillhouse Avenue, 1871, Russell Sturgis, New York; 1934, Kimball and Husted, New York. In 1934 no one had a good word to say for Victorian architecture. Today this poor house testifies to the lengths people were willing to go to express their dislike. Henry Farnam had first come to New Haven as engineer of the Farmington Canal and later of the railroad. He subsequently made a fortune and became a great benefactor of the city and of Yale. He settled here in the '70s, pleasantly in sight of his onetime canal and railroad, and built the finest house the avenue, or indeed New Haven, had yet seen. After the architectural doldrums of the '60s, this reestablished the prestige of both. Sturgis at roughly the same time was at work on Farnam Hall for Yale. Since 1937 the house has been the home of Yale's presidents.

K 14   Aaron Skinner House, 46 Hillhouse Avenue, 1832. Alexander J. Davis. Aaron Skinner was a young man in his thirties who decided to open a boys' school on Hillhouse Avenue. As usual James Abraham, concerned with providing a suitable ornament for the avenue, took an active part, and plans were reviewed both by him and his father-in-law, who was doing the financing. Skinner wistfully hoped to build something rather modest (his only resource, he explained, would be the income from his sixteen pupils). But Davis was persuasive and Hillhouse was firm and in the end the contract, signed with Nahum Hayward in September 1832, approached the frightening sum of $6300. Thus came into being one of New Haven's most distinguished houses. A remodeling in the '50s (often attributed to Henry Austin) filled in the second story in the angles flanking the portico, changing the cruciform plan to a more conventional rectangle (the original shape may be traced by following the entablature around); Austin-like window heads and brackets were also added. Around 1910 a large stair hall and dining room were created, with a wing on the west and a bay on the north, changing the scale and style of the interior. The front rooms however still belong to the Greek Revival.

No. 38 next door, **the Henry F. English House** (1892, Bruce Price, New York). The last private house built on the avenue brings its architectural history full circle, from classicism to classicism. But the differences are great—sedentary repose instead of action and tension, horizontality instead of dynamic balance. Contrast the furrowed shadows and highlights of the Skinner house with this bland surface. Interior recently remodeled for Yale offices and considerably cut up.

K 15 John Graves House, 51 Hillhouse Avenue, 1862. Conservative Hillhouse Avenue hung onto the Villa formula through the '60s but clearly was in several minds about how to spruce it up. The frenzied carpentry of the Graves house seems to have been an isolated experiment. See the Fisher house for an alternative idea (K 10); also no. 37 (K 11). On Prospect Street a more progressive version appeared (K 51).

K 16 John P. Norton House, 52 Hillhouse Avenue, 1848–49. Henry Austin. An early version of the towered Italian villa, closely following a design published by Andrew Jackson Downing six or seven years before. This was a novel building. In New Haven—and on the avenue of all places— its mysteriously shadowed arcades and wild, free silhouette must have been a shock. But Puritan New Haven was loosening up, and the Norton House was a prophecy of other towers to come. Today it is hard to recapture the excitement, for later events have made it tame. Also later owners have been draining the magic out by bits and pieces. A mean third floor now mires the energetic rise of the free vertical forces, and the south wing breaks the tripartite balance. With its once perky oriental canopies and balconies removed, the walls are flat and dull—someone even went to the trouble of stripping the moldings off the window surrounds. For all that, this remains a house one looks for whenever one happens to pass this way.

K 17 Peletiah Perit House, 55 Hillhouse Avenue, 1860. Sidney Mason Stone. Modeled on the Ezekiel Trowbridge House (I 8), this is one of the few remaining examples of Stone's work—fortunately a fine, full-blown one. Contrast the carefully disciplined design and the finesse of the Renaissance detail with the more personal style of Austin. Also notice the unexpected Victorian opulence of the arched door, with great ropey moldings. A splendid Tudor library, big as a ballroom, was added at the rear sometime after 1888, carefully designed to match the exterior. Both outside and inside the Perit House today is one of the avenue's best historic specimens. Needless to say, it was not originally purple.

K 18 Elizabeth Apthorp House, 56 Hillhouse Avenue, 1837. Alexander J. Davis. Mrs. Apthorp, whose earlier house has been mentioned in K 11, soon moved to a bigger one, occupying it by early 1838. The design is sometimes attributed to Town and Davis, but probably, following the pattern of young Hillhouse's other projects, was personally designed by Davis. Today the house has been so much and so eccentrically altered that it provides a field day for architectural detectives. Originally it was a cube with a pair of symmetrical wings on the rear connected by a veranda, and with exposed rafters under the eaves in the Tuscan manner. Isolated against the plain facade, the focus of the design was the oversized Egyptian porch (the funny box now on top is obviously later). All other protrusions are subsequent accretions, including a Renaissance solarium, an exceptionally handsome Eastlake library of polished woods in black and brown, and the window heads on the front. The pilasters on the south wall were salvaged by an antiquarian owner from a celebrated Federal house demolished in 1909, the DeForest house by David Hoadley (did the owner know that they belonged to a remodeling of the 1860s?). Inside, more pilasters and a number of thin columns are standing around in curious places with a very Hoadley-like look, and these too are part of the salvage. Original elegant stair rail remains, slender and fluid as a whip, with ivory button on the newel. A single lush marble mantel of the mid-century appears suddenly on the top floor. Door lights may be a Federalizing reproduction, set in the Greek Revival frame. On top of all this, Yale has recently contributed some oddities of its own. All in all, Mrs. Apthorp's house is the Old Curiosity Shop of Hillhouse Avenue.

K 19 Yale Computer Center, now Watson Astronomy Center, 60 Sachem Street, 1961. Skidmore, Owings and Merrill, Chicago. Taking advantage of a sharp change of grade, the building is a floating island, connected to the land with a narrow bridge—an effective way of isolating the geometric form in space, as modern architects like to do, without consuming a lot of ground.

Opposite: **Osborn Memorial Laboratories,** 1913, Charles C. Haight, New York. The towered gatehouse recalls A. J. Davis's Alumni Hall which had been demolished just two years before (J 10).

K 20 Pierson-Sage Square. This was the last property held by the Hillhouses, the square of approximately 40 acres on which Sachem's Wood stood. It was acquired for Yale by the same expansive administration that had opened University Quadrangle as a link to the north in 1901 (J 28). The fact that the land was impracticably remote, and that many of the faculty were opposed, was no deterrent. The move is hard to explain except as sheer Beaux-Arts imperialism: this was the most superb piece of property in New Haven, standing at the head of its most splendid avenue—Yale should have it. A vision of radiant domes and towers presiding over the entire city must have been in the Corporation's mind, and such a dream was in fact later drawn up by John Russell Pope. After many delays the land was conveyed to Yale in 1910, excepting only a square plot in the middle where Mr. and Mrs. Hillhouse continued to reside in Sachem's Wood.This was one of the few times that Yale had ever had a large unencumbered acreage, a *tabula rasa* on which to plan any way it might desire, and many ideal plans were in due course made—by Frederick Law Olmsted, Jr., by Pope, by James Gamble Rogers, and no doubt others. But freedom proved hard to handle. When it came time to build, the plans were set aside, and by the early '60s a mere handful of buildings seemed to have blanketed all the space: on its most magnificent site Yale had produced its most poorly integrated, inefficient, and incoherent complex. To Philip Johnson in 1962 fell the job of making order out of this sprawl, and his subsequent deployment of the three buildings of the Kline Science Center, in order to minimize the damage already done and focus attention on what was good, repays attention. (Shown here: the site as laid out by Pope in 1919.)

K 21 Kline Biology Tower, 1964. Philip Johnson Associates, New York. The choice of color at once relates the Kline buildings to the older buildings on Whitney and Prospect and drops out the ones in the middle. At the foot of the hill the Kline Geology building (1962) acts as a podium for the group above. The courtyard brilliantly provides the tower with a loose link with the eastern buildings without, so to speak, compromising it. It also screens out some dismal works behind while keeping the open feeling of the great sweep of the land and the satisfying sight of the Chemistry labs climbing the hill with huge measured steps. Inside, the lobby of the tower is suddenly barren and inhuman like an office building, but the library (to the right) is a handsome room, and on the top floor is a penthouse restaurant with a view of all New Haven and Long Island Sound—not only a breathtaking sight but a wonderful way to study the patterns of the city and its topography.

The buildings on Whitney Avenue are mentioned in Itinerary E. Part way up the hill, in marble and green glass: the **Josiah Willard Gibbs Laboratories** (1955, Paul Schweikher with the Office of Douglas Orr); behind it the **Accelerator Laboratories** (1953, Office of Douglas Orr) and **Nuclear Structures Laboratory** (1963, Office of Douglas Orr, deCossy, Winder and Associates). If you leave the Kline Tower by the back door, the **Sloane Physics Laboratory** is in front of you (1911, Charles C. Haight, New York), and the majestic pile of the **Sterling Chemistry Laboratory** is on the right (K 52).

K 22 St. Ronan and Prospect Streets (K 22–K 55). New Haven's top display of domestic architecture. No set course need be followed—it is pleasant walking wherever you go. The houses noted here have been chosen as a sampling of different trends and different architects, both out-of-towners and the home team. Development begins around 1895, the main thrust is from 1900 to 1920. The most palatial estates were built on Prospect Street, overlooking the view to West Rock. Smaller gentry, including a large Yale population, settled nearby. Growth virtually ended with the Depression, although the establishment managed to hold fast until World War II. But since the war the neighborhood has followed the now familiar urban pattern, the more magnificent houses falling to institutions (chiefly Yale and Albertus Magnus College) and to cheap developers. Today the area as a whole is still green and fair, but its western border, along Prospect Street, is being eroded by some of the most depressing postwar housing in New Haven. Shown here: **190 St. Ronan Street** (1920, Heathcote Woolsey, New York), a good introduction to a neighborhood that blends images from the past with modern comfort. The house is a reproduction of a Federal house that stood on High Street, but in scale and texture it is pure American 20th century.

Edwards Street, bordering the Hillhouse park, was built up with large houses, many now gone. **No. 309,** 1905, Allen and Williams. **No. 299,** 1896, Lamb and Rich, New York. **No. 291,** 1896, R. Clipston Sturgis, Boston: under the city's most monumental wisteria, brick wings flank a wood center section.

K 23 Walter Malley House, 305 St. Ronan Street, 1909. Grosvenor Atterbury, New York. At the rear: **Bethesda Lutheran Church,** 1958, Office of Douglas Orr. Across the street, the iron fence is all that remains of the Winchester-Bennett house by McKim, Mead and White, which stood on Prospect Street. The Yale Divinity School now fills the site (K 46).

K 24 Loomis Place and Autumn Street. Two short streets that make pleasant detours. Shown here: **55 Loomis Place,** 1967, Sidney T. Miller. Opposite: **the Foote School,** 1957–60, Perkins & Will and Carleton Granbery; 1966, north addition, Davis Cochran and Miller. **Autumn Street** is a mews-like street, originally running along the backs of large properties. **No. 21** (1960, Office of Carleton Granbery): a remodeled carriage house, sheltered from the road by a pretty court.

Back on St. Ronan Street: **No. 345** (1934, Norton and Townsend)—a Tudor house astringently handled in the stripped style of the '30s. **Nos. 340** and **346** (both 1909)—Georgian Revival in full bloom. **No. 352** is a later version by R. W. Foote, 1913.

K 25 389 St. Ronan Street, 1889. A prototype Shingle Style model of the turn of the century, part Queen Anne, part Colonial—here in an unusually impressive version, combining shingling, wood panels, and windows in a subtle pattern. A skillful paint job heightens the effect.

K 26 396 St. Ronan Street, 1910. Brown and VonBeren.
Much of the individuality of this house lies in the deliberate historicism of using local seam-faced traprock, recalling New Haven architecture of the early 19th century. Compare the design with 50 Edgehill Terrace (K 30).

Opposite: **401 St. Ronan Street,** 1965, William Petchler. **No. 421,** 1905, Leoni Robinson.

K 27 450 and 460 St. Ronan Street, 1913. James Gamble Rogers, New York. No. 460 is shown here. Built for members of the same family, the two structures are identical, dressed up to read as a pair but not as twins. Georgian at its most patrician.

K 28 3 Edgehill Road, 1917. Brown and VonBeren. An eloquent example of the low-slung cosy cottage, vaguely suggestive of picturesque Colonial simplicities, which was so appealing to an increasingly affluent and complex society.

K 29 9 Edgehill Road. This is one of New Haven's few Gothic houses (another is at 210 St. Ronan, hidden behind evergreens). Its background is a mystery, for Edgehill Road was not opened until the turn of the century and the house is obviously older than the street. Apparently it was built first as a cottage on the Eli Whitney Jr. estate in the 1850s. When the road was opened it may have been moved slightly to face the street.

K 30 50 Edgehill Road, 1905. Brown and VonBeren. 50 Edgehill, 3 Edgehill, and 396 St. Ronan Street are variants on the same plan by the same architect. Here cobblestones suggest the popular Edwardian image of the rustic cottage. The attempt to make the house look low and earthbound leads to an almost total obliteration of the wall: the seeming roof comes down so far it almost joins the seeming foundation. Diamond-paned windows, dark stain, and the ornamental use of the gambrel outline are other trends of the times—all in all a nice example.

K 31 67 Edgehill Road, 1909. This tour might well be a study in the variety of the Georgian Revival. Here is an early version of the "authentic" phase, recreating the 18th-century mansions of Massachusetts or Virginia—in this case given a personal flavor with the enriched texture and warm color harmonies of brick mixed with stone trim. **No. 64:** 1901, Grosvenor Atterbury, New York. **No. 82:** 1902, Mantle Fielding, Philadelphia.

K 32 Elizabeth Hooker House, 123 Edgehill Road, 1914. Delano and Aldrich, New York. In a highly sophisticated design, ornament is replaced by elegance of materials, workmanship, and color. Complexity of form takes the place of ostentatious size, requiring an ensemble of outbuildings, walls, and courts to complete the extended composition. Even the well-clipped bushes play a necessary part.

Down the hill, **Ogden Street** was cut through the Eli Whitney estate and opened relatively late. It is probably the neighborhood's most stylish cross street—though bereft of most of its big trees, still a vivid evocation of the chic of the 1930s. **No. 87,** 1930, Delano and Aldrich, New York. **No. 107,** 1930, Douglas Orr. **No. 120,** 1938, Carina Eaglesfield Mortimer. **No. 140,** 1930, Douglas Orr.

K 33 Hayes Q. Trowbridge House, 100 Edgehill Road, 1907. Peabody and Stearns, Boston. New Haven's most elaborate Shingle Style design. As you go up Ogden Street notice the carriage house, in some ways more satisfying to look at than the house. (Photograph 1937.)

K 34 269 Ogden Street, 1972, William deCossy. Built as the architect's own house.

K 35 10 Briar Lane, 1962, Frank Winder. Built as the architect's own house.

K 36 75 Edgehill Terrace, 1967. A refreshing variation on the modern walled-house idea, the in-and-out movement of the masses giving some exposure to windows and glimpses of garden—the effect is welcoming rather than exclusive. Sidney T. Miller, architect.

K 37 6 Prospect Court, 1923. Gray and Lawrence. George H. Gray, listed in the city directory in the 1920s as "architect and community planner," was interested in city planning and public housing at a time when these were relatively unfamiliar ideas. This was his own house, built as part of what he intended to be a model mixed-income suburban development. Plans were exhibited and promotion begun as early as 1923, but it was not until 1942 that work got under way on the projected lower-income section beyond Prospect Court, and 1947 before houses were actually built. Sample blocks will be found on Morse and North Sheffield Streets and Homelands Terrace. "Homelands" at one time was the name Gray used for the development. (Photograph 1942.)

871 Prospect Street, 1917, Charles O. Whitmore, Hartford.

K 38 George Berger House, now part of Albertus Magnus College, 810 Prospect Street, 1927. Douglas Orr. Today almost all the large houses at this end of the street, having lost their onetime owners, have found a refuge in Albertus Magnus College which generously upholds the spirit of the neighborhood.

K 39 Austin Cheney House, 755 Prospect Street, 1918. Rossiter and Muller, New York. The neighborhood's most full-blown specimen of that hardy perennial, the Tudor manor house, here given an added fillip with 18th-century gates.

K 40   275 East Rock Road, 1920. George S. Chappell, New York. After the repetitive historical images of the surrounding streets, this interesting house with its recessed porch and strongly rhythmic columns strikes an individual note.

K 41   Louis Stoddard House, 700 Prospect Street, 1905. Peabody and Stearns, Boston. New Haven's grandest house, the only time the city ever attempted the Palladian style in the great 18th-century English tradition. Superbly sited, richly detailed. The view across the plain to West Rock was one of the most beautiful in the city until recent buildings came into the foreground.
Victor Tyler House, 760 Prospect Street, 1906, Peabody and Stearns. **No. 711:** 1925, J. Frederick Kelly. All three of these houses now belong to institutions—Albertus Magnus and Trinity Church.

K 42   594–600 Prospect Street, 1926. As an approach to multiple housing in an established neighborhood, compare this U-shaped apartment of the '20s with the style of the '50s across the street. Two big pieces of land long held empty were sold off here en bloc after the war—hence the blasting of the neighborhood fabric with cheap developments between here and Canner Street.

K 43   500 Prospect Street, 1905. Brown and VonBeren. A princely-seeming house built of "artificial stone." The trim used to be painted gray, matching the wall as if it too were stone: somehow it made the pretense less noticeable, the effect smoother and richer. VonBeren, as has been noted before, was a jack of all styles—from Roman mansions like this to a beer baroness's extravaganza on Sherman Avenue (G 52) or to tenements in the Hill district (H 9).

These two blocks from Highland to Division Street, dropping down to the bottom of the hill, were once **Highland Park**—a "park for residences" laid out in the 1850s by a merchant from New York named Charles Elliott. Elliott started the ball rolling by building a house of his own on Division Street. But lots were slow to sell, money ran short, and Elliott soon gave up and went back to New York. The curving tree-planted drives of Highland Park remained one of the pleasant spots of the neighborhood until they disappeared into the ordinary grid of the city in the 20th century. A few aberrant twists remain on Mansfield Street.

K 44   406 Prospect Street, 1903. At the turn of the century half-timbering was out ahead even of Georgian and Colonial. Here is a particularly forthright example. Grosvenor Atterbury, New York, architect.

K 45 400 Prospect Street, 1901. Donn Barber, New York. A fresh design, enhanced by quietly unusual colors.

K 46 Yale Divinity School, 1931. Delano and Aldrich, New York. Of all Yale's new buildings, this quadrangle was probably the most admired during the '30s and '40s. The scheme is based on Jefferson's University of Virginia, but the handling is distinctly personal. A rising site has been used to intensify a quite un-Jeffersonian expression of verticality. Edges are hard, and the steeple—in contrast to Jefferson's dome—is sharp and tense.

At this point we reenter Yale country. From here on almost everything but the Grove Street Cemetery is owned by the university.

K 47 John M. Davies House, 393 Prospect Street, 1868. Henry Austin and David R. Brown. The most lavish of Austin's remaining domestic commissions and the only known instance in which he was not bound by a city lot but was free to compose pictorially in a larger setting. The romanticism—the love of irregularity and movement—which were latent in much of his earlier work is here freely realized in a supply-jointed composition of towers, bays, and porches. From the street, the sweep of lawn and drive are all one movement, reaching a climax in the sharp outline of the single off-center tower. In 1964 the house was recorded by the Historic American Buildings Survey, and its sumptuous interior at that time was found to be still intact. The report speaks of the notable plaster ceilings decorated with wreaths and moldings; of mantels in marble, brass, and varicolored woods with inlaid arabesques; of parquet and marble floors. There is no doubt that this was one of New Haven's most splendid houses in its time, and it is a fortunate survival— one of the few souvenirs that the city can now claim of the Gilded Age. Recently used for a school for restaurant chefs, it is now owned by Yale and boarded up.

K 48 Othniel Marsh House, now Marsh Hall, 360 Prospect Street, 1878. J. C. Cady and Company, New York. One of the more individual houses of the '70s, product of the high style of the big-city architects and the taste of a cosmopolitan client. It makes an interesting contrast with local work of the same period, as for example the Adler house (N 23) or the house built by Russell at 131 Sherman Avenue (G 50). Marsh bequeathed his house to Yale in 1899 and it became the first building of the Forestry School. The celebrated grounds were maintained as the Marsh Botanical Garden.

Out back, the modern building with the patterned roof is the **Greeley Lab**—see M 7.

K 49 Alexander Catlin Twining House, 314 Prospect Street, 1880. Brown and Stilson. This house was described at the time as "Queen Anne," but it is quite distinct from the jagged silhouettes and narrow verticality that characterized most Queen Anne work in New Haven. Brown by this time had already been working for Donald Grant Mitchell, and the Twining House may show his influence. As you come up Edwards Street from Whitney, it is a marvelous sight to see the great roof lifting itself slowly up out of the hill. Original colors were probably warmer and earthier.

K 50 John Schwab House, 310 Prospect Street, 1896. R. Clipston Sturgis, Boston. Compare this Yale professor's house with some of its more aggressive contemporaries on Whitney Avenue.

K 51 William Trowbridge House, 210 Prospect Street, 1871. Rufus G. Russell. On Hillhouse Avenue we have already seen three variants on this theme—the old Italian Villa Style tricked out with a central pediment. Russell's version seems the most purposeful, all the elements of form and ornament organized to transform the sedentary cube of the villa into something vertical and active. An interesting and handsome house.

K 52 Sterling Chemistry Laboratory, 1922. Delano and Aldrich, New York. Descend the street then look back at the impressive streetscape of the Science Buildings. The Chemistry Lab rides the hill like a fortified medieval town. Inside: a grand stair hall.

No. 205, with a logger carved above the door: **Sage Hall,** main building of the Yale Forestry School—1923, William Adams Delano, New York. Next to it: Sloane Physics Lab (K 21); on the corner, Osborn (K 19).

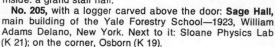

K 53 Ingalls Hockey Rink, 1957. Eero Saarinen. This was the building that launched Yale's patronage of modern architecture. It was not, in actual fact, Yale's first modern building—there had already been Kahn's Art Gallery (G 13) and Schweikher's laboratory (K 21). But it was with this one that President Whitney Griswold's imagination caught fire, and Yale and much of New Haven followed his lead. The rink, of concrete with a suspended aluminum roof, provides an enormous unbroken interior space, seating 3000—a breathtaking sight the first time you see it. Around town the rink is fondly known as the Yale Whale.

The buildings in the next block, on the west side, belong to the **Berkeley Divinity School,** now part of Yale.

K 54 Sheffield Laboratory of Engineering Mechanics, 1894. Cady, Berg and See, New York. A four-square, no-nonsense science building of unpretentious grandeur, lightened with slim arches, terra cotta garlands, and a wonderful skyline.

K 55 Becton Engineering and Applied Science Center, 1968. Marcel Breuer and Associates, New York. Breuer describes the visual effect of the facade as a wall that is folded horizontally and vertically, with pipes and ducts in the folds. The arcade was designed to relate the building to the human scale and invite the pedestrian, but some have found it overbearing and far from welcoming. Tunnels connect Becton with the other buildings of the engineering complex, and at the rear an open space is one of the main routes and distribution points of the foot traffic that flows among the Science Buildings from Prospect Street to Hillhouse Avenue. This space, as it was initially, Breuer described as "a lot of messy ground on various levels." It is interesting to compare his handling of it with Rogers' approach in similar situations. Where Rogers might have maximized the possibilities of the different levels, and where he might have seized on the irregularities of shape to create a sense of movement—hooking around at the south end to highlight the picturesque enclosure made by Strathcona, narrowing at the center to screen out the unappealing rear of Dunham, and at the upper end focusing on the exhilarating sheer rise of the Sheffield Lab's red wall—Breuer has taken the opposite tack and eliminated all irregularities with a rectangular platform suspended in space that makes no contact with its neighbors at any point. "The area behind the building had to be cleaned up, organized, and made purposeful," Breuer said.

L Orange Street

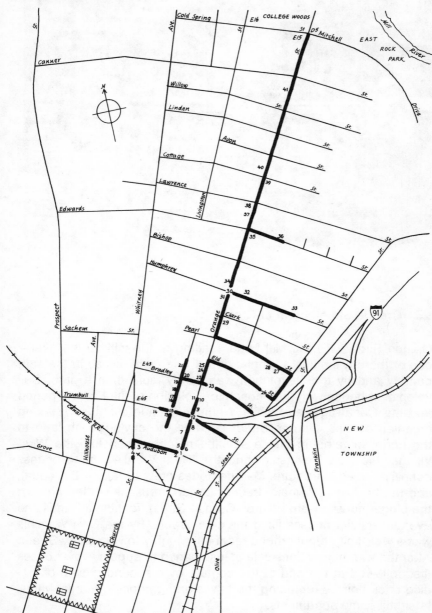

Turn-of-the-century churches and a modern Arts Center, the rest mostly residential—some antebellum, some 1890s. One-way streets make difficulties—this tour is better on foot.

153

L **Orange Street, north of Grove.**

Orange Street was the Mill Lane, leading to the mill on the river—
one of the city's oldest Colonial roads. It fell into disuse in the 18th
century and by the Revolution was hardly more than a path. Development began with the economic explosion of the Federal period
and the Canal age, and while Whitney Avenue slumbered among
arcadian estates, Orange Street became the city's growth lane to
the north, developing into a satellite neighborhood like the West
Village, the New Township, and the Third Ward—a more or less
cohesive village structure. Manufactories grew up along the canal,
and the houses of owners, tradesmen, and artisans settled nearby:
the bigger houses were built on Orange Street, forming a handsome
avenue; smaller houses filled the side streets. By the Civil War this
was a well-knit neighborhood reaching roughly to Humphrey Street.
After the war, higher density land-use began to appear—row houses
first, followed at the end of the century by a second growth of cit-
ified brick houses replacing the lawns and gardens of earlier villas;
later still came apartments.

All this was the beginning of an urbanization that never in the end
took place, for in the '90s fashion moved over to Whitney Avenue
and Orange Street became a backwater, with incomplete urban

154

blocks jutting up among surviving villas. At the same time, out beyond Humphrey, a new community suddenly materialized, an eruption of carpentry confections that swept up the outer avenue, reflecting the new wealth of an industrial age and a rising middle class. The pattern is the same as in the West Village: big, showy houses, all built within about a decade, springing up on the outer rim of an older, cohesive community. The older community in turn faded, gradually letting the old villas go to seed.

Today despite decay (and sometimes even more disastrous improvements), something of the quality of an antebellum neighborhood can still be glimpsed in these lower blocks: the modest scale, the orderliness of fences. Also still visible is the interpenetration of economic levels represented by the difference between avenue and side streets—an ancient urban pattern that would be increasingly replaced at the end of the century by the large class enclave.

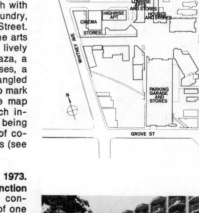

L 1 Audubon Street and the City Arts Center. Audubon Street bordered the Farmington Canal (later the railroad), and it grew up as one of the city's many small early manufacturing nodes. Prosperity later faded, and after the Depression the street was abandoned to decay. It is now in the process of redevelopment as an arts center, one of the Redevelopment Agency's more ambitious projects. The program is notable for combining the usual blitz approach with adaptive reuse of buildings of historic character—a foundry, a synagogue, and some Victorian houses on Orange Street. The resulting package has had a wide appeal, and the arts center, although unfinished, is already generating lively activity. The plan shows elderly housing, garage, plaza, a high school and arts and music schools, town houses, a movie theater, restaurants, offices, and shops. The angled face of the Creative Arts Workshop (L 3) is designed to mark the plaza. The planned breakthrough shown on the map from the center of the plaza to Lincoln Street, which involves the removal of an existing building, is currently being questioned by residents and others as a weakening of cohesive and presently meaningful spaces at both ends (see L 15).

L 2 McQueeney Apartments, 358 Orange Street, 1973. Frank Chapman, Architects and Planners, in conjunction with Franklin Construction Company. Post-tension concrete slabs were poured on the site, stacked on top of one another, and raised into place together—a method of construction still little tried in Connecticut. This was the prize-winning entry in a competition for a multipurpose building—shops on the ground floor, offices on the next two, and public elderly housing above. Exposed edges of the floor slabs make an in-and-out movement of horizontals across the facade while hexagonal balconies with see-through rails give a honeycombed surface, breaking up and lightening the long block of the building. The balconies are angled to provide maximum space with views in more than one direction.
348 and 352 Orange Street: two mid-Victorian houses that are to be remodeled for offices, shops, and a restaurant as part of the Arts Center project (Gilbert Switzer, architect).

155

L 3 McLagon Foundry, 33 Whitney Avenue, 1870. Established c1848, this was one of several foundries that grew up near the canal. The present building was built later, after the canal had been filled in for the railroad, whose tracks adjoin it on the south. Well scrubbed to bring back its tomato red color, the foundry has been remodeled for shops, offices, and a cafe as part of the Arts Center (1973, Charles Brewer; rear wing on Audubon Street, John Fowler).

Next door: 100 Audubon Street, **Neighborhood Music School,** 1968, Charles Brewer (the facade is shown here, the rear elevation in L 4); no. 80: **Creative Arts Workshop,** 1972, Orr, deCossy, Winder and Associates. Looking south down the proposed mall, the blank brick wall of the telephone company closes the view (1968, Sherwood, Mills and Smith, Stamford).

L 4 The Farmington Canal. Turn down Whitney Avenue below the foundry and pause on the bridge for a sentimental observance of the bed of the canal that gave New Haven one of its most golden moments. This was "the ditch, through which a torrent of prosperity was to flow": for a few brief years through here water ran from Massachusetts into New Haven Harbor. A financial failure, the canal was bought and converted to a railroad in 1846.

From the bridge the rear of the Neighborhood Music School (shown here—also see L 3) makes a striking composition of black and white. Below the bridge, **27 Whitney Avenue** (1928, Harold H. Davis): built for a small expensive shop, a gem of architectural salesmanship.

L 5 Temple Mishkan Israel, now Educational Center of the Arts, 1896. Brunner and Tryon, New York. A building of great presence, at once awesome and delicate. The architects described the style as Spanish Renaissance, but there is a cleanness in the handling of cubic forms that is Edwardian—note the sheerness of the towers, the use of square piers for columns, the linear simplification of the windows. Arnold Brunner is known today for a number of major works in New York: Lewisohn Stadium, Montefiore Hospital, and Congregation Shearith Israel of 1897. In New Haven, Temple Mishkan Israel was the first important building built by the Jewish community, which until then had worshiped in hand-me-down or modest quarters, and it fittingly symbolized their new prestige in the life of the city. The design seems to have made a strong impression locally, being emulated by the Presbyterians and the Catholics (L 36). The interior has now been reamed out and converted to a theater (1971, Charles Brewer), but the great golden windows have been allowed to remain, at least on one side. The west window also is preserved.

L 6 383 Orange Street, 1889. Here at the neighborhood's start a few houses show the beginning of its second growth: **nos. 383, 385, and 392,** all built within a few years of each other. Stock Queen Anne features (jutting gables, textured surfaces of brick, terra cotta, molded shingles, and fancy woodwork) are combined with Romanesque arches and Japanese spindle rows—the taste of the day was for a bit of everything. **No. 377,** built in 1905 and Edwardian rather than Victorian, joins them amiably while showing the new feeling for clean mass and flat plane. These houses combine well with the colors of the Arts Center, adding a bit of fantasy and richness to the modern group.

L 7 400 Orange Street, c1857. A group of Italian villas, badly kept and drearily painted, still evokes the antebellum style of the street: **nos. 389, 396, 406,** and **412** show typical variations. The importance of the fences in giving unity to the streetscape is still seen—note that they match across the street. Also notice the pretty gates—it is rare to find gates still in existence. Third-floor windows are later. Nos. 396 and 400 once had Greek Revival porches like the one still up the street at no. 445 (L 10). No. 412 was once quite grand—originally stuccoed or painted sand color. Inside: paneled doors and a mighty newel post. Carriage house out back. A modest architectural specialty of the Orange Street neighborhood is small touches of ornament in relief, applied to lintels and doors—the softly modeled swags on no. 400 are a good example.

    No. 399: Willis Smith House, 1866. Under new stucco, the ghost of the old mansard roof can be seen. Willis Smith and his brother-in-law Nehemiah Sperry were among New Haven's top builders after the Civil War, and much of this neighborhood is probably their work. Perhaps Orange Street's distinctive ornament was their trademark. Sperry's house is just up the street (L 22).

L 8 Row Houses 405-15 Orange Street, c1864. Smith and Sperry, builders. In a garden neighborhood, row houses are the first sensitive sign of a turning point, and the first arrivals usually took pains to make themselves acceptable. Here the easy pitch of the steps had a graciousness that later rows skimped on, while basements of fine outsize ashlar gave the front areas dignity. Notice the use of overscaled detail, establishing the unified effect of a single facade, also the rhythm of the strong stair rails and pediments, and the matching pattern of cornice and doors (all six doors amazingly still there). Out back, on no. 405, a wonderful cast iron balcony on scrolly brackets.

L 9 Timothy Lester House, 431 Orange Street, 1846. Before the tower lost its finial and the walls were shingled, this was one of Orange Street's best houses. If it is all original, it is New Haven's first known towered Italian Villa, that specialty of Henry Austin's which would soon be seen again in the Norton house on Hillhouse Avenue (K 16). The arcades, which may have been added later, give it a fluid grace that is lacking in the stiffer Norton house.

L 10 445 Orange Street, c1855. Another block of antebellum houses, several now badly disguised under aluminum siding. No. 445, the best preserved, provides us with a classic specimen of the small, tasteful antebellum villa, still retaining much of the detail that originally gave it dash: the shutters are still here, and the Greek Revival porch still has its vigorous balustrade, giving height and enrichment. Even the color is close to the original (it would have been slightly lighter). The lines made in the stucco to resemble ashlar blocks can also still be seen. This was a common practice of the day: more than just a pretense it was a means of articulating the wall and giving it scale.

    No. 441: note the baroque window heads, a far-off echo of Borromini that made itself at home in Puritan New Haven.

L

L 11   John C. Anderson House, now St. Mary's Convent, 444 Orange Street, 1882.   Anderson was a millionaire tobacconist from New York who retired to New Haven and built a house that set the town agog—the newspaper breathlessly guessed that it cost $100,000. But, alas, within six years Anderson left, complaining of "excessive taxation," and the house was sold for $30,000. Architecturally it is surprisingly *retardataire* for so lavish a commission, its mansard roof and quoins recalling the Second Empire palaces of the 1860s in New York, here given an unexpected turn by being done in bright red brick and brownstone. Also unexpected is the astonishing fleshy carving on the front steps combined with the drier Eastlake treatment of the walls. Inside: ceilings of great height and quantities of carving, stained glass, frescoes, and rich plasterwork—all but the frescoes well preserved. Out back is the carriage house, making a formal termination to the garden. A contemporary account gives the architect as John Seeley of Brooklyn.

No. 436: **William Converse house,** 1887. Converse was president of Winchester's, and his house was elaborate. The interior is a fine period piece, showing the late Victorians' sensuous pleasure in the colors, grains, and surfaces of varied woods. The dining room has a ceiling of polished mahogany.

L 12   Trumbull Street.   Opened by the younger Hillhouse and others in 1828, Trumbull Street first grew up as part of the antebellum community (**no. 18** is shown here). In the '90s, the western end began a new life as fashionable overflow from Whitney Avenue, and although some of the earlier houses survived (they can be easily spotted), its aspect became turn-of-the-century. The house of Yale's President Hadley on the corner set the tone (E 45), later capped by the **John Slade Ely House** (51 Trumbull Street, 1901, by S. G. Taylor, New York). By the 1940s decline had set in, and doctors' offices were moving up from Elm. Today a major traffic route, Trumbull's days are probably numbered, as the ramp of I 91 seems to indicate. Meanwhile, the glorious lane of sycamores makes this one of the city's more distinguished blocks.

Nos. 40-48: one of Smith and Sperry's rows, c1864.

L 13   John Sanford House, 50 Trumbull Street, 1842.   This shows what a determined Colonial Revivalist can do with a Victorian house. The original building seems to have been a standard Greek Revival type with its gable end on the front and a wing on the east. In 1904 it was all wrapped around with additions to give the illusion of a Colonial house with its roof ridge parallel to the street. The interior was remodeled at the same time with woodwork salvaged from an 18th-century merchant's house on Water Street.

L 14 Chaplin-Apthorp House, 58 Trumbull Street, 1806. Young James Abraham Hillhouse's fondness for moving houses has been mentioned in Itinerary K. Of all his mobile homes, this is the most traveled. It began on Whitney Avenue, built by James Chaplin and financed by the elder Hillhouse. In 1820, after some financial mishaps, it was back on Hillhouse's hands and was rented briefly to his son's friend, Samuel F. B. Morse. In 1827 the house was vacant. At the same time a connection of the Hillhouses, a widow named Mrs. Apthorp, came to New Haven hoping to start a prestigious young ladies' school. Young Hillhouse, ever alert to promote his real estate at bargain rates, gallantly took charge and in a complicated maneuver (described more fully in K 11) moved the house off to Hillhouse Avenue where, with a schoolroom added on behind, it was set up for Mrs. Apthorp. But the old-fashioned Chaplin house must have struck a false note in the burgeoning high style of the Avenue, and in 1838 it was again packed off, this time to Trumbull Street, the schoolroom having been lopped off and sent elsewhere (Mrs. Apthorp also went elsewhere—see K 18). Young Hillhouse died soon after, and the Chaplin house stopped wandering. Modernized in Victorian times, it was unmodernized in the Colonial Revival. It is not known if the doorway is original. Metal roof and wings later.

No. 54: local lore has it that this is Mrs. Apthorp's schoolroom. But other evidence indicates that the schoolroom alighted on Grove Street and was later demolished. No. 54 is a straightforward design of the mid-century.

L 15: Lincoln Street. Opened in 1836, Lincoln Street was quickly dotted with good but unpretentious Greek Revival houses. The east side, belonging mostly to the backs of the grander places on Orange, gave the street something of the air of a private road. A dead end at both ends until the 20th century, Lincoln today still retains a sense of hiddenness and quiet that makes it almost unique among the city's streets (shown here: **no. 18**—see L 18).

Little Theater Guild, 1 Lincoln Street (1924, Gray and Lawrence). The Little Theater movement was an active element in the artistic currents of the '20s. George Gray, one of the most interesting of the local architects of the period, designed this unpretentious building with sensitivity to form a backdrop at the end of the charming street. Later converted to a movie theater, the facade was given the plastic-and-neon treatment. Plans by the Redevelopment Agency now call for its demolition in order to open the street through from the Arts Center (L 1). Residents are protesting that this will destroy the essential thing that gives Lincoln Street its character—the cul-de-sac. Others have questioned the merit of breaking open the Arts Center at its midpoint.

L 16 10 Lincoln Street, c1840. A diminutive variant of an elegant model such as the Benjamin house up the street (L 19). The north corner of the porch, which may have once existed, evidently lost out some time ago to the tree. The clapboards are probably not original, for in other cases of this classic design, the wall is elegantly flushboarded. The south bay was added after 1890, its underpinning obviously later removed. For an interesting insight into Early Victorian design, compare this house with no. 12 next door.

L 17 12 Lincoln Street, c1840. This house should be looked at with no. 10. One a chaste Grecian villa and the other a picturesque Gothic cottage, they stand at the two poles of 19th-century taste. But look twice—they are the same house. Only the roof and the accessories differentiate them. Under today's asphalt shingles, this one has walls of vertical flushboarding. No. 10 was probably painted white or a delicate cream with white trim, and no. 12 was probably a sand or honey color with beige trim—a beguiling pair.

Across the street: Mr. Anderson's **carriage house**, practically a mansion in itself (L 11). White mortar seems to belong to a modern repointing.

L 18 16 Lincoln Street, c1852. The basic formula for a respectable but unpretentious house, built all over New Haven from the Federal period to the Civil War. In this block and the next, nos. 14, 18, and 22 show variations at different dates and different prices. On **no. 18** the Doric porch and rectangular window in the gable give the date away as relatively early (1830s or early '40s). **Nos. 14 and 22** show typical later modifications, probably of the '50s. **No. 24** seems to be another early one, to which a reproduction of a Colonial-Federal door has been added.

L 19 Everard Benjamin House, 232 Bradley Street, 1838. This house was built on Orange Street and moved here about 1870. It marks the divide in New Haven architecture between the era of Ithiel Town and the era of Henry Austin. To Town's influence it owes the cross plan and portico, the Venetian windows, and the austerely classical Ionic order. But the wide-brimmed roof hints at the extravagant outlines that would soon characterize Austin's style. On its first site, set back from the street on a broad lawn, the house had a kind of miniature majesty, making a serene classical statement in the landscape. The walls then were smoothly flushboarded, and this contributed to its classical poise and abstract clarity. The Lincoln Street side is the front, although the address is now on Bradley.

L 20 Casa Bianca, 223 Bradley Street, c1848. This was the home of George Dudley Seymour, the great leader of the City Beautiful movement in New Haven in the early 20th century, and also one of the first to make New Haven aware of the existence of its antebellum architecture. It seems an appropriate monument to his memory that this charming example of the mid-Victorian villa should be one of the few now left in New Haven that still has its finial gallantly flying on top. Once the Victorian skyline was full of these exotic little spires.

Bradley Street, a block farther north than Trumbull, runs a generation behind it. Like Trumbull, it was settled first from the Orange Street side then resettled after 1900 from the Whitney Avenue side. Specialists of the later period will be interested in the attempts to Colonialize (or Federalize) the earlier Victorian buildings. **No. 239** was once a stuccoed Italian villa, **no. 258** a double house of the 1870s. For **no. 265** see E 43.

L 21   Serge Chermayeff House, 28 Lincoln Street, 1962.
Serge Chermayeff. A new concept of urbanism (or perhaps we should say a very old one), where privacy takes precedence over the life of the street. Pictures of this much-published house show a total lot use inside its palisade, the open spaces shaped with the same precision as the enclosed ones, making a sequence of alternating indoor and outdoor rooms. The abstract formality of the design is a foil for sculpture and planting.

L 22   Nehemiah Sperry House, 466 Orange Street, 1857.
Sperry, in partnership with his brother-in-law Willis Smith, was a prominent builder (see L 7). His own house and the Rowland house on Wooster Square (N 26) were twins, and the Rowland house today still shows us some of the detail now missing here. Once light in color with black stair rail and dark shutters, the Sperry house was a festive and elegant accent on the avenue. An open balustrade edged the roofline.

L 23   Bradley Street East of Orange. Today the neighborhood east of Orange has a special charm and also a special historical interest—one of the few places left that give us a glimpse of the all but vanished 19th-century world of the skilled artisan and small tradesman. Bradley, Eld, and Pearl Streets, even more than the West Village (G 19), still preserve the memory of a way of life—the fabric is barely ruptured, and the relationship both to the fashionable world of Orange Street and to the developing laboring-class tenements on State Street is still visible. With their miniature versions of Orange Street villas and with their appealing little vagaries of ornament, these streets make fascinating walking. Development on the whole is chronological, moving outward from town. Bradley is the oldest, and like the West Village it reflects the urban expansion of the Canal age. The street was opened sometime after 1830 and by the end of the '40s was well stocked with Greek Revival cottages. **No. 183**, shown here, is typical of the scale. **No. 184** is more elaborate, a hopeful reflection of the Benjamin House (L 19) which at that time stood at the head of the street (porch and front window altered).

L 24   478 Orange Street, 1866. Italian villas continued even after the Civil War. Note Austin's Indian columns, first seen in 1845 in Wooster Square (N 3), still going strong twenty years later. Especially nice carving on the bases. Inside, the plasterwork is a good surviving example of the opulent ornamental style of the mid-century.

L 25 484 Orange Street, 1867. A late-lingering member of the Villa style, overgrown but still trim.

    No. 495 on the northeast corner of Eld: a particularly satisfying example of Queen Anne (1884), holding the corner well; more purposeful and less capricious than some, except for an irresistible flight of whimsy in the north balcony. Trim used to be cream color, brightening up the red of the brick with a light but gentle contrast. Architect, Rufus G. Russell. **No. 503:** one of the earlier settlers, a simple vernacular Greek Revival house with Doric porch. South side added on later.

L 26 Eld Street. Development of Eld Street begins mainly in the antebellum period. Like Bradley and Pearl, the street is enlivened by the decorative fancies of the local carpenter. **No. 4,** shown here, must have knocked everybody's eye out. The date is c1865.

    At the foot of the street: The Roman Catholic Church of **St. Stanislaus** (1912)—surely the most immaculately kept church in town, center of what is now mainly a Polish neighborhood. Good maintenance must be a Polish trait, for all the public buildings in these few blocks are in conspicuously good condition and contribute handsomely to their surroundings. Inside: a rich and dimly lit nave, with polished marble columns, gilded capitals, and embroidered banners. Chickering and O'Connell, Boston, architects. At the corner of State and Franklin: **Swedish Lutheran Church,** now Glad Tidings Tabernacle, 1904, Brown and VonBeren—recently cleaned and restored. Down State Street at Grove: the German Roman Catholic Church of **St. Boniface,** 1923, George Zunner, Hartford.

L 27 14 Pearl Street, c1875. The development of the "flat" house—i.e. the two-family house divided horizontally rather than vertically—is discussed in the Sherman Avenue itinerary (G 54). This house, with its narrow, tentative balcony, is one of the early experimental models. The idea did not take hold at first, and it was not until the '90s that the two-family house burst forth in all its glory all over town.

L 28 24 Pearl Street, 1848. The memory of Alexander J. Davis lingers on. The "pretentious" porch that he designed for Mr. Dean on Dwight Street in the 1830s (G 60) gave New Haven one of its favorite embellishments for the next two decades.

L 29 Row Houses, 545–51 Orange Street, c1871. Though small, this is one of the most lushly designed rows in town. Juicily carved lintels and cornice, gorgeous doors. As in other rows, the unity of the group is stressed as a single facade. Note the encompassing roofline and the rhythmic shadows of the door hoods (before the pigeon repellers), binding the parts together.

L 30 Upper Orange Street. From Humphrey Street out, Orange Street belongs mainly to the end of the century. High style had moved to Whitney Avenue, and although Orange Street continued to flourish, its architecture becomes less "correct." Compared to Whitney Avenue there is less solemnity in brick, more fantasy and folly in wood, reflecting the joyous taste of a newly rich generation suddenly swept up into the middle class in the expansive McKinley era. As in the equivalent neighborhood in the west end, around Sherman Avenue (G 48), the names of Anglo-Saxon home owners are now for the first time mixed at random with Irish, German, and Jew. A riot of Queen Anne and Colonial Revival features makes this a stimulating walk. Be sure to notice the change of scale that occurs at Humphrey Street: the road is wider, lots are larger, houses are higher, the building line is set farther back. Also fences go out of fashion, giving a greater sweep to the lawn. In a word, everything is bigger. It is all very indicative of the new life style of the late Victorians.

Orange Street is one of the few residential sections where the neighborhood store still flourishes. Shown here, the corner drugstore, a local institution **(767 Orange Street).**

L 31 St. John's Episcopal Church, 1895. W. Halsey Wood, New York. A good example of the Episcopalian style in well-to-do suburban sections at the turn of the century, strongly evoking the image of an English parish church.

Humphrey Street and Edwards seem to have had a magnetic effect on churches. All the leading denominations gathered here within a few blocks at the turn of the century— Episcopalians, Congregationalists, Methodists, Baptists, and Catholics, presently followed, over toward State Street, by German, Swedish, and Polish churches.

L 32 Humphrey Street Congregational Church, now Seventh-Day Adventist Church, 1882. A curiously astringent design for the period, distinguished for sharp lines and sheer planes at a time when architecture in general was running to rich textures, sonorous color effects, and deep modeling.

Down the block: **German Emanuel Lutheran Church,** 1927, Brown and VonBeren.

163

L 33 Humphrey Street School, now Polish National Home, 1877. Rufus G. Russell. One of the last surviving public buildings of this colorful period in New Haven today—it is gratifying that a private organization has not only saved it but restored it so well. The embroidery of the surface has come to life after a good cleaning, reminding us that this period was originally one of vivid and often strong color effects. It is the dirt of our own century that has created what we think of as Victorian gloom.

L 34 Swedish Emanuel Congregational Church, now Evangelical Covenant Church, 1925. A small tastefully handled design of the Federal Revival, with a somewhat incompatible later cupola. Pleasant white simple interior in the period style.

L 35 Epworth Methodist Church, now Gospel Tabernacle of the Assembly of God, 1892. The filled-in arch with the cross was originally an entrance, altered in 1945. The most satisfying view of this church is from up the street, looking back at the north elevation with its patterns of circles and rectangles.

On the corner of Edwards and Livingston: **First Baptist Church,** 1903, Leoni W. Robinson; interior, C.H. Blackall, Boston.

L 36 St. Joseph's Roman Catholic Church, 1904. Joseph A. Jackson, New York. The design is reminiscent of Mishkan Israel down the street.

L 37 Henry Herz House, 666 Orange Street, 1895. Brown and VonBeren. The three houses from here to the corner were built simultaneously by the same architect.

L 38 Moritz Spier House, 678 Orange Street, 1895. Brown and VonBeren. VonBeren here varies the sequence with an early and rather tentative experiment in the Georgian-Colonial style. It seems a bit subdued after Herz's bulbous columns and cave-like window, but white railings around the roof and the top of the porch originally made it more ebullient.

L 39 711 Orange Street, 1889. Complexity of massing deliberately heightened by white trim. Fortunately the color scheme is preserved, for these flamboyant wooden houses lose much of their intended excitement when their intricate composition is washed out by a monotone color.

L 40 726 Orange Street, 1883. The *ne plus ultra* of Orange street, happily being well maintained today in exactly the manner to which it was accustomed. This house and the one next door were owned by two brothers. One wonders if the brothers were identical twins like their houses. (Two-decker porch a later addition.)

L 41 820 Orange Street, c1905. As in the Sherman Avenue neighborhood and similar parts of town that experienced a flash growth at the turn of the century, the backbone of Orange Street's new community was the two-family house, here seen in an unusually restrained version (compare G 54).

M The Winchester Triangle

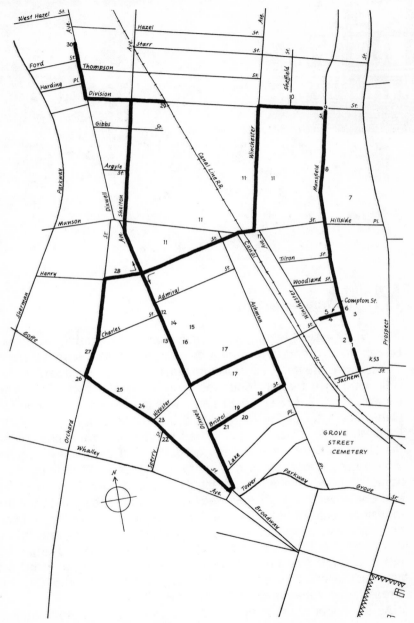

A century of industrial life: factory, houses, tenements, slum, redevelopment.

M The Winchester Triangle.

The Winchester Repeating Arms Company was established in New Haven in 1870 and before long became the city's biggest industry. The site was the thinly settled plain that stretched west from Prospect Hill, lying in a triangle bounded roughly by Mansfield Street and Dixwell Avenue. A lowland, this area was the route of the Farmington Canal and later of the railroad laid along the canal's bed. By the Civil War a few manufactories had settled along the line, chiefly the Newhall Carriage Company around which a hamlet had grown up—today its memory is preserved in the vaguely defined place name of Newhallville. Winchester's soon absorbed much of this and converted the early manufacturing plant of the plain to the new industrial scale of the American imperialist age. A world of workers' homes began to spread across the triangle, occupying first the old established antebellum neighborhood at its apex in the angle between Dixwell Avenue and Goffe Street and fanning outward with new middle-class houses in the '70s and, in the '90s and '00s, with three-decker tenements and multiple dwellings.

As the importation of unskilled foreign labor increased, later arrivals moved into the older houses while the new ones farther out were taken by the established ranks of the skilled and semiskilled. The farther from work, the better the job; the higher up the hill the higher the income. On the flat, on Winchester Avenue, were the tenements; one step up the ridge, on Mansfield Street, substantial two-family houses marked a white-collar strip; and on the summit, Oliver Winchester himself presided over the plain from his house on Prospect Street.

By World War I, names listed in the Directory show a mixture of Yankee, German, Irish, and Jewish. At the same time, in the old quarter at the apex of the triangle, a black community crystallized. Blacks had long had a small colony here, but this was only one of several, and by and large the black population in the 19th century was scattered. Massive immigration at the end of the century, however, had the effect of regrouping the city around national or ethnic identities, and the black constituency in the other wards began to decrease and to consolidate in the lower Dixwell area. By 1910 Dixwell Avenue had become known as the Harlem of New Haven.

The Winchester Repeating Arms Company reached a peak around World War I and the '20s and has since declined in size. But the plain has continued to expand, its outer rim filling with houses of the '30s, '50s, and '60s. At the same time the triangle has widened, until it comprises roughly the whole wedge from Mansfield Street to Sherman Parkway. The black community has grown outward along the spine of Dixwell Avenue and now occupies most of the new streets of the early 1900s. At the apex of the triangle, the old antebellum quarter, which by the Depression had become one of the city's three major slums, has today been almost totally demolished and rebuilt, and is one of New Haven's foremost exhibits of urban redevelopment.

For a contrast between the urban patterns of pre-Civil War manufacturing and post-Civil War industry, it is interesting to compare the Winchester triangle with the New Township (N)—one a village organism, with factories grouped along the streets and with owners and workers living closely around them, the other a sprawling complex strung out along the railroad, surrounded by dormitories following the trolley lines and organized to a large extent in class enclaves.

M 1 Mansfield Street. Around the time of the Civil War a few substantial houses settled on lower Mansfield Street near the Sachem Street corner as overflow from the Hillhouse Quarter, but for the most part, although it had been laid out in the '60s, the street remained rural and empty until the end of the century. In the '90s a tidal wave suddenly swept up from Winchester's, filling the upper street almost solidly within about a decade. This will account for the uniformity of the house fronts from Compton out. Mansfield today merits a serious look. Not the architecture, but the street itself. The movement of the roadway as it rises up the hill in an effortless flowing line; the sycamores leaning inward at a magical angle, as if in a dance; the strong enclosing rhythm of old-fashioned porches make this one of the most beautiful streets in the city. Uniformity, repetition, fluid movement, a long perspective, and dappled light to shed grace over homely things—these are the elements of good 19th-century street design. Hillhouse Avenue, on a similar slope, once looked like this.

When these blocks were developed, lots were drawn parallel with the side streets and thus at an angle to Mansfield. Because a deep house can only fit on a narrow lot if it lies parallel with its side lines, the unusual pattern of angled house fronts results.

M 2 72 Mansfield Street, c1875. A sprightly souvenir of the street's more fashionable days.

M 3 101 Mansfield Street. The nosey tourist who ventures down the alley beside 97 Mansfield Street will find a surprise. This handsome Gothic house was built c1875 and recently moved here—clearly it once belonged to the high society of the Sachem Street corner.

No. 99 was also part of the Sachem Street set, built in 1861 (originally it would have been a less melancholy color). It too has been moved here.

A lovely feature of the east side of Mansfield Street is the big back yards that flow together with the yards of the Prospect Street houses, making a hidden interior parkland. But, alas, nothing is more irresistible to a university hungry for parking lots than a lovely interior parkland, as demonstrated here.

M 4 14 Compton Street, c1870. Compton Street belonged in the Sachem Street orbit, and several of its houses date from the pre-Winchester period. This one is distinguished by a pretty porch with cut-out quatrefoils. The design seems to be a neighborhood trademark, and many others like it can be seen along the way on this tour.

M 5 19 Compton Street, c1872. An interesting design, showing the preoccupation with the language of wood construction and with a supposedly rustic effect which characterized this period. (Over the city line and hence beyond the limits of this tour but not far from the last stop is the **Bassett House** at 484 Newhall Street, the major example of this style in the area. Built in 1870 on Shelton Avenue, the main portion of the house was later moved. Architect, Henry Austin.)

M 6 Two-Family House, 109–11 Mansfield Street, 1901. The two-family house swept New Haven at the turn of the century and seems to have exemplified the American dream. Spacious, well planned, with a separate kitchen, porch, and stair for each family—even a separate "art glass" window, glazed-tile fireplace, and golden oak overmantle—it offered a high standard of privacy and of graceful living to a newly rising middle class. Subsequently scorned, these houses are today being revalued by a generation starving for space, large windows, well-proportioned rooms, good construction, and soundproof walls. The genre flourished until after World War I when it was replaced by the later American dream of a saltbox in the suburbs, singly owned and having its own garage. Samples of this later growth may be seen out toward the end of Winchester Avenue and Newhall Street (for more about two-family houses see G 54).

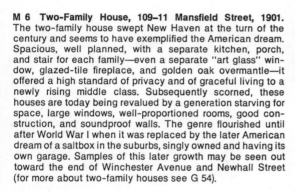

M 7 Yale Forestry School, Greeley Laboratory, 1959. Paul Rudolph. It is frequently said that the branched columns are metaphors for trees, but the architect's description of the building indicates a more abstractly architectural intention: "The building is conceived as a pavilion with a single hovering roof supported on precast concrete columns. These 'Y' shaped columns, which exploit some of the possibilities of form inherent in precast concrete, are placed in front of a glass and marble chip spandrel wall to gain the maximum amount of play of light and shadow, and to give a measured rhythm to the facade. The ceiling is exposed precast concrete panels designed to express the nature and direction of the roof stresses .... These precast concrete panels are joined to the precast columns by means of a poured in place beam which is widest at the columns where the shear stresses are greatest and narrowest at the center of the bay. This pattern is repeated in grey and white marble chips directly above on the roof surface."

M 8   Yale University, Mansfield Street Apartments, 291–311 Mansfield Street, 1960. Paul Rudolph. Rudolph is here putting modular apartment units together like blocks, piling them up the hill in a stepped composition of interlocked solids and voids. The effect has often been likened to a pueblo village or a Mediterranean town, but this should not be taken to mean that the design is intentionally picturesque or allusive. On the contrary it is a methodical, additive scheme, prefiguring Rudolph's later work with prefabricated units at Oriental Gardens (F 17).

M 9   Upper Mansfield Street. The bend in the road beyond Division Street is all that is left of the curving drives of Highland Park, a "park for residences" laid out here by a landowner in the 1850s (K 43). The park is now almost entirely filled by apartments: 1950s-style up the hill, 1960s-style, shown here, at **55 Division Street** (Alden Berman and Associates, 1969).

M 10   Sheffield Street. Two-family houses came in many sizes and prices. Here, one rung down the hill from Mansfield Street, is a less pretentious version, still forming an enclosed, congenial street. The date is mainly 1912–13.

M 11   Winchester Repeating Arms Company. Winchester's, now a division of Olin Industries, was founded in 1866. The company moved to New Haven in 1870, building a factory which was described in the newspaper as "mammoth" and which was almost immediately enlarged. Originally a three-part composition with central pediment and classical cupola, the complex stood on Winchester Avenue, backing up to the railroad and facing the house of Oliver Winchester across a great sweep of open hillside. Soon thereafter trees (sycamores for the most part) were planted along nearby streets, and these have long given this industrial neighborhood its special character. The north and central sections of the original complex, shorn of the cupola, still stand on the west side of the avenue between Division and Munson Streets. Numberless additions have been made over the years, and, in recent times, subtractions. Despite the latter, Winchester's today still offers a useful survey of the industrial architecture of a century. In general the 19th-century buildings are brick; steel and concrete are first mentioned in building permits in 1902. Expansion reached a crescendo at the start of World War I, more than 12 new buildings being added in 1915 and '16. Little new construction took place thereafter until the mid-'50s, when miscellaneous modernizations (much of it concerned with refenestration or blocking up window walls with concrete), additions, and cosmetic redecorations occurred. Chief architect from at least 1892 (and probably earlier) until his death in the '20s was Leoni Robinson. For the recent work no architect is listed. (The plant is shown here in 1936.)

M 12 235 Dixwell Avenue, c1875. In an area of massive redevelopment, this once-important house has been left, giving some historic depth to the bright new scene.

M 13 Dixwell Plaza. The old antebellum quarter at the apex of the Winchester triangle between Dixwell and Goffe has been the Redevelopment Agency's biggest target in the city. More than simply a matter of new housing, this has been a program to rebuild a neighborhood completely, wiping out the memory of the past with its decaying hand-me-downs and creating an image of a brave new world—new streets, new centers of public life, new symbols of community. Now nearly complete, this transformation is whole enough to suggest the urban scene of the future. Here modern buildings are no longer isolated bits of dramatic architecture supported by the fabric of the old city around them, they *are* the fabric of the city. A new kind of street, a new scale, a new kind of space appear.

The Plaza is the hub of the new community, pulling together shopping, institutional and cultural functions. Shown here: **public library** (1968, Douglas Orr, deCossy, Winder and Associates) and **shopping arcade** by the Redevelopment Agency. The design attempts a difficult balance between the need for urban definition of the street and the popular modern imagery of the highway, the shopping center, and the flat suburban skyline.

M 14 United Church of Christ, 217 Dixwell Avenue, 1968. John M. Johansen, New York. Shaped like a crystal, the centralized form detaches itself from the plaza around it to dominate its own space. This Congregational church is the descendant of New Haven's first black church, founded in 1824 by William Lanson, Prince Duplex, Scipio Augustus, John Lisbon, Bias Stanley, and other black leaders, aided by Simeon Jocelyn, who served as first minister.

M 15 Community Center, 197 Dixwell Avenue, 1967. Herbert S. Newman and Edward E. Cherry, Collaborating Architects. Like a stage set, there is great dramatic effect with economy of means. Notice the ceremonial power of the piled-up steps, diminishing to a distant point at the top where an imaginary space is suggested beyond.

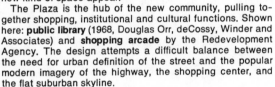

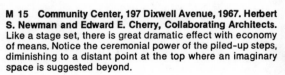

M 16 One Dixwell Plaza, 1965. Gilbert Switzer. Of contrasting color from the rest of the group, this apartment block firmly holds the plaza in shape at its lower end.

At 87 Webster Street: **East Rock Lodge, IBPOE,** 1967; Granbery, Cash and Associates.

M 17 Elm Haven Housing, Webster Street and Vicinity, 1939. Douglas Orr and R. W. Foote, Associated Architects. It is interesting to compare this prewar project with the many postwar varieties around it. Along with Farnam Court (N 42) and Quinnipiac Terrace (O 9), this was New Haven's first venture into slum clearance. The project covers an extensive area and involved the redesign of several streets. Foote and Eaton Streets were removed and four angled interior drives put in their place. Additions in the immediate postwar period on Ashmun Street include a brief experiment in high rises— the bleakest moment to date in the city's housing history.

M 18 71 Bristol Street, c1875. Of the cluster of streets that formed the older neighborhood at the apex of the Winchester triangle, Bristol is almost the only one left. It is an interesting, faded place, once obviously colorful like the side streets off Orange (L 23, 26–28) or in the New Township (N 35–41). In streets like this carpentry has a special flair, and porches and cornices offer small unexpected delights. Here they belong mainly to the '70s.

M 19 101 Bristol Street. Another handsome porch, of a rather unusual design. The date is probably in the '60s.

M 20   Edith M. Johnson Towers, 114 Bristol Street, 1971. Herbert S. Newman Associates.   Notice the tranquil expanse of garden behind and the splendid backdrop made by the Yale Gym. The low side buildings with sharp shed roofs, which house a community room and outdoor band shelter, bring the big brown tower down to neighborhood scale. Parking is handled tidily.

M 21   Kolynos Company, 130 Bristol Street, 1915. McClintock and Craig, Springfield.   Boisterous and unforgettable, with a sort of carnival-industrial air—buildings like this, as they mellow into history, become the landmarks that give certain neighborhoods a special flavor. Now vacant.

M 22   Goffe Street Special School, 106 Goffe Street, 1864. Henry Austin.   Begun in 1854 as a small school conducted by Sally Wilson, a black teacher, in her own house, the enterprise was so successful that it attracted the attention of civic improvement groups, and in 1864 money was procured for a building and an enlarged staff. Henry Austin, the record recalls, donated a plan. He must have rummaged in his drawer and pulled out something that came to hand, for the building standing here today was surely once destined to be a church—note especially the side elevation. The front porch, so unlikely for the 1860s, may be a later addition from the enthusiastic era of Federal reproductions around World War I.

M 23   Firehouse, Goffe and Webster Streets, 1973. Venturi and Rauch, Philadelphia.   Fire-engine red provides a bit of pageantry for the neighborhood: public imagery can hardly be more vivid than this. Webster Street was widened and splayed at the corner to make it easier for fire trucks to swing out fast. This dramatizes the excitement of emergencies but is less serviceable for daily pedestrian life or for the psychological cohesion of urban spaces. Venturi's continuous curve and blazing color help to hold things together.

M 24 Florence Virtue Homes, 1964. John M. Johansen, New York. A moderate-income co-op, this was one of the Redevelopment Agency's first major developments and a showcase project. Along with Columbus Mall in the New Township (N 30), built at about the same time, it epitomizes the suburban ideal as it has increasingly come to dominate urban imagery. Notice the many devices both of siting and of architecture used to disguise the essentially urban module of the rectangular building units. The result is an inviting oasis, with delicately frosted colors, dark pine trees, and free-flowing open spaces. The emphasis is on the movement toward the interior rather than on the traditional relationship to the street.

The three housing projects that come together here on Goffe Street (M 25, M 26) reinforce this non-urban approach to urban planning. Each is identified as an entity rather than as part of the city fabric, its separateness stressed by uniform design and a conspicuous individuality that asserts its difference from, rather than its connection with, the others. The widened street is treated as an artery, becoming a divider rather than a meeting place, and the neighborhood as a whole is fragmented into subneighborhoods. Again the imagery of the suburb and the village is plain.

M 25 Helene W. Grant School, 1964. Caproni Associates; John M. Johansen, Design Consultant. The building lies low and flat, close to the ground. A band of smooth concrete emphasizes the level cornice, dramatizing the eruption of active shapes on the roof and giving elevation to the bell tower. Again the village imagery appears in this nostalgic symbol of old-fashioned small-town life, serving here as a banner for the new housing around it. Its role is purely heraldic and sculptural—the bells do not ring for school.

Opposite: **St. Martin DePorres low and moderate income co-op,** 1968, Polak and Sullivan.

M 26 Goffe Street Town Houses, 1970. Edward E. Cherry. Natural-colored siding and a clustering of sharply pitched roofs again play on the village theme, although the village is here given a clean urban perimeter along the street.

M 27 Eastern Press, 654 Orchard Street, 1965. Carlin, Pozzi and Associates. Two units (the southern section is later), visually tied together by a dominating red-and-white sign-board.

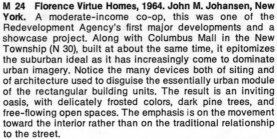

M 28   127-47 Henry Street, c1875. Remodeled by the Redevelopment Agency with no pretense of emulating the original architecture, the repetition of heavy handrails on the steps nevertheless continues to make this row a strong statement in a somewhat fragmented neighborhood. Part of one original porch remains, suggesting the enrichment of light and shadow on the surface that once carried out the rhythmic theme of the carved window heads. Remodeled 1967.

M 29   220-24 Division Street, c1875. Row houses usually belong to the inner city, inside the fire zone, and hence are of masonry. This little frame row is an oddity, appealing in its diminutive scale and simple ornament. The equally diminutive chapel next door was a picturesque accompaniment before it lost its spire. Both buildings suggest some now forgotten community growing up here on the outer fringe of town beside the railroad tracks. This, together with **Lincoln School** at the corner, seems to be all that remains of **Newhallville.** The school (no longer used as such) was built in 1870 and is perhaps the earliest still recognizable school building in the city. It was a stirring sight before its surface got flattened with paint, washing out the color contrast between red brick and ornate brownstone trim on which visual interest had centered.

M 30   Martin Luther King School, 1967. Damuck and Babbitt; Charles Brewer, Design Consultant. With a windowless facade, spreading one-story plan, contrasting textures of warm gray brick and concrete, this school exemplifies many trends of recent school planning in New Haven. The contrast with Lincoln School of a century before is interesting. Where Lincoln expressed civic importance by monumental height, King does the same thing with monumental space, occupying a whole block on the avenue and surrounding itself with a wide ceremonial lawn. This use of ornamental green space, as in many of the new housing developments around town, poses a problem of maintenance that the city seems not yet to have fully faced up to.

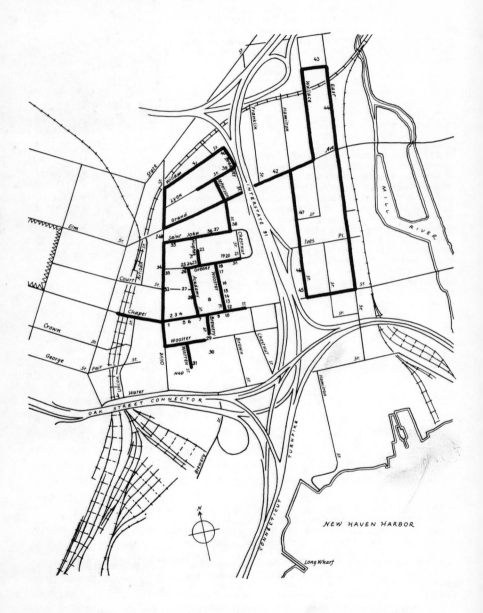

In the city's early manufacturing district, its best remaining concentration of antebellum houses and its best new industrial park—a balance of history and redevelopment.

N The New Township.

When the city first began to grow, it jumped the East Creek and moved eastward along the harbor. With the Creek as Main Street and with the Long Wharf at its base, the eastern side of town became the center of the seaport, and in the maritime prosperity of the later 18th century the cross-creek area flourished. By the Revolution it had acquired the name of the New Township. The name is illuminating, revealing both the maritime community's confidence of future growth and also a sense of separateness from the rest of the town.

In the Federal period, as the port experienced its hour of glory, expansion came fast, and the promise of the canal in 1825 set off a real estate boom. Symbolizing the new community's sense of status, a handsome square was opened at the head of one of the streets leading up from the harbor. It was named Wooster Square after General David Wooster, a hero of the Revolution and a native of the neighborhood, and there seems little doubt that the maritime community foresaw it as their own counterpart—even perhaps a rival—to the Green of the "old" township.

The failure of the Farmington Canal and the panic of 1837 brought this phase of development to an end, and the New Township never materialized as the great seaport its promoters had envisioned. But the lull was short. In 1839 a carriage maker named James Brewster built a railroad (the first in the state) along the eastern edge of the township, coming down the Mill River to join the steamboat pier at its mouth. Here Brewster built a large carriage factory and around it, in the Collis Street section, laid out what today would be called an industrial park, encouraging other factories to settle nearby. A manufacturing community quickly grew up, and by 1850 the New Township, which only 25 years before had been a mercantile town, had become the manufacturing center of New Haven. Brewster's and other carriage companies; the New Haven Clock Company; the Candee Rubber Boot Company; later Sargent's and other hardware companies; manufacturers of melodeons, daguerreotypes, bentwood chairs, and a host of others founded the fortunes of New Haven's golden age from 1835 to 1865.

In structure the community continued to keep some of its self-contained character, like the satellite village-clusters that have been noted in other parts of town: the West Village, Orange Street, and the Hill (Itineraries G, L, H). Along Chapel Street and around the square were the houses of the manufacturing aristocracy while on the smaller streets were the homes of skilled artisans, supervisors, and tradesmen, and rented houses of laborers. On the edge of the open fields two small subcommunities appeared briefly in the 1820s: New Guinea, operated by the black king, William Lanson, and a straggling group of buildings called Slineyville, inhabited by a band of Irishmen who had come to town to dig the canal and later stayed on to build the railroad. For the growing laboring class, in the 1830s, a model development was hopefully laid out on the riverside (N 43).

Outwardly the New Township changed little until the end of the century. But the new scale of post-Civil War industry brought many stresses. Old factories became outmoded and new industrial centers grew up elsewhere—principally Winchester's (M). As the importation of foreign labor skyrocketed, immigrants arrived in enormous numbers that could no longer be absorbed. In the '90s a flood of Italians arrived, pushing out the Irish, swelling the already overloaded tenements. Abruptly, around 1890, the factory owners and the upper ranks of the middle class fled, leaving the New Township to become the capitol of New Haven's Little Italy. In 1899 the shift was solemnized when St. Michael's Catholic Church assumed possession of the First Baptist Church on the square.

For the next 80 years poverty and absentee landlords accidentally preserved the architecture of a once brilliant past. Change came only in the form of attrition: the loss of paint, shutters, cast iron fences, elegant balustrades, fanciful balconies and canopies, the Ionic and Doric columns of porches—all the finery slowly wore away. By the Depression the New Township ranked as one of the city's three principal slums, and early renewal plans in the 1940s called for its almost total demolition: a heliport at one time was proposed for Wooster Square, and early plans for I 91 were designed to cut right through it. However when renewal finally came, around 1960, attitudes had changed, both toward the destruction of neighborhoods and toward Victorian architecture, and the New Township became one of the Redevelopment Agency's most interesting programs of rehabilitation and reconstruction. With the line of the new highway as a divider, residential preservation took place on one side and industrial modernization on the other. Both programs are among the most widely publicized and successful of New Haven's redevelopment.

N 1 St. Paul's Episcopal Church, 1829. Founded as a chapel of Trinity, St. Paul's became an independent church in 1845. This two-towered design was a popular model in the early Gothic Revival, and St. Paul's was a precocious example in New England—perhaps the first. Compared to the churches on the Green of a generation before, it is distinguished by its great size and solemnity, and it must have been an awesome building when it was new. It stands at the entrance to the New Township, marking the bend in Chapel Street with its paired towers (as Rudolph's towers mark the similar bend at the other end of the street—G 15): a gateway building. An old photograph is used here, showing the original towers and the openwork crenellation that dressed up the roofline. The upper parts of the towers were of wood and were ambitiously removed in 1893 to be replaced with stone, but only one got done. The builder was Sidney Mason Stone. Who drew the plan is uncertain. The cornerstone attributes it to the minister's son, Sherman Crosswell. The minister himself, in his diary, attributes it to the assistant minister, Francis Hawks. At the same time he mentions a number of informal consultations with Ithiel Town. Interior remodeled in 1845, 1875, and later.

N 2 Nelson Hotchkiss House I, 621 Chapel Street, 1850. Nelson Hotchkiss began as a builder, went into manufacturing window sash and blinds and into high-class real estate development. He worked with Henry Austin on more than one occasion, and in the 1840s the two undertook an ambitious suburban development called Park Row in Trenton, New Jersey. Back in New Haven in 1850 Hotchkiss plunged into a rather similar program here on Chapel Street, building with his partner William Lewis the three houses now standing at 621, 613, and 607; he may also have had some promotional connection with No. 604. The architecture of Chapel Street reaches a high point in this brief stretch, and the personality of Henry Austin seems to emerge clearly. Austin's connection with the whole group cannot be documented, but circumstantial evidence is strongly suggestive. The attribution in the present case rests on an Austin drawing in the Beinecke Library which seems to be for this house.

N 3 William Lewis House, 613 Chapel Street, 1850. Lewis was Nelson Hotchkiss's partner and together they bought these three adjoining lots. They built their houses simultaneously, and it is possible that Austin was the architect of this one as well as the other. However it is equally possible that Lewis's house is a builder's adaptation of a popular Austin design, already visible in the English house down the street and in the Dana house on Hillhouse Avenue (N 7, K 6). Here the same Indian plant columns are used to give an exotic flavor to the plain basic cube of the Italian Villa style. The side balcony is a typical touch of Austin fantasy, although probably added later.
    No. 614: 1873. **No. 612:** 1882, Henry Austin and Son.

N 4 Nelson Hotchkiss House II, 607 Chapel Street, 1854. After Hotchkiss had lived in his first house a while, he moved into this one, stayed two years, then moved back. Again the design strongly suggests Austin. The double-bow front seems to have been a prestigious symbol in New Haven, and five examples were built in this expansive decade (see N 26 around the corner for another). Originally there was a balustrade around the edge of the roof. It dressed the house up (Austin was nothing if not festive, whenever the client's budget allowed) and gave it more life, carrying the vertical lines into the skyline instead of having the great wide eaves pressing down on the walls like a lid. Porch and balcony are original but not the glass enclosures.

N 5   604 Chapel Street, 1852. Henry Austin.   This is generally called the Oliver B. North House, but it now appears that
a Cincinnati merchant named Jonathan King had been living
in it for 16 years before North. This towered Italian villa is
one of Austin's most important domestic works. Compare it
with the Norton House on Hillhouse Avenue of three or four
years before (K 16) and note the new freedom and swing.
Here the tower is in the center—it rises with unimpeded
vigor while all the other elements of the design revolve
around it. An old photograph is used here, showing the house
before various misfortunes befell it—principally the added
third floor and the new windows of the west wing. Notice the
role of fences and railings in the design. Originally the roof
of the tower would never have been white but a strong
earthy red, evoking an image of the red tiled roofs of Italy:
for a good idea of what the color scheme probably was, take
a look at Raynham on Townsend Avenue (H 47).

N 6   Henchman Soule House, 600 Chapel Street, 1844.
The design belongs to the afterglow of the high period of
New Haven's Greek Revival, the use of an austerely simple
and majestic porch to dramatize a plain cube recalling
houses by Town and Davis on Hillhouse Avenue. A crisp
parapet originally edged the roof, giving the building a bit
more swagger.
  No. 601: a survivor of the New Township's seaport era,
built perhaps around 1810. It is hard to realize it now, but this
house once looked like the Pinto and Griswold houses (I 42,
J 39). Under asbestos shingles in the gable is a Palladian
window.

**N 7   Willis Bristol House, 584 Chapel Street, 1845. Henry
Austin.**   Austin must have got this one out of one of the
books in Ithiel Town's library, for to his basic villa-style cube
he has added some ornament of very distinguished pedigree:
from the Royal Pavilion at Brighton, before that from the
palaces and temples of India. In staid New Haven the Bristol
House makes a startling appearance, but the new manufacturers of the booming '40s were apparently ready for anything.
Originally the effect was more vivid, sand-colored walls
providing a light background for the accent of delicately
drawn windows, rich porch, and black iron railings. Bay
windows added 1872.
  No. 592: **James English House,** 1845, Henry Austin.   Alterations have made this an architectural oddity. Originally much
like the Lewis house (N 3), it had its roof raised, cornice and
all, in the '70s to make a third floor, giving a strange, steep
proportion; later the columns were streamlined. James English, who became one of New Haven's most eminent manufacturers and citizens, began as a builder (see N 14). Years
later, when he became governor of Connecticut, he said
that he was the first governor to walk on a state house floor
that he had laid himself.

N 8 Wooster Square. In 1825 a group of New Township landowners led by Abraham Bishop—political radical and owner of extensive property in the area—deeded a six-acre field to the city for the creation of Wooster Square. Bishop contributed 2½ acres, the rest was paid for by subscription. Although ostensibly intended as a public ornament, the square was also seen as the focus for a new boom in real estate which the promoters expected would follow the opening of the Farmington Canal. This merging of public interest and private speculation, so characteristic of its time, produced one of the notable achievements of the great age of New Haven urbanism. The promoters had an almost clean slate to work with, for only Academy Street was already built on, and they set about building and laying out lots with an extraordinarily disciplined sense of design. Houses were built in facing pairs across the green, large square masses weighted the corners, terminal accents were placed on axis with the ends of streets. Much of the original effect is now gone, and today if you would know what the square once looked like, you must use your imagination. Stand by the statue of Columbus and recall that at the foot of Brewery Street the harbor was brightly visible, framed between two strong Greek Revival mansions that flanked the entrance to the square like gateposts. Opposite, at the other end of the square, Hughes Place gave a responding vista to the north, and here against the backdrop of East Rock stood a church on axis with the street. The square itself was shaped with precision by an iron fence, with an oval path laid out inside it. The ground was leveled and sown to hay (the proceeds were used for upkeep), and around the perimeter the classical houses took their appointed places. No record survives of who planned this distinguished composition, but the names of a number of committee members stand out: Abraham Bishop, Samuel Wadsworth, Joseph Barber, and Philip Galpin (who is said to have designed the fence).

N 9 Row Houses, 552–62 Chapel Street, 1871. Unquestionably the most posh row in town, as befitted the first intruder in a precinct of stately houses. Notice how the six separate units have been designed as a single palatial facade, under an encompassing roofline with a climactic mansard and fancy crested windows in the middle; notice how the lights and shadows made by the heavy moldings flow across the house fronts and weave them together into one composition. Architect, David R. Brown.

The hole next door to the west was once a solid Greek Revival mansion, holding down the corner and balancing an equally solid mansion on the other corner: the two of them made a gateway down to the harbor. **No. 576:** look twice—this is the other Greek Revival mansion. Built in 1841, it has been stripped down and entirely refaced (1935, Lester Julianelle). You can still recognize the old sash and fence—that's all. Notice the door and elegant Art Deco glass transom.

N 10 546–48 Chapel Street, c1842. Double houses were used in a number of key places around the square to strengthen the design. This handsome porch, raised on a stoop like the houses of Washington Square in New York, was placed on axis with Wooster Place, responding to a similar double porch at the other end of the street, now gone. Originally a substantial white cornice across the top bound the two halves of the house together as a single facade (a section of cornice remains on the west end). The third floor is obviously of recent date. Bay window added in the '70s.

No. 542: another good Greek Revival porch, another lost cornice. Compare this house with **no. 538** next door, noting the similarity of proportions, fenestration, and plan. They were built within a few years of each other (c1845), and both have since added third floors—one carefully, one not. **No. 532:** this was the third member of the group, also built about the same time. The bland porch columns look like later alterations.

N 11 Rectory, Church of St. Louis; now Society of St. Andrew the Apostle, 515 Chapel Street, 1924. Richard Williams. In the great tide of immigration at the turn of the century, a colony of French Canadians settled in New Haven. Local francophiles raised a subscription, and a small but elegant church was built, designed in 1905 by Richard Williams in a style described as French Renaissance. The church burned in 1960 and the congregation moved away, but this charming rectory remains.

Paul Russo Building, 533 Chapel Street, 1905. Paul Russo was one of the early Italians to settle in New Haven. He began earning money as an Italian interpreter, became a lawyer and proprietor of an Italian newspaper, and, following a pattern we have noticed before among rising immigrant groups, went heavily into real estate in his own neighborhood. He became a political leader and an eminent figure in the Italian community of the early 20th century.

N 12 541 Chapel Street, 1832. The architectural design of Wooster Square as a *square* has already been mentioned. This house is a conspicuous example of the discipline it imposed on the individual owner. On a critical corner location, where frontality on the square was needed to respond to the house across from it and balance the bottom of the green, a side elevation has been designed which acts as a facade—an unusual and sophisticated solution. Originally the effect was more imposing. A white carved parapet surrounded the roof, and a Doric porch faced Chapel Street where the enclosed vestibule is now. It is a welcome sight to find the house still painted white, as most of the early houses of the square would have been. (This house is generally called the Matthew Elliott house but it had been in fact built by a former owner two years before Elliott bought it.)

N 13 Russell Hotchkiss House, 7 Wooster Place, 1844.
Many things have happened here since 1844. When they
started out, no. 7 and no. 9 next door seem to have been much
alike—both unusual examples of a side-entrance plan, an
experiment of the Greek Revival period designed to permit
a full-width room of stately proportions across the front
of the house. Later came the cast iron balconies. The date
is not known, but the manufacture of this sort of iron lacework begins around 1850. It was popular all over the country,
in the North as well as the South, and there is no need
of a romantic legend about southern families summering
in Wooster Square to explain its presence here. Compare
the lacy design with the simple geometry of the earlier
fence (and incidentally this is as good a place as any to
notice, if you have not already, that these first houses of
the square all have the same fence). In 1873 a third floor
was added and with it the ornamental cornice. Despite
these radical alterations and other lesser ones the house
wears its history lightly and today is one of the square's
most cherished landmarks.

N 14 9 Wooster Place, 1833. James English, builder. English, whose later rise to wealth and eminence as a manu-
facturer has already been mentioned (N 7), was known in
the building trade for his ability to draw and design, so
perhaps the plan of this house with its unusual side entrance
is his. It is his only known work. Wings were added in the
rear in the '60s, the mansard roof came in 1872, and the
porch probably came along with it. But the delicate iron
veranda over the doorway, imitating a tent or silk canopy
in the manner of English Regency designs, seems to be
original. This house is generally called the Stephen Jewett
house but was in fact built by a shipping merchant named
Theron Towner and promptly sold to Jewett.

N 15 11 Wooster Place. Here is another early Davis-like
porch clearly related to the one on Mr. Dean's "house
of considerable pretension" on Dwight Street (G 60)—this
one of even more pretension, with six columns instead of
the standard four. As far as is known, this is a unique example
of such an imposing facade. The date is not known but is
either around 1836 when the lot was first sold or 1844 when it
was bought by Theron Towner, who lived here thereafter.

**N 16 Conte School, 1960. Skidmore, Owings and Merrill,
Chicago.** A restrained design that manages to capture in
concrete something of the classical spirit of the square,
with its cool arcades and serene courts. Notice as you approach from the bottom of the street the rhythm of columns
running up the block.

N 17 Wooster Square Congregational Church, now St. Michael's Roman Catholic Church, c1855. Only by a technicality can this still be called the church of 1855, designed by Sidney Mason Stone with a Corinthian portico and tall steeple. Its history has been one of many owners and many vicissitudes. The building has burned twice, the steeple blown down once. Built by a group of Congregationalists who went bankrupt, it was acquired by the Baptists in 1856 or '57 and by the Catholics in 1899. A remodeling after the first fire, in 1874, created an almost completely new design, and a second remodeling (1904, Brown and Von-Beren) after the second fire created the Italian Renaissance building that is seen today. The three windows on the front survived the fire and the remodeler and are souvenirs of 1874. Only the side walls and tall arched windows preserve the memory of 1855.

N 18 John Robertson House, 37–39 Wooster Place. Robertson bought the lot in September 1833 and probably built the house straightaway. It is a different version of the double house from the one just seen at the foot of the street (N 10). Here both units are contained within the outline of one dwelling, with a single porch and a traditional five-bay facade. Only the paired doors and the blind window above, which marks the partition between the two households, give it away. In design the Robertson house should be compared with the Ingersoll House on Elm Street (I 7). Note the similar high basement and the majestic assurance of the commanding porch. Today the house has had many alterations. Windows have been cut into the basement, a wing added on the side; a chain link fence replaces cast iron, and the white parapet around the roof is gone. These changes of detail add up to a considerable change of style.

N 19 Greene Street. The smaller streets that grew up in the orbit of Wooster Square between 1835 and 1875— Greene, St. John, Lyon, William—carried on its general tone but on a smaller scale. Prosperous and modestly stylish, they must once have had great charm—this can still be discerned in spots. The picture used here is of **257 Greene Street,** built in 1847 and an example of the classic Greek Revival town house that is one of the most characteristic building types of the New Township. Because scarcely one has survived today with its detail intact, an old photograph is used here as a handy reminder of what many of the faded brick houses that you will see on nearby streets once looked like. **No. 257** and **no. 237** down the block, built a few years later, have fared better than most. Though both have lost their balustrades and original porches, no. 237 still has its dentiled cornice and no. 257 its dainty little metal canopy on the side.

    Towne House Apartments, Greene Street and Hughes Place, 1963, William Mileto.

N 20 Phebe Wallace House, 251 Greene Street, 1854. A popular mid-century model which may be seen in profusion all over town. The return to a gable front after a generation of villas and of roofs screened by horizontal balustrades marks the beginnings of the urge to verticality and peaks that would characterize the second half of the century. The paired arched windows breaking the cornice line are typical of the style. This house is a particularly crisp and well-finished example, with a good Ionic porch and a delectable balcony on the east side. Beautifully maintained, it adds pleasure to the street.
245 Greene Street, c1870.

N 21 Joseph Bromley House, 231 Greene Street, 1849 and Later. A marriage of two periods, with a few little affairs on the side. First there was a villa of three bays, with Austin's favorite eared window surrounds. The third story probably came in the '60s and with it the bay window and rear addition. At the turn of the century came the climax, when (with considerable care) the whole thing was enveloped in a grand new concept of corner tower and wide veranda with Colonial Revival detail. Probably at first the tower had some sort of peak or crenellation finishing it off at the skyline. The house fell on hard times soon after this, and a brick storefront was built into it. Happily a new owner has recently restored it to its former style.

N 22 13 Hughes Place, 1971. Caswell Cooke. Hughes Place was opened after Wooster Square and played its part in the overall design. Balancing Brewery Street, which at the south end led to the waterfront, it provided a backstop—a short vista soon closed by a Methodist church placed on axis with the opening. The street itself, like Brewery, was kept mostly as gardens and stables belonging to the houses on the square and on St. John. The church is now gone, and the east side of Hughes Place has been gradually filled, but intimacy is retained. This modern building preserves the narrow module of the neighborhood housefronts.

N 23 Max Adler House, 311 Greene Street, 1879. An interesting house and an interesting owner. Max Adler belonged to one of the early Jewish families who immigrated to New Haven in the '40s. Starting in a tailor shop, he worked his way up to ownership of the corset factory that still operates a block away on Olive Street and became a leader in New Haven civic and cultural affairs. His house was an example of the most advanced and sophisticated architecture of its day and was probably considered spectacular by some of its neighbors and outrageous by others. It shows both the characteristic concern of the Stick Style of the '70s with structural articulation and the embroidered brick and terra-cotta surfaces of the incoming Queen Anne. Inside, the downstairs rooms have ebonized overmantles with paintings and tiles by J. Moyr Smith that follow the latest fashion of the Aesthetic Movement in England. Not yet common in this country, they may have been imported in toto. Today the Daughters of The Holy Ghost Convent, this valuable house is fortunately in good hands. Architects, Brown and Stilson.

N 24   323 Greene Street, c 1870.   A very late version of the Villa Style, conservatively carrying on the tradition of the square's great days. To the simple villa cube are now added elaborate bracketings and moldings and an oversized porch almost as powerful as the house. The original effect was even more sumptuous, with an open balustrade around the top of the porch and a flamboyant monitor on the roof. The interior is rich in plastered ceilings, door moldings, and marble fireplaces—much of this well preserved by careful owners. Notice the voluptuous arch of the door framed in the entry arch of the porch.

N 25   Davenport Congregational Church, now St. Casimir's Church, 1872. Rufus G. Russell.   Like the Calvary Baptist Church (G 16) which it much resembles, the building was designed as a base for an imposing steeple, now gone. St. Casimir's is the Roman Catholic church of the Lithuanians. They acquired the building in 1927. Before that it was an Italian Baptist church for a while.

No. 345–47, behind a later porch and pots of flowers, is probably the oldest house in the neighborhood, a Late Colonial design basically rather like the Chaplin-Apthorp House on Trumbull Street (L 14).

N 26   Edward Rowland House, 42 Academy Street, 1857.   Built by Smith and Sperry, this is a twin of Sperry's own house on Orange Street, built at the same time. Compare these descendants with their prototype, Austin's house built for Nelson Hotchkiss on Chapel Street (N 4), and notice how the lines have become more vertical, the two wide bows now turning into tubular stacks. As usual, today some of the finery has been lost, principally the fence and balustrade and front steps.

40 Academy Street: another house of many transformations. Built c1846, it probably began as a Greek Revival townhouse (N 19) or a flat-topped villa. In 1872 it got a third floor with rippling window heads and cornice, in the 20th century it lost the columns of its porch (see 351 and 352 Greene Street around the corner for probable examples of the original); and finally it was prettily renovated in the 1960s and given shutters. Be sure to notice the door—few early doors are left on the square. This house was also Edward Rowland's. He lived here before moving into the grander bow-front. It is shown on the left in the photograph.

N 27   Court Street, 1869–70.   Court Street was first named Home Place after the developer, the Home Insurance Company. Originally the long side of Academy Street had had no opening in it. It must have caused quite a stir in stately parlors around the square when the protective wall was suddenly broken open for a low-priced row development, and this event may perhaps be taken as a turning point in the social history of the neighborhood. But although the houses were modest, the company made an effort to maintain the urbanist standard of the square that it was about to fasten onto, and as a formal entrance from downtown (assuming that an entrance from downtown was wanted) the group was well designed. This is better seen from the Olive Street end where the gateway buildings are (N 32). In 1961 Court Street, which by then had become gloomy and dingy, became one of the Redevelopment Agency's most dramatic rehabilitation projects. Houses were spruced up, the street was closed off, and planting installed (1961, James L. Skerritt).

N 28 12 Academy Street. Academy Street was first built up in the Federal period before Wooster Square existed, and three or four of its early houses are still standing, but this is the only one now recognizable. The date is probably c1810. The corner bay appears to be an addition of the '60s, the Queen Anne south wing (with fine interior woodwork and tiling) of the '80s. The porch has been the battleground of many owners. Whatever the original Federal porch may have been, it was replaced c1865 by the present one, resting on square columns. Around 1960 the square columns were replaced by metal trellises. In the 1970s these in turn were replaced by Greek Revival columns salvaged from a house on Trumbull Street. What next?

20 Academy Street, 1885. The last private house built on the square. **No. 10,** originally adorned with baroque window heads and an opulent porch in the manner of the mid-century. **No. 8,** 1817. This is the house of Samuel Wadsworth, one of the small group who created Wooster Square and guided its first growth. Although his is one of the early Federal houses, it has taken on a wholly different personality with a Greek Revival porch and a 20th-century roof. **No. 2:** another personality change. Built c1835, this was one of the most brilliant mansions on the square.

N 29 Wooster Street. The Redevelopment Agency widened Brewery Street with a strip of park. The little counterpark on the edge of the real park seems distracting, but the idea was to give the new housing on Wooster Street a sense of being related to the square. In the square's original design a strong corner building stood here, matching the one on the opposite corner and giving definition to this important opening (N 9).

Wooster Street is (or was) Main Street. Long celebrated for Italian restaurants, today it is a pizza paradise.

N 30 Columbus Mall, 1962. Earl P. Carlin. The gate is placed on axis with Brewery, providing a formal termination to the view—it is interesting to see how a modern designer, using his own idiom, still preserves the earlier urbanist concept (compare the apartments on Greene Street, N 19, where no attempt is made to reestablish the accents or rhythmic module that originally shaped the space.) Inside, the flow of lawn and the partial delineation of fences make a relaxed interior park. This was one of New Haven's early low-moderate income co-ops. Peter Millard, Design Associate; Paul Pozzi, Associate.

Brown Street to the east is the only place in the New Township today where any of the fabric of the seaport town of the Federal and Greek Revival periods remains, but the houses have been so changed that they have not much interest.

N 31 Harmanus Welch House, 59 Warren Street, 1849.
Henry Austin's drawings reveal a frustrated hankering to
load up lintels with piles of foliage, which seldom materialized
on the executed design—this was evidently where the client
always decided to economize. Welch's otherwise plain house
is the only known example where the architect won (unfortunately the upper garlands, which rested on top of the
windows, have recently been removed). Whether the design
is actually by Austin cannot be documented. We know
that he built a house for Harmanus Welch, but Welch, we
also know, built two houses. This one, however, is unmis-
takably close to Austin's style of the '40s and '50s.

For the apartment at the foot of Warren Street to the west,
see H 40.

N 32 83, 85, 87 Olive Street, c1870. The tall houses
flanking the entrance to the new development on Court
Street (N 27) were designed as gateway buildings facing
the Green—impressive height accentuated by elegantly
dressed high basements, symmetry emphasized by octag-
onal bays paired across the entry. Notice how they and the
attached row houses behind them are tied together with
the same cornice and fenestration, though of simpler ornament. Today, front and rear groups have been decorated
somewhat differently, and the connection is less obvious
than it used to be. Shutters a recent addition.

Nos. 95, 97, 99 (all c1885): Queen Anne houses of brick
and terra cotta make an ornamental lineup (note the unusual
fence at no. 95). The parking lot across the street is one of
several by the Redevelopment Agency, demonstrating
with what simple means car yards can be civilized.

N 33 101–09 Olive Street, 1965. Simeone and Wendler.
By using a color related to the colors of traditional building
materials around it and by breaking the block down into
bays which read as separable vertical units, this apartment
building fits itself into the private-house module of the
street without a jarring break.

**N 34 Friendship Houses, 100–26 Olive Street, 1967. Gran-
bery Cash and Associates.** Built solidly on the building
line, this is an example of the urban (as opposed to the more
usual suburban, broken-form) type of housing project: all
open space is reserved for the interior, away from the street.
Arcading and stucco provide an Italianate allusion for a
traditionally Italian neighborhood.

On the corner of Grand Avenue the strong form of the
firehouse marks an important intersection (I 48).

N 35 St. John, Lyon, and William Streets. The bloom has long since faded from these streets, but their basic structure remains a nearly perfect specimen of the small side streets that grew up around the core of a grander avenue or square in the village clusters of the early city. Here in the affluent New Township, they were a cut above the equivalent streets of the West Village (G 19) or the Orange neighborhood (L). They must once have been trim and starchy under the dappled light of luxuriant foliage, with clean lines and spotless paint. Only a few items will be noted now, but connoiseurs will find much that is suggestive.

324 St. John Street, the **Charles Osborn House,** c1840. Osborn was a builder. He built houses for Henry Austin from the 1830s through the '50s, and his own house is either an Austin design or a good imitation. Inside, a diminutive spiral stair with a domed skylight above. The walls of the hall still have their original finish: plaster scored like dressed masonry, stone colored. The rear part of the building and probably also the porch with Austin-like columns (compare N 2) seem to be later additions, as also the especially volatile monitor. Porch railing obviously recent.

St. John Street in the city's seafaring days was a ropewalk. It was opened as a street in the 1830s.

N 36 257 St. John Street. Traces of Austin's style are everywhere in these streets; witness the curious thick columns of the porch here and next door. This block has a number of houses of the 1850s, but most of the street was built in the '40s. Porches may be later embellishments.

N 37 245 St. John Street. To an ordinary Greek Revival house, probably built in the '30s or '40s, someone with dreams of glory in the Gilded Age added a super porch. One can imagine his pride.

No. 227 at the foot of the street. Another fanciful addition, this one of the 1870s, popped on top of a sober Ionic porch of the '40s or '50s. Well maintained and handsomely painted, this makes a good-looking house.

N 38 Lenzi Park, 1970. Dan Kiley, Charlotte, Vermont. One of the New Township's stylish new playgrounds. Whether children enjoy playing in it as much as adults enjoy looking at it is perhaps a question that should not be asked. Notice especially the strip that runs on along Jefferson Street—a garden fantasy of concrete stumps, poplar trunks, and shadows against a concrete wall. In winter it is as engaging as in summer—a composition of gray on gray.

N 39 Nos. 17 and 73 Lyon Street. No. 17 is another example of that useful enlarger of old houses, the mansard roof, here topping a villa of the '40s which, if one may judge by the distinctive porch columns, may once have looked like George Mason's house on Whitney Avenue (E 21). No. 73 had a similar career. Today the two houses offer a useful study of the effects of aluminum siding. Notice on the aluminum house the stronger horizontal made by the wide clapboard, the elimination of the taut vertical corner boards, and the disappearance of the delicate shadow lines formerly made by the projection of window moldings. The result is broader, blockier, and plainer.

Lyon Street was opened in the 1830s by the architect Sidney Mason Stone who, we are told, had made a "fortunate" purchase of a pasture in the New Township. Probably after the custom of builders at the time, he built a number of the houses on the street. The neighborhood was known as **Stoneville.**

N 40 58–62 Bradley Street, 1967. Thomas Rapp. In a cul-de-sac at the end of the line, white stucco triangles and dark stained walls make arresting shapes. This is one of the few private houses built in the New Township in the last hundred years.

N 41 73 William Street. The carved Aeolian capitals of the porch were a popular symbol of elegance in the Greek Revival vernacular. Conspicuously well maintained today, this house is an attractive interlude on the street.

N 42 DeLauro Park, 1971. Dan Kiley, Charlotte, Vermont. From William Street the route goes out Grand Avenue. At Franklin, I 91 crosses, dividing the New Township in two, and beyond lies a different world. This was the manufacturing heart of the old city, now almost entirely demolished and rebuilt. The barrier of the highway has been used by the city as a demarcation of its redevelopment programs: west of it, residential rehabilitation; east of it, blitz and the creation of a new industrial park along wide tree-lined boulevards. This is an impressive performance, and those interested in the problem of fitting light industry into an urban setting will find a tour of Grand Avenue, Hamilton, Wallace, and East Streets worthwhile. DeLauro Park is the most elaborate of the distinguished series of pocket playgrounds which the Redevelopment Agency has been putting on vacant lots around the New Township. It borders **Farnam Court** (1941, Douglas Orr and R. W. Foote, associated architects), which along with Elm Haven and Quinnipiac Terrace (M 17, O 9) was the city's first trailblazing venture into public housing.

N 43 Franklin Square, now Jocelyn Square, 1835. The Jocelyn brothers, Nathaniel and Simeon—artists, social reformers, and real estate speculators—have been mentioned before in connection with Spireworth Square and the African Church (H 32, M 14). One of their boldest ventures was the purchase and development of the entire northeast end of the New Township, from Grand Avenue to State Street between Hamilton and the river. Intended for the artisan class, the development was typical of the expansive schemes and urbanist idealism of New Haven's Canal Age. A pattern of wide straight streets was laid out around a large square, all streets were planted with trees, and on Hamilton Street an added mall or promenade was provided, named Hamilton Place (today the poor remains of Hamilton Place will be found just north of Grand, the stumps of its noble trees still standing in a row.) The Jocelyns advertised the sale of lots in New York and chartered a steamboat to bring potential investors up to choose their sites. But the sale was only moderately successful, and the crash of 1837 soon ended further development. The little house above is one of the few built before the Civil War. Today the desolate square has been renamed in honor of the Jocelyns. What an ironic tribute.

N 44   426 East Street, 1961. Perry and Travers.   The streets of the new industrial park seem to be the heirs of the urbanist ideals of the 19th-century: the tree-lined boulevards, the measured rhythm of spaced buildings, the strong sense of building lines and order perpetuate the tradition of street architecture in the grand manner that seems to have almost disappeared from modern residential work. Individual buildings are of a rather uniform level. Those shown here are chosen merely as examples.

N 45   60 Hamilton Street, 1967. Gilbert Switzer.

N 46   80 Hamilton Street, 1964. Richard F. Heyer.

N 47 New Haven Clock Company. Now a complex of various manufacturing enterprises. It seems fitting to end this tour of the early manufacturing center of the city with the old New Haven Clock Company. Like most of the first manufactories, the company had its birth in the inventiveness of a resourceful Yankee, later built up (mostly by others) into an enormous business with a worldwide market. It was on a host of enterprises like this that New Haven's fortune was built in its great days before the Civil War. The Clock Company, founded in 1817 by Chauncey Jerome and called the Jerome Clock Company, was one of the first to flourish and one of the last to die. The remains of its once extensive plant are almost the only factory now left standing in the New Township to remind us of its history. The first building was located on this site in 1844. It was rebuilt in the 1870s and today is almost intact—a U-shaped structure fronting on St. John Street with wings extending a short way up Wallace and Hamilton.

O Fair Haven

A streetcar suburb of the 1870s, an old oystering village, and the ghosts of some vanished country estates. Along the way: a century of public school architecture.

O Fair Haven.

The spit between the Mill and the Quinnipiac Rivers was called the Neck by the early colonists, and the far shore of the Quinnipiac was given the name of Dragon. No one now knows why: some will tell you that seals used to snooze on the bank and the settlers thought they were dragons, others that there was a tavern there named The Dragon.

The growth of this riverbound land has been shaped by fords, ferries, bridges, and by the highways leading to them. The two main arteries are Grand Avenue and Ferry Street, both (in part) as old as the colony itself. Grand Avenue has been the main growth lane, running out from town to the ford across the Quinnipiac, later the site of the Dragon Bridge built in 1793. At the two ends of the bridge the village of Fair Haven grew up.

Going out Grand Avenue today you go through a spiral of time. First comes the New Township (Itinerary N), the earliest part to be built and the earliest to be destroyed and rebuilt. Across the Mill River and the railroad you come to a streetcar suburb of the 1860s and '70s, precipitated by the opening of the Fair Haven and West-ville Horse Railroad in 1861. This was in part an Irish neighborhood of socially rising immigrants from the New Township, its development promoted by a quarryman and land speculator named Francis Donnelly. After the Civil War the whole area grew fast, and today it is the city's major concentration of the vernacular of the 1870s.

Beyond the streetcar suburb you come to the Quinnipiac River and step backward in time to the oystering village of Fair Haven. Starting soon after the Revolution, oystering began to develop into a major New Haven industry, and by the mid-19th century the port of Fair Haven (with its small satellite at Oyster Point—H 28) had an extensive coastal trade and ranked second only to Baltimore in volume of business. The village prospered and grew fast, building up in the Federal period with oystermen's houses along the river-bank and later with more substantial houses on the higher slopes. Spreading back from the river, this growth met the streetcar suburb coming the other way, and the two merged somewhere around Ferry Street in the '80s.

Across the river, on the heights, still another community appeared —a chain of large properties running along the ridge and northward up Quinnipiac Avenue. Fair Haven Heights—commanding a famous view of the river and Sleeping Giant mountain to the north—had a great day after the Civil War, becoming one of the city's earliest affluent suburbs.

Fair Haven and the Neck flourished until sometime around World War I, but in the industrial growth of the early 20th century—lying too close to the railroad and the factories—they started to fade. The Irish began to move on to farther suburbs, and their place was taken by others coming out from the New Township. New tenements appeared, and old houses were converted to multiple use. At about the same time the oyster industry began a slow decline, caused in part by economic changes, in part by hurricanes, starfish, and pollution. By the Depression the soft edges along the railroad and the waterfront were developing into slums, and in the 30 years since World War II physical deterioration has come on fast.

Nevertheless today there are still pleasant neighborhoods and many streets of good vernacular houses that might yet be rescued. Fair Haven is presently a Redevelopment target area, but so far only scattered projects have been undertaken.

O 1 Power Plant. Somber, huge, mysterious—seen only from a distance beyond locked gates—this building towers over the dark river. Futurist fantasies, reveries of medieval strongholds, and electric minarets in a white cloud of smoke combine to produce one of the city's most haunting architectural images. Parts of the complex have been built at various times, principally 1927 and 1947, by Westcott and Mapes.

O 2 Christopher Columbus School, 1966. Davis Cochran Miller Baerman Noyes; Victor Christ-Janer, Design Consultant, New Canaan. This school provides a refreshing approach to its surrounding grounds—hillocks, serpentine paths, and carefully placed trees creating a miniature landscape that serves as a neighborhood park. The eye-catching pattern of window shapes is designed to admit less light on sunny exposures, more on shadier exposures.

Fair Haven is a good place to observe public school architecture, for examples of many periods remain: Woolsey (1878, O 4), Ferry Street (1881, O 5), Ezekiel Cheever (1896, O 6), Clinton Avenue (1911, O 9), Strong (1915, O 9), the Junior High (1928, O 8), Quinnipiac (1964, O 22). What is most striking about the progression, aside from increase in size and decrease in windows, is the change in land use. Woolsey, following the urban tradition, is built close to the street and originally accommodated 14 rooms on one-third of an acre. Columbus by contrast is set back from the street and accommodates 14 rooms on 3 acres.

O 3 Blatchley Avenue and Vicinity. High style in the 1860s and '70s flowed along the main thoroughfares—Blatchley Avenue, Ferry, and Lombard, with offshoots to the side on smaller streets like Exchange and Woolsey. Little will be singled out here because the area today has lost much of its spirit, either from neglect or improvement. Blatchley Avenue, once a lively show, is giving way to aluminum and pastels, while the side streets are less changed but shabby. Nevertheless people who like to explore will find things that are interesting. **226 Blatchley Avenue** is probably the best-preserved specimen of the '70s. **Nos. 220** and **219** show other typical work of the day, though the latter now looks a bit subdued without its roof cresting and porch. Illustrated: **241 Exchange Street** of the same period.

O 4 Woolsey School, 1878. A pleasant short street under the majestic shadow of the school. The building has lost its ornamental iron rail atop the porch, and the high coloring of the fancy brickwork is dulled by dirt, but it is still an exciting sight in a neighborhood already characterized by ebullient architecture. Architect, Rufus G. Russell.

O

O 5 Ferry Street. The corner of Ferry Street and Grand Avenue is the crossroad of the community, fittingly solemnized by a dignified **bank** (1914, Brown and VonBeren), its clock (added in 1924) a well-known neighborhood landmark. On the right as you go north: **St. Francis Church,** nucleus of the early Irish Catholic development (begun in 1867, much altered and enlarged since). **Nos. 414 and 418:** a once sprightly pair of Victorian Gothic cottages of the '70s, with pierced work still in one gable. At **547 Ferry Street:** behind a row of stores, the carcass of what must have been a sensational Victorian extravaganza, built by the minister of the First Church in 1876. The truncated tower once had a fish-scale or shingled peak, topped with an ironwork crest like the Lancraft house on the Heights (O 28). **No. 334 Lombard:** now wrapped in a becoming air of melancholy, this shapely mansard house began life on Ferry Street, was later demoted to the rear of the lot. 611 Ferry Street: another venerable school, its impressiveness presently diminished by paint (**Ferry Street School,** 1881; no longer in use).

O 6 Hiram Camp House, 9 Fox Street, 1864. The section at the head of the Neck was called Cedar Hill. The streets near here had a rather separate growth from the rest of Fair Haven, having begun to develop before the Civil War with a group of large suburban villas along Ferry Street. In an extensive urbanist program in the '50s, new streets were projected, upper Ferry Street was laid out as a straight avenue (displacing the old diagonal Ferry Path), and a broad cross-axis was opened through to the river in the form of a mall named Clinton Park (O 9). Only fragments of all this remain today. The mall (a bleak place, bare of the tall trees it was surely meant to have) may be seen between Peck and English Streets, and a sharp eye will find a few traces of early mansions along upper Ferry Street. The Camp house, hidden behind the delicatessen standing on its front lawn, was once imposing, its grounds running nearly to Peck Street (Fox Street is a recent incision). If the design is not by Henry Austin, it is a close imitation. The exterior is now painted landlord gray and the front porch has been cut down from four columns to two, but the interior preserves much original detail. Southeast bay a later addition.

Those interested in schools may make a loop around Peck and Fillmore Streets, passing **Ezekiel Cheever School,** 1896, on the corner of Fillmore and Lombard.

O 7 Ruoppolo Manor, 1969. Gilbert Switzer. Balconies make a play of horizontal planes against vertical planes, enhanced by vertically striated walls with smooth banding. Generous attention to landscaping, especially the preservation of a great tree, gives this public housing for the elderly an air of elegance.

O 8 169 Grand Avenue, 1852. A graceful villa from the antebellum days when the Neck was still rural, and another design strongly suggestive of Henry Austin. Fine proportions and a monumental porch make this a classic of the Villa style.

With the **Grand Avenue Congregational Church** next door, this block still holds on to some of its former dignity and spaciousness (originally built in 1853, the church acquired a whole new forepart in 1878; the tower has since lost its top stage, spire, and corner pinnacles). Opposite: **Junior High School,** 1928, Brown and VonBeren. **No. 134:** a striking side elevation, its pile-up of pyramidal roofs sliced by the towering chimney. The date is c1890, perhaps the last substantial house built in this area.

O 9 Fair Haven Cemetery, 1885. At the foot of a lane (now blacktopped and merged into a parking lot) this High Victorian Gothic gate made a solemn processional entrance from the street.

Those interested in schools, housing, or urban design may make a side trip up Atwater Street, crossing **Clinton Park** (O 6) along the way, to the **Clinton Avenue School,** 1911, Brown and VonBeren—one of the most monumental of the city's schools, reflecting the Neo-Classicism of the Edwardian era. At the foot of Clinton Park is **Quinnipiac Terrace,** one of New Haven's three early housing projects (M 17, N 42) and the most ambitiously conceived (1940, Douglas Orr and R. W. Foote, associated architects). On a superb site, the architects sought to maximize the views of the river and also to dramatize the urbanist intention of the early planners of the neighborhood, carrying the park down to the river and defining it with landscaping and with architectural massing (the sweep of the mall is now broken by ballfields, and the landscaping is not apparent). Down Clinton Avenue at the corner of Grand: the **Strong School** (1915, Brown and VonBeren). After Neo-Classicism came Collegiate Tudor—workmanlike shells with lots of glass, easily decorated with diapering on plain brick walls. Strong was one of the most elaborate of many built through the '20s. You have to go into the vacant lot across the street to get the effect of the facade with its little chapel-like structure on top. The design was published in the *American Architect* in June 1922. At 118 Clinton Avenue: **The Home for the Friendless,** 1888, Henry Austin and Son; built when Austin's practice had been largely taken over by his son Fred.

O 10 North Front Street. As Grand Avenue drops down to the river you come into the **village of Fair Haven** (notice no. 37–39 as you go by, an interesting Greek Revival double house with recessed Doric porch). This oystering port until a few years ago was one of the important architectural sites of Connecticut, a rare case where something of the texture of a Colonial–Federal streetscape could still be seen. Some of this has recently been demolished, the rest is dwindling away, either through neglect or modernization. North and South Front Streets have a few desolate remnants. These typical oystermen's houses, raised on high cellars dug into the bank at the tide line, are historically significant as evidence of a building type that seems to go back to the founding of the colony—living examples of the "cellars" which early colonial records mention as the first shelters built by the settlers. This is an ancient European form of waterfront architecture—boats and goods below, dwelling above—which lasted on the Quinnipiac and also at Oyster Point (H 29) into the 19th century. Front Street used to be lower, and at high tide oyster boats floated almost to the cellar doors. From the river docks, the bowsprits of ships projected over the road.

No. 182–184: **Rowe's Tavern,** built not long after the opening of the bridge in 1793 and center of the oystering community's business life. With its steep roof pitch the tavern is still Colonial in outline. **No. 186** may be somewhat later (on the blurry vernacular borderland of Late Colonial, Federal, and Greek Revival), while **no. 188** is a once chic Italian villa probably of the '40s, and **no. 192** (shown here) combines a delicately molded Federal cornice with a Greek Revival door. Despite asbestos shingles, this foursome still gives a capsule history of the architecture of the riverfront. Dates can no longer be precisely determined, but the bulk of the waterside houses seem to have been built between c1795 and c1830.

O 11 196 North Front Street. The traditional Colonial one-and-a-half story house with central chimney long persisted on the waterfront. Here the low roof pitch suggests a date in the Federal or Greek Revival period. The building is turned sideways to the street, its door facing south. Many other south-facing doors will be found along the river. The entry porch is a later addition, probably of the '70s.

No. 204: a little Federal half-moon window smothered in asbestos shingles still tells of early elegance.

O 12 270 North Front Street. Two-tiered porches came to Fair Haven with the Greek Revival. Combined with the terracing of the bank and with stairs and steps, they made picturesque compositions. This example probably belongs to the Henry Austin era. Characteristic banding still remains on the rear columns. The photograph, taken two or three years ago, shows a later jigsaw railing, now gone.

Along the way notice **no. 231** (c1855): a reassuring reminder that a fresh coat of paint can make a lot of difference.

O 13 17 Pine Street, c1861. Pine Street became a fashionable spot in the '50s. It is gratifying to find one of its mansions well preserved and still presiding over the hillside with a queenly air. **No. 32,** now dark gray, is of the same vintage. **No. 36** next door was probably built as a twin. **No. 25,** on a high basement of finely dressed stone, is the oldest house in the neighborhood.

O 14 South Front Street. Shops congregated at both ends of the bridge. On the corner of South Front Street is **King's Block,** built probably in the 1820s or early '30s (traces of a half-moon window may be seen in the north gable). Compare this typical late Federal commercial building (the only survivor of the type, as far as we know) with the newer style then appearing downtown, in the Exchange and the Street Building (I 30, I 49). Past King's Block, on South Front Street, a Federal house of some elegance stood until last year, and beyond stretched a streetfront of Federal and Greek Revival waterfront houses. The street today probably represents one of New Haven's major lost opportunities. Had restoration been undertaken, this might have been made into a historic locality of architectural importance and considerable charm. But a planned new bridge has wiped out the upper end, many of the best houses were demolished in the '50s, and Redevelopment has cleared most of the rest for future apartments and housing. On the water side a scrap metal enterprise has been removed, and a marina and park are planned. The photographs show South Front Street as it looked in 1938 and the corner house as it is today **(no. 76).**

O 15 86 South Front Street. This was originally one of a row of similar houses extending south to the corner. It is another example of the traditional waterfront house of the one-and-a-half-story, central chimney type (compare it with O 11), here dressed up with a porch probably added in the '80s. Additions to the waterfront houses are rather rare after the Civil War, suggesting that the more prosperous oystermen were moving elsewhere. *Demolished, fall 1975.*

O 16 66 South Front Street. This once elegant stuccoed house with Doric doorway was here by the mid-40s. The pitched roof and arched window, to which goods were evidently lifted by a hoist, seem to be a later change.

The tour now swings around the foot of South Front Street. On River Street: the **Quinnipiac Brewery,** typical of the boisterous architecture that beer seemed to give rise to after the Civil War. The front on River Street is dated 1896. Behind it most of the buildings are of the '80s, evidently incorporating the earlier Robinson Company factory of the '70s with mansard roof and tower. Robinson manufactured "Oyster Tubs, Kegs, and Extension Tables." This building is best seen from the Ferry Street side. Architect of the later section, Leoni Robinson.

O 17 East Pearl Street. As the village prospered, more prestigious houses came to be built back from the waterfront, and in the antebellum era East Pearl Street became the oystering community's most elegant address. **No. 37** was one of the finest places, with spacious grounds descending behind to the river (the handsome fence still marks the original frontage along the street). The house began as a stuccoed Grecian villa in the '40s, was later transformed with mansard roof, porch, and other additions, probably in the '60s or '70s. **No. 42,** also of the '40s: tattered remnants of fringe on the eaves are a reminder that fancies of this sort were common in the Villa style, most since removed. An old photograph shows the fringe all around the roof and over the tops of the windows, and porch columns like the remarkable ones still remaining at no. 59. **No. 48:** another good fence; in fact, notice the line of fences up and down the street and the part they play in scaling down the roadway. **Nos. 58–68:** four tidy Greek Revival facades which once read as a unified row when all were painted white. Every one now has lost its porch (58 and 60 still have the roof but not the Doric columns visually needed to support it). **No. 59** (shown here): another villa of the '40s, with plantlike columns and an iron rail that now seem to be unique in New Haven.

O 18 76 East Pearl Street. We have seen these columns, which are associated with A. J. Davis's work, many times already (see G 60). Here they are topped by a giddy cornice and brackets of the 1870s. Probably the house began as a small villa (built around 1851) and later acquired a new roof, top floor, and all the trimmings.

No. 69: an Austin-like design of the 1850s whose original colors probably gave it the same sort of sparkle that the mansion on Pine Street has (O 13).

No. 100: the Queen Anne style brings East Pearl Street's architectural history to a close. This was built as the Methodist parsonage in 1882.

O 19 East Pearl Street Methodist Church, 1871. A local sally into Victorian Gothic that achieves a quite awesome effect.

At **106 Exchange Street:** behind evergreens and asphalt sheathing a villa on a high stone basement with a distinguished porch. To return to Grand Avenue, drop down the hill on Exchange Street. Small versions of the waterfront houses perch on the slope.

O 20 Dragon Bridge, 1896. Due to be soon replaced by a new bridge. The path for a bigger and higher approach may already be seen cutting through the houses on the south side of Grand Avenue.

O 21 Quinnipiac Avenue. Quinnipiac Avenue originally was much like Front Street but today has been considerably denatured. The intersection with East Grand Avenue, at the head of the bridge, was the crossroad of the village and until recently had a certain formal importance, with large buildings standing squarely on the corners. Now, with a gas station, a taxpayer, and a vacant lot, it is no longer a place at all.

On the water's edge several of the oyster docks remain. Shown here **Brown's Seed Oysters** at 494 Quinnipiac Avenue. **No. 512–514:** on high ground above the dock stands the house, another example of the late Colonial type, with a porch added perhaps in the mid-century. Inside, a Colonial interior can still be found: central chimney, beams, beaded wainscotting of 15-inch boards, and ceilings scarcely more than 6 feet high—an almost perfectly preserved specimen of an oysterman's house.

O 22 Quinnipiac School, 1964. Perkins & Will and Carleton Granbery. This well-sited building makes use of a steep slope to present an imposing front to the avenue below while gaining seclusion for the school and its entrances above (access is both from Runo Terrace and Lexington Avenue). Landscaping enhances the sheltering enclosure of the upper hillside, giving a feeling of intimacy and of a child-scaled world.

O

O 23 Upper Quinnipiac Avenue. Those who wish may make a loop up along the river. The view past the city dump up the valley to Sleeping Giant was once celebrated, and after the Civil War upper Quinnipiac Avenue became a long procession of stately Victorian houses. The line-up today is ragged, but suggestive bits remain. Near the North Haven line **no. 1706** (shown here) is a sole survivor of the large farms which in Colonial times filled the river plain. If the attributed date of 1771 is correct, this is one of New Haven's best remaining Colonial houses, with arched windows on the first floor and molded brick watertable. **1314 Quinnipiac Avenue:** housing (1961, Carl Koch and Associates Inc., Cambridge). **No. 1212:** a flamboyant mansion of the 1870s. **No. 1190:** another one—earlier and quieter. At **Foxon Road:** four corner gas stations distinguished by good planting and maintenance (the Mobil station a variant of Eliot Noyes' prototype model on Whalley Avenue—Itinerary F). **No. 1134:** low-rent public housing (1970, Alden Berman and Associates), with fine landscaping and pleasant interior paths separating the units. **Nos. 972–984:** condominium (1972, Herbert S. Newman Associates). Returning to Hemingway Street, the gray apartments looming ahead are elderly housing (**Bella Vista,** 1971, Henry Schadler, West Hartford).

O 24   Charles Ives House, now Fairmont Park. With Clifton Street we come to the top of the hill and to the land of the country estates. North of the road is the former Ives property, sold to the city for a park in 1923. We know that there were once more places like this along the Heights, a loose chain of suburban estates running, with interruptions, all the way to Morris Cove (others are mentioned in H 45–49). People who enjoy the ghosts of the past can still spot the telltale redstone walls and overgrown gates. The Ives gates, shown here, will serve as a monument to this vanished world. At 151–53 and 159–61 Clifton Street: the dismembered remains of the mansion itself, moved across the street and turned into two two-family houses. Architect, Rufus G. Russell. Inside the park: plane-spotting station from World War II.

Below the park: **80 and 84 Clifton Street,** a pair of Greek Revival houses raised on high cellars, faithfully preserving the waterfront style way up the hill; also an agreeable pair of Gothic cottages at **nos. 106 and 112 Sherland Avenue.**

O 25   James F. Babcock House, 89 Sherland Avenue, 1862. Opposite the Ives house, the Babcock estate originally covered 30 acres. It was sold and subdivided around 1870, and two more houses were built next to the original mansion. Lined up side by side facing Sherland Avenue across a great slope of lawn, they must have been an imposing trio. One has now been torn down, two remain. As you go down Summit Street, you will find Babcock's carriage house on your left, still gallantly painted to match the house though now separated from it by new development.

O 26   154 East Grand Avenue, c1875.   Along with the Babcock house, this is one of the few that remain from the great days of Fair Haven Heights—a fine full-blown specimen of carpentry Victorian Gothic, with sharp gables and a wild skyline. Porches and bays, struts and rails and openwork dissolve the walls into light and shadow with deep openings drawing the outsider in. It is hard to look at a house like this without imagining the tall cool rooms inside and the view out of the windows to the gleaming river. The house has evidently kept itself alive by selling off its land for building lots. Its barns will be found on the other side of Summit Street.

Across East Grand Avenue, the **upper end** of **Summit Street** is one of the few good examples in the city of post-World War II vernacular: a streetscape based on extreme horizontality and a strong rhythm of garage doors. Downhill, **Sherland Avenue** is a pleasant older street, reflecting the prosperity of the Heights in the years before World War I. **133 East Grand Avenue:** the 1870s again, this time a Swiss variation, with a strong jutting profile and a pattern of intricate carpentry against brick, presently enhanced by good contrasting colors.

O 27   Firehouse, 1927. Brown and VonBeren.   Like its partner in Westville (F 24), a perfect expression of suburban good taste in the 1920s. The firehouse joins the churches to make a break in the movement of the avenue, defining a small genteel civic center.

O 28   Pilgrim Church, 1851.   On one side of the street a Congregational echo of Center Church, on the other an Episcopalian echo of Trinity (**St. James Episcopal Church,** 1844). The allusion which this little oasis makes to the New Haven Green is clear.

Next door, **no. 61:** one of the earliest houses on the hill, built between 1836 and 1847, spruced up with stylish balustrades and shingles around 1880.

Down Lenox Street, past Oxford, on your left: another redstone gate and ruined grounds, another towered confection of the '70s. This is the **Henry Lancraft house,** a sample of the life style of an oyster dealer and builder after the Civil War (entrance now at 120 Lexington Avenue).

207

Chronological List

Colonial	H 44, H 46*, H 49 I 3, I 5 J 2 0 23
Federal (1790–c1825)	B 3* D 1 E 11 H 47 I 4, I 12, I 13, I 14, I 19, I 42, I 45, I 46 J 18, J 24, J 35*, J 39 K 9*, K11 L 14 N 25*, N 28 O 10, O 11*
Vernacular Borderland	G 22, G 23, G 24, G 25, G 31, G 37, G 38, G 39 N 30* O 10, O 11, O 13*, O 14, O 15, O 21
Greek Revival (c1825–c1845)	E 1, E 41 F 16*, F 20, F 23 G 1, G 6, G 20*, G 21, G 36, G 37, G 39*, G 40, G 60 H 6, H 32, H 50 I 1, I 7, I 30, I 47, I 49, I 52* J 3, J 21*, J 24, J 34 K, K 4, K 6, K 8, K 12, K 14, K 18 L 13, L 15, L 16, L 17, L 19, L 23 N 1, N 6, N 8, N 9*, N 10, N 12, N 13, N 14, N 15, N 18, N 28*, N 35, N 37, N 41, N 43 O 12, O 16, O 17, O 24*, O 28*
Antebellum (c1845–c1860)	E 3, E 21, E 42 F 6, F 31 G 3*, G 11, G 56 H 2, H 5, H 21, H 27*, H 29, H 32, H 33, H 47 I 2, I 8, I 51, I 52 J 9, J 10 K 4, K 16, K 17, K 29, K 43* L 7, L 9, L 10, L 12, L 14*, L 18, L 20, L 22, L 28 M 3* N 2, N 3, N 4, N 5, N 7, N 17, N 19, N 20, N 21, N 26, N 28*, N 31, N 36, N 39 O 8, O 10, O 12, O 13, O 17, O 18, O 19*, O 28

*Subsidiary entry

1860s	E 24
	F 21*, F 28, F 29
	G 5, G 32, G 34, G 47, G 53, G 59
	H 12, H 13, H 19, H 27, H 32, H 51*
	I 20, I 33
	J 4, J 37
	K 10*, K 11*, K 15, K 47
	L 7*, L 8, L 12*, L 24, L 25, L 26
	M 19, M 22
	N 24, N 27
	O 5, O 6, O 24, O 25
1870s	D 2
	E 7
	G 10, G 16, G 35, G 41, G 42, G 46, G 50, G 51, G 56*
	H 7, H 10, H 11*, H 14*, H 15*, H 25, H 27*, H 32, H 48
	I 25, I 33, I 41, I 43, I 44
	J 5, J 6
	K 3, K 7*, K 9*, K 13, K 48, K 51
	L 3, L 20*, L 27, L 29, L 33
	M 2, M 3, M 4, M 5, M 11, M 12, M 18, M 28, M 29
	N 3*, N 9, N 17, N 20*, N 23, N 25, N 26*, N 32, N 47
	O 3, O 4, O 5, O 8*, O 16*, O 19, O 23*, O 24*, O 26, O 28*
1880s	D 6
	E 45
	F 37
	G 3*, G 20*, G 61
	H 7*, H 8, H 11, H 14, H 19*, H 20*, H 23, H 26*, H 32
	J 3*, J 4*
	K 2, K 3*, K 7, K 9, K 10, K 25, K 49
	L 6, L 11, L 17*, L 25*, L 32, L 39, L 40
	N 3*, N 28*, N 32*
	O 5, O 9, O 16*, O 18*
1890s	E 30, E 31, E 32, E 34*, E 36, E 38
	F 4, F 14, F 19
	G 2*, G 4, G 17*, G 44, G 52, G 54, G 55
	H 9, H 22, H 25, H 26*, H 41, H 45*, H 46*, H 51
	I 6, I 50
	J 1, J 36
	K 14*, K 22*, K 50, K 54
	L 5, L 31, L 35, L 37, L 38
	O 6*, O 8*, O 16*
1900-WW I	E 2, E 12, E 15, E 17, E 18, E 20*, E 22, E 25, E 26, E 27, E 28,
	E 29, E 30, E 33, E 35, E 37*, E 46

*Subsidiary entry

F 5*, F 7, F 8, F 9, F 10, F 16*, F 24, F 25, F 26, F 33, F 36
G 3, G 7, G 11*, G 37*, G 49, G 55*, G 56*, G 57, G 60*
H 2, H 3, H 16, H 18, H 24, H 27*, H 38, H 42, H 45
I 2, I 9, I 15, I 16, I 25, I 26, I 27, I 29, I 31, I 36, I 53
J 3, J 5*, J 7, J 8, J 9, J 10, J 13, J 21, J 25, J 27*, J 28, J 30,
J 31, J 32, J 33*, J 36*, J 38, J 39*
K 2, K 3*, K 4*, K 19*, K 20, K 21*, K 22*, K 23, K 24, K 26,
K 27, K 28, K 30, K 31, K 32, K 33, K 37*, K 39, K 41, K 43,
K 44, K 45
L 6*, L 12*, L 26*, L 35*, L 36, L 41
M 6, M 10, M 21
N 11, N 17
O 5, O 9*, O 20, O 26*

1920s
D 5
E 13, E 19, E 20, E 37*, E 39, E 40, E 44
F 11, F 21, F 29*, F 30*, F 32, F 35, F 37*, F 38
G 2*, G 7*, G 8, G 12, G 17, G 26*, G 45, G 57*
H 32*, H 50, H 51*
I 11*, I 15, I 32, I 37, I 39, I 53*
J 2*, J 11, J 12, J 13, J 15*, J 16, J 17, J 20*, J 26, J 27*,
J 31, J 39*
K 22, K 37, K 38, K 40, K 41*, K 42, K 52
L 4*, L 15*, L 26*, L 32*, L 34
N 11
O 1, O 8*, O 27

1930-WW II
E 4, E 43
F 12, F 30, F 34
G 26, G 27, G 28, G 29, G 57*, G 59*
I 16, I 38
J 8, J 10, J 11, J 13, J 14, J 15, J 20, J 22, J 23, J 27, J 31*,
J 33, J 35
K 13, K 24, K 32*, K 46
M 17
N 9*, N 42*
O 9*

1940s
E 27*
F 17*
H 51*
J 6*
O 1

1950s
B
C
D 5*, D 6*

*Subsidiary entry

E 6*, E 23
F 14*
G 13, G 18, G 58*
H 15*
K 4*, K 21*, K 23*, K 24, K 42*, K 53
M 7
O 26*

1960s   A
B 2, B 3, B 4
C 1, C 2, C 3, C 5
D 1*
E 5, E 8, E 9, E 23*, E 34, E 37
F, F 3, F 15, F 16, F 19, F 22, F 26*, F 38*
G 9, G 15, G 31*
H 11*, H 15, H 34, H 36, H 37, K 39, H 40*
I 1*, I 8*, I 17, I 20*, I 21*, I 22, I 23, I 24, I 28, I 48
J 10, J 19, J 23*, J 26*, J 29
K 3*, K 5, K 19, K 21, K 24, K 26*, K 35, K 36, K 55
L 1, L 3*, L 21
M 8, M 9, M 13, M 14, M 15, M 16, M 24, M 25, M 27, M 30
N 16, N 19*, N 29*, N 30, N 33, N 34, N 40, N 44, N 45, N 46
O 2, O 7, O 22, O 23*

1970s   B 1, B 3*
C 3*, C 4, C 6
D 2, D 4
E 6, E 37, E 45*
F 2, F 14*, F 17, F 18, F 27
G 14, G 32*, G 49*, G 51*, G 57*, G 58*
H 15*, H 20, H 28*, H 31, H 40, H 51*
I 10*, I 16*, I 18, I 21, I 26*, I 34, I 35, I 38*, I 40
J 10*
K 34
L 2, L 3
M 20, M 23, M 26
N 22, N 38, N 42
O 23*

*Subsidiary entry

Index of Architects, Builders, Planners, and Artists

General Index

Chaplin-Apthorp House, K 11, L 14, N 25
Cheney, Austin, house, K 39
Chermayeff, Serge, house, L 21
Churches and Synagogues, 8, 15, G, G 19,
L 5, L 31
African Church, D 1. *See also* United
Church of Christ, Dixwell Avenue
All Saints Episcopal Church, H 23
Bethesda Lutheran Church, K 23
Bikur Cholim Sheveth Achim. *See* First
Church of Christ Scientist, *1909*
Calvary Baptist Church, G 16
Center Church. *See* First Congregational
Church
Christ Church, *1859*, F 1; *1895*, F 4
Church of the Ascension (Episcopal).
See All Saints Episcopal Church
Church of the Epiphany (Episcopal),
H 45
Church of the Redeemer (Congregational)
1870, I 41; *1949*, E 27
Churches on the Green, 4, I, I 9, I 10,
I 11, I 14, I 37, N 1
Davenport Congregational Church, N 25
Division Street Church (The Taylor
Church), M 29
Dwight Place Congregational Church,
G 42
East Pearl Street Methodist Church,
O 19
Epworth Methodist Church, L 35
Evangelical Covenant Church. *See*
Swedish Emanuel Congregational
Church
First Baptist Church, *c1855*, N, N 17;
1903, L 35
First Church of Christ Scientist, *1909*,
G 57; *1950*, E 23
First Congregational Church (Center
Church), I 2, I 11, I 12, I 13, O 28
First Methodist Church, I, I 2
First Presbyterian Church, E 23
Forbes Chapel. *See* Church of the
Epiphany
German Emanuel Lutheran Church, L 32
Glad Tidings Tabernacle. *See* Swedish
Lutheran Church
Gospel Tabernacle of the Assembly of
God. *See* Epworth Methodist Church
Grace Methodist Church, H 19
Grand Avenue Congregational Church,
O 5, O 8
Howard Avenue Congregational Church,
H 19
Howard Avenue Methodist Church, H 25
Humphrey Street Congregational Church,
E 37, L 32
Italian Baptist Church. *See* Davenport
Congregational Church
Mishkan Israel, I 42, L 5, L 36
New Light Holy Church. *See* Howard
Avenue Methodist Church
North Church. *See* United Congrega-
tional Church
Oyster Point Church. *See* Howard
Avenue Methodist Church
Pilgrim Congregational Church, O 28
Plymouth Congregational Church, G 46,
G 49
Sacred Heart Church. *See* South
Congregational Church
St. Anthony's Roman Catholic Church,
H 16

St. Barbara Greek Orthodox Church, G 59
St. Boniface Roman Catholic Church,
L 26
St. Casimir Roman Catholic Church.
See Davenport Congregational
Church
St. Francis Roman Catholic Church, O 5
St. James Episcopal Church, O 28
St. John's Episcopal Church, L 31
St. John's Roman Catholic Church, H 12
St. Joseph's Roman Catholic Church,
L 36
St. Luke's Episcopal Church, *1844*, F 5,
G 19; *1905*, F 5
St. Mary's Roman Catholic Church,
K 1, K 3
St. Michael's Roman Catholic Church.
See Wooster Square Congregational
Church
St. Michael's Ukrainian Catholic Church,
G 58
St. Paul's Episcopal Church, N 1
St. Stanislaus Roman Catholic Church,
L 26
St. Thomas's Episcopal Church, E 13
Seventh-Day Adventist Church. *See*
Humphrey Street Congregational
Church
South Congregational Church, H 32,
H 33
Swedish Emanuel Congregational
Church, L 34
Swedish Lutheran Church, L 26
Taylor Church, M 29
Third Congregational Church, E 1
Trinity Episcopal Church, I 11, I 14,
K 41, O 28
Trinity Lutheran Church. *See* Church of
the Redeemer, *1870*
United Church of Christ, Dixwell
Avenue, M 14. *See also* African
Church
United Church of Westville. *See*
Westville Congregational Church
United Congregational Church, 4, I 11,
I 12, I 37, I 46
Wesley United Methodist Church. *See*
Grace Methodist Church
Westville Congregational Church, F 23
Whitneyville Congregational Church, E 1
Wooster Square Congregational Church,
N 17
Zion Lutheran Church, H 11
Churches on the Green. *See* Churches
and Synagogues
Church Street, 14, I, I 15, I 21, I 26, I 28,
I 30, I 39, K; no. 55, I 26; no. 157, I 32;
no. 195, I 35; no. 205, I 37; nos. 221, 227,
and 234, I 38; no. 258, I 40
Church Street South, C 1, H 20, H 35, H 37
City Arts Center, L 1, L 2, L 3, L 5, L 6, L 15
City Hall, I, I 33, I 34, I 41
City of Elms, 6
City planning, 9, 10, 11 (Colonial), 17,
H 35, H 38, I 34, K 37, M 17, M 24.
See also Redevelopment; Urbanism
City Point. *See* Oyster Point
Civic Improvement Committee, 9, I 9.
See also Gilbert-Olmsted Report
Clark, Massena, estate, E 32
Cliff Street, E 11
Clifton Street: nos. 80 and 84, O 24; nos.
151–53 and 159–61, O 24

Photographic Credits

Hervey Townshend
O, O 12.

Yale News Bureau
G 12–13, G 28, H 15, I 6, J 2, J 5, J 7–8, J 11–15, J 17–18, J 22–23, J 27, J 29, J 31, J 33, J 35, K 13b, K 52, K 54.

Yale University Archives, Yale University Library
G 2, G 5, K, K 4.

Yale University Art Gallery, the Mabel Brady Garvan Collection
E 10.

Yale University Press
K 5.